UNDERSTANDING CHILDHOOD

an interdisciplinary approach

This book is the first of four which have been prepared as the core teaching texts for The Open University course U212 *Childhood*. The growing field of childhood and youth studies provides an integrative framework for interdisciplinary research and teaching, as well as analysis of contemporary policy and practice, in, for instance, education, health and social work. Childhood is now a global issue, forcing a reconsideration of conventional approaches to study. Childhood is also a very personal issue for each and every one of us – scholars, policy-makers, parents and children. The books therefore include children's and parents' voices as well as academic discussion of childhood in diverse societies and points in history. The recognition of childhood and youth as a focus of study, debate and personal reflection provides the starting point for this introductory series.

Book 1 *Understanding Childhood: an interdisciplinary approach* asks 'What is a child?' and introduces a range of perspectives within childhood and youth studies. Topics in this book include the history of beliefs about childhood, the growth of scientific approaches to studying children, the significance of gender, debates around children's rights and how far children are seen as innocent or knowing.

Book 2 *Childhoods in Context* examines the interplay between family, work, schooling and other influences in the daily lives of children and young people. Topics include changing family patterns, debates about school versus work, and current concerns about child labour. Issues in early childhood are discussed, as well as the transition from child to adult.

Book 3 *Children's Cultural Worlds* looks at the distinctiveness of children's cultural worlds by exploring the everyday activities of young children through to teenagers. Topics include friendships and the significance of play, how children use language to construct relationships and identities, the role of print literature, other media and information technology in children's lives, and their growing power as consumers.

Book 4 *Changing Childhoods: local and global* considers the status of children in society, and the significance of children's rights. Topics include the effects of poverty, ill-health and violence on children's well-being. Finally, the book illustrates the ways in which children and young people become engaged with social issues, including issues surrounding their status as children.

Further details on The Open University course U212 *Childhood* and other courses in the BA Hons *Childhood and Youth Studies* degree can be obtained from the Student Registration and Enquiry Service, The Open University, PO Box 197, Milton Keynes, MK7 6BJ, United Kingdom. Telephone +44 (0)870 333 4340, e-mail general-enquiries@open.ac.uk, web site http://www.open.ac.uk/courses.

WILEY

The Open University

UNDERSTANDING CHILDHOOD

an interdisciplinary approach

edited by Martin Woodhead
and Heather Montgomery

The Open University
Walton Hall
Milton Keynes
MK7 6AA
United Kingdom
www.open.ac.uk

John Wiley & Sons Ltd
The Atrium
Southern Gate
Chichester
PO19 8SQ
www.wiley.com

Other Wiley editorial offices

John Wiley & Sons Inc., 111 River Street, Hoboken, NJ 07030, USA

Jossey-Bass, 989 Market Street, San Francisco, CA 94103-1741, USA

Wiley-VCH Verlag GmbH, Boschstr. 12, D-69469 Weinheim, Germany

John Wiley & Sons Australia Ltd, 42 McDougall Street, Milton,
Queensland 4064, Australia

John Wiley & Sons (Asia) Pte Ltd, 2 Clementi Loop #02-01, Jin Xing
Distripark, Singapore 129809

John Wiley & Sons Canada Ltd, 6045 Freemont Blvd, Mississauga, ONT,
L5R 4J3

Library of Congress Cataloging-in-Publication Data

A catalog record for this book is available from the Library of Congress.

British Library Cataloguing in Publication Data

A catalogue record for this book is available from the British Library.

ISBN 978 0 470 84692 6

Edited, designed and typeset by The Open University.
Printed in Malta by Gutenberg Press Limited.

1.4

Contents

Contributors

Rachel Burr is a lecturer in Childhood Studies at The Open University. She has worked as a social worker and trainer in England, Ireland and Vietnam. Between 1996 and 1998 she lived in Vietnam where she did child-focused research for a doctorate in anthropology at Brunel University. Her research interests are in child-focused human rights, the role of child-focused international aid agencies, and children of the streets and orphanages in Vietnam (she is currently investigating the effects of HIV/AIDS on the lives of those children). She has taught anthropology in the US. Her recent publications include 'Global and local approaches to children's rights in Vietnam', *Childhood*, vol. 9(1), and 'Ethics of doing anthropological fieldwork', vol. 3, *Anthropology Matters*.

Mary Jane Kehily is a lecturer in Childhood Studies at The Open University. Her background is in cultural studies and education and her research interests are in gender and sexuality, narrative and identity, and popular culture. She has published widely on these themes. Her most recent publication is *Sexuality, Gender and Schooling: shifting agendas in social learning* (Routledge, 2002). She is also director of a research project exploring the cultural meanings of drugs and drug use in young people's lives.

Heather Montgomery is a Lecturer in Childhood Studies at the Open University. She is an anthropologist who has conducted fieldwork in Thailand among young prostitutes and is the author of *Modern Babylon? Prostituting Children in Thailand* (Berghahn, 2001). She has held post-doctoral positions in the USA, Norway and Oxford and is the author of several articles on children's rights, abuse and the anthropology of childhood including 'Imposing rights? A case study of child prostitution in Thailand' in *Culture and Rights* (edited by Cowan, Dembour and Wilson, Cambridge University Press, 2001) and 'Abandonment and child prostitution in a Thai slum community' in *Abandoned Children* (edited by Catherine Panter-Brick and Malcolm Smith, Cambridge University Press, 2001).

Wendy Stainton Rogers is a senior lecturer at The Open University and is also head of its Research School. A psychologist by training, she has carried out extensive research within the area of childhood, particularly into the social policy, law and practice issues around child protection. She has published (with Jeremy Roche) 'Child protection in England' in *Child Abuse: international perspectives* (edited by Schwartz-Kenny, McCauley and Epstein, Greenwood, 1999). She has also written and carried out research on children's sexuality and the application of postmodern theory to child-care practice. Her publications in this field include 'Word children', in *Children in Culture: approaches to childhood* (edited by Lesnik-Oberstein, St Martin's Press, 1999) and 'What is good and bad sex for children?' in *Moral Agendas for Children's Welfare* (edited by Michael King, Routledge, 2000) (both with Rex Stainton Rogers).

Martin Woodhead is a senior lecturer in the Centre for Childhood, Development and Learning at The Open University. He has contributed to courses in child development and education, as well as carrying out research in child development, early education, the sociology of childhood, child labour and children's rights. He has been a Fulbright scholar in the US as well as a consultant to international organizations including Council of Europe, Save the Children and OECD. His publications include 'Psychology and the cultural construction of children's needs' in *Constructing and Reconstructing childhood* (edited by James and Prout, Falmer, 1997), and, with Dorothy Faulkner, 'Subjects, objects or participants?' in *Research with Children* (edited by Christensen and James, Falmer, 2000). Martin chaired the course team for The Open University course U212 *Childhood*, for which this book is one of the core texts.

Introduction

Common sense suggests a child is someone who is young, who is smaller, more immature and vulnerable and in many other ways different to human adults. The pioneer anthropologist of childhood Margaret Mead believed children everywhere are:

> pygmies among giants, ignorant among the knowledgeable, wordless among the articulate ... And to the adults, children everywhere represent something weak and helpless, in need of protection, supervision, training, models, skills, beliefs, 'character'.

(Mead, 1955, p. 7)

Half a century later there's good reason to challenge this universal prescription for young humanity. Children share in common that they are growing, changing and learning, but they differ in innumerable ways in the expression of growth and change, as well as in the circumstances, goals and extent of their learning. And the idea that children represent the same to all adults is equally questionable. Children are not seen universally as weak, wordless or ignorant. Childhood is viewed very differently depending on the geographical area under investigation, the period of time under study as well as the standpoint of the person studying childhood.

As Allison James and Alan Prout explain:

> The immaturity of children is a biological fact but the ways in which that immaturity is understood and made meaningful is a fact of culture ... It is these 'facts of culture' which may vary and which can be said to make of childhood a social institution. It is in this sense, therefore that one can talk of the social construction of childhood and also ... of its re- and deconstruction ... Childhood is both constructed and reconstructed both for and by children.

(Prout and James, 1990, p. 7)

This book is as much about studying the cultural beliefs, representations and discourses of childhood as about studying children's immaturity, growth and development. Of course these two ways of approaching childhood and youth studies are linked. In so far as diverse and changing images, representations and discourses shape cultural practices, they influence the treatment of children and young people and in turn shape their growth and development. Key questions are raised about the status of young humanity – their needs, competences, responsibilities and rights. Put simply, how far are children seen as innocents who need protection, nurture and training, and how far as social actors who engage with and contribute to their development, and who have a right to be heard? The near universal adoption of the United Nations Convention on the Rights of the Child (1989) has come to symbolize a profound and challenging shift in perspective, especially its emphasis on children's participatory rights. This is reflected in a small way in the preparation of this book, which includes perspectives of children and young people on many of the issues being discussed.

The United Nations Convention defines a child as anyone under the age of eighteen, which is also consistent with much national and international legislation. We have taken this as a starting point for the chapters that follow, at the same time recognizing respects in which it is problematic. What does this vast cross-section of the world's population – in some countries nearly half the population – have in common that justifies a single formal designation? This is not just an issue of diversity between societies. It is also about the varieties of childhood within the broad age span nought to eighteen years. How far are children united by their immaturity and innocence – how far by their dependency and powerlessness? The child of five months is worlds apart from the child of five years, as is the five year old from the fifteen year old. In many ways a fifteen-year-old 'child' has more in common with a twenty-five-year-old 'adult' than with a five-year-old 'child', even though the age gap is the same.

Developmental psychology has provided detailed descriptions of the many stages and transitions that take place within Western childhoods, which are also reflected in everyday distinctions in the English language, for example between babies, toddlers, school children, teenagers and young people. Distinguishing kinds of childhood by finely divided ages is not universal. In some societies, traditionally children's ages have not been recorded; their status has been determined by their abilities, their social class or caste and their gender, not by their age. Defining childhood as a distinctive life phase is also premised on assumptions about adulthood. There is good reason to challenge the contrast between the dependent, vulnerable, developing child and the autonomous, mature, knowing adult, for example by acknowledging situations where adults may be vulnerable and children may be resilient. In many societies, children take on adult responsibilities long before they reach the age of eighteen. Defining the beginning of childhood is equally problematic. A case can be made that childhood starts before birth and that the unborn too are children. Each of these difficult issues are tackled in this book, which takes the beginning and end of childhood as a starting point for enquiry, analysis and debate.

Since the systematic study of childhood began in Europe and North America in the nineteenth century, numerous disciplines have contributed to the field, each with their own set of theoretical assumptions, research questions, methodologies and internal debates. Sociologists look at childhood as a social phenomenon, analysing children as a particular group of people in society; linguists look at the way that children learn and adapt language; psycho-analysts study the effects of childhood on adult personality; anthropologists examine the cultural beliefs of different societies about children; psychologists analyse stages in the personal, social and emotional development of children. Childhood is also a major area of applied study. Concerns about childhood are evident in medicine, in politics and economics, in law and social policy and in education. The book's authors represent a wide range of disciplinary approaches to childhood, notably sociology, anthropology, psychology, and cultural studies. Short readings at the end of each chapter provide additional perspectives by drawing on, for instance, literature, economics and the law.

While some chapters introduce particular disciplines, the book is not organized on disciplinary lines. Our aim instead has been to span conventional academic boundaries in order to achieve a more interdisciplinary understanding, as well as to acknowledge the unresolved tensions between different approaches to childhood. We have concentrated on examining childhood from three broad perspectives. These are:

1   a scientific approach which seeks empirical knowledge about children, especially by devising theories and testing them through observation and experimentation;

2   a social constructionist approach which studies childhood as a cultural construction, examining beliefs, images and ideas about children especially through the study of representations and discourses, including those generated by scientific approaches;

3   an applied approach which looks at the ways children and young people are defined in terms of the law and children's rights, as well as through policies and professional practices as these affect the experiences of children themselves.

These ways of approaching childhood bring particular sets of assumptions and attitudes towards childhood and each approach is examined in a separate chapter (Chapters 2 to 4). The book then goes on to apply an interdisciplinary approach to two topics, 'gender' and 'innocence'. There is no attempt to reconcile all the varying points of view expressed or to smooth out the tensions between them. There are inevitable clashes, as will become apparent throughout the chapters. Ideas about childhood are contested not only between academic disciplines but also within them.

Chapter 1 'What is a child?' takes the issue of when childhood ends in order to explore the complex nature of childhood. Immediately the problems inherent in defining childhood as a stage of life become apparent. There are no universally agreed criteria for deciding when someone has reached the moment when she or he stops being a child and becomes an adult. In fact contradictions abound in different areas of social practice. Children of the same age may be treated as competent and responsible in one area of life but immature and dependent in another. This chapter explores how the three approaches of social constructionism, science and the law deal with the end of childhood. The chapter focuses on one particular debate, about the age of criminal responsibility, illustrating how studies within scientific, social constructionist and applied approaches can shed light on how children who commit serious crimes are treated, so revealing complex and sometimes contradictory issues.

Chapter 2 'Childhood in time and place' elaborates on the idea of childhood as a social construction. This chapter draws on sociology, anthropology, cultural studies, philosophy and history to look at how childhood is understood in various places and at various times. By looking cross-culturally as well as historically, we can see that ideas about childhood have changed over time and that they vary between cultures. In contrast to the previous chapter, this one looks at the question of when childhood begins. Once again, it problematizes what, at first, might appear to be a very straightforward question. However, by showing that beliefs about the beginning of childhood differ radically from society to society, it raises questions about universality of beliefs about childhood. Later sections of the chapter elaborate on some major influential themes in Western discourses of childhood and asks how far these are being exported as part of a new globalized image of childhood.

Chapter 3 'The child in development' explores scientific approaches to childhood, taking developmental psychology as its main example. The chapter traces the origins of developmental research and illustrates some of the early attempts to describe universal stages of physical, social and mental development. Besides introducing some examples of theory and research, the chapter questions the significance of studying the child as a developing being and considers how developmental theories have influenced child care and education. The chapter goes on to look at theories of intellectual development, especially those associated with the work of Jean Piaget and Lev Vygotsky. By revisiting two of Piaget's classic experiments described in Chapter 1 and showing how ingenious variations have produced rather different results, the chapter demonstrates how scientific theories about children's competences have been modified to take greater account of the way context and cultural meanings shape children's understanding.

Chapter 4 'Children and rights' turns to applied approaches to childhood, in particular the significance of children's rights in policies and practices. The chapter asks what rights children have, how far these rights are universal and whether having rights improves children's welfare. It looks in particular at the United Nations Convention on the Rights of the Child and the influence this has had in setting the age of eighteen as the boundary between adulthood and childhood. It examines the distinction between protection, provision and participation rights and explores the concept of the 'best interests of the child'. This chapter looks closely at the ways age is used as a criterion to judge children's competence, drawing attention to complexities and contradictions in deciding whether children are capable of participating fully. It also analyses the contradictions between universal standards of children's rights and the local reality of children lives.

Chapter 5 'Gendered childhoods' examines a fundamental aspect of children's lives and experiences, that of gender. Although children are often spoken of as a homogenous group, gender is a critical distinction within it. It is one of the first and most important markers in a child's life. Children are assigned a gender from birth (and even before birth where modern medical technologies are used). They are treated differently according to that gender throughout their upbringing, gain awareness of gender early and use it in their interactions with others. This chapter looks at how and why this distinction is made and what the three approaches can tell us about childhood and gender. It explains the biology of sex differences and summarizes some major approaches to children's acquisition of gender. It examines the impact of gender on the expectations, choices and opportunities for children and asks how far differences between boys and girls are caused by biology and how far by social construction, and touches on the legal and bureaucratic issues these considerations raise.

Chapter 6 'Innocence and experience' picks up many of the issues found in the previous chapters by discussing one of the most enduring beliefs in Western cultures – children's innocence. It focuses on images and representations of childhood. It revisits Chapter 2's discussion of the social construction of children as naturally innocent and looks at its implications. If children are naturally innocent, how can we understand children who behave in ways that appear not to be innocent? Have they been corrupted? Are they no longer children? Beliefs about children's innocence are often tied to sexuality, and the authors use this as a starting point for asking how much children know and whether innocence (and its opposites) are in the eyes of the beholder. Finally, the chapter returns to one of the topics of Chapter 1, how the concept of innocence applies to children who commit crimes. Two much-discussed cases in Britain and Norway reveal competing views of children's innocence and guilt and their capacity to understand the difference between right and wrong.

A guiding principle for the course team in planning this book has been to acknowledge wherever possible that knowledge, beliefs and understanding about childhood are culturally situated. Much scientific research on childhood, especially in developmental psychology, has been criticised for presenting its conclusions as universal truths, even though that research was based on children and young people growing up in industrialized societies, especially in Europe and North America (discussed in Chapter 3). In the same way, dominant discourses of childhood innocence need to be understood in the context of Western history and cultural traditions (Chapters 2 and 6). This issue applies even more strongly in relation to the study of children's rights, where one of the key debates is about how far the UN Convention projects a universalized image of the individualized child which fails to take account of competing cultural traditions (Chapter 4).

Making comparisons between childhoods according to cultural tradition or world location is itself fraught with difficulties. Numerous terms are in circulation, losing and gaining popularity according to their symbolic power as much as their descriptive accuracy. Examples of these include Third World, industrialized countries, developing countries, or most recently minority world and majority world. In an attempt to distinguish between parts of the world that are different in material terms we have for the most part used the labels 'North' to denote the richer, more industrialized countries, and 'South' to denote the poorer, less industrialized ones. We have adopted these labels to replace the terms 'developed' versus 'underdeveloped' or 'developing', in order to avoid the implication that 'developed' countries are superior to 'developing' countries. However, some of the readings and quotations use terms such as Third World, non-industrialized world and developing world. Also, while we have generally avoided terms such as 'the West', we use the label 'Western' to denote the cultural beliefs and practices associated with highly industrialized societies, which have their roots in the philosophy that developed in Europe and North America during the historical period sometimes called the 'Age of Enlightenment'.

In preparing this book, we aimed to draw on issues and examples from a wide range of geographical locations, including the beliefs of many different societies, both small and large. We have tried as far as possible to avoid treating childhoods in the countries of the North as the norm against which other societies might be compared and contrasted. This book (and the others in the series) have been linked to the production of audio-visual case studies of childhoods in three locations – Cape Town (South Africa), Chittagong (Bangladesh), and Oakland (California) (the books and audio-visual material together make up the Open University course U212 *Childhood*). Many of the themes of the book were explored with children, parents and communities in these three locations, and quotations from them are included in several of the chapters, especially the perspectives of individual children and young people on the experience of being a child.

This book raises more questions than it answers, but its aim is not to provide comfortable or simplistic solutions to some very complex questions. It also cannot be comprehensive. Of necessity, the authors have simplified this introduction to childhood studies by concentrating on three very different ways of thinking about and researching childhood, within an interdisciplinary approach. Overall, this book aims to stimulate critical thinking and awareness about the issues involved in studying childhood. Where do beliefs about childhood come from? What is their provenance and their history? How do these beliefs vary from one society to another? We cannot ever fully answer the question 'What is a child?' but we can begin to see ways of studying childhood and begin to understand some of its complexities.

We would like to thank all those who contributed at each stage in the preparation of this book, especially Dr Christine Griffin (University of Birmingham) and Dr Allison James (University of Hull).

Heather Montgomery and Martin Woodhead
The Open University, 2002.

References

MEAD, M. (1955) 'Theoretical setting – 1954' in MEAD, M. and WOLFENSTEIN, M. (eds) *Childhood in Contemporary Cultures*, Chicago, University of Chicago Press.

PROUT, A. and JAMES, A. (1990) 'A new paradigm for the sociology of childhood? Provenance, promise and problems' in JAMES, A. and PROUT, A. (eds) *Constructing and Deconstructing Childhood: new directions in the sociological study of childhood*, Basingstoke, The Falmer Press.

Chapter I

What is a child?

Wendy Stainton Rogers

CONTENTS

1 INTRODUCTION

Of course, you know what a child is, don't you? Everyone was a child once upon a time, after all. You almost certainly know children – your neighbours' children, those of family and friends, perhaps the children you care for or work with, and, possibly, your own children. So 'childhood' and 'children' are not obscure theoretical ideas for you: they are things you have experienced and, quite probably, play a part in your everyday life. But in some ways this familiarity is a disadvantage. When studying something abstract like physics or music, it's not hard to realize that there are things about these subjects that you know nothing about and that you need to learn. But first-hand experience of children and childhood can make people think that they know what a child is already.

Allow 15 to 20 minutes

ACTIVITY 1 What is a child?

Look at pictures 1–6. Which ones do you think definitely look like children? Which ones do not look like children? Which ones are you unsure about? Think about the choices you made. Make a list of the criteria you used in deciding which ones seem to you most 'childlike', and which ones seem least 'childlike'. From this, write some notes about what, to you, constitutes 'being a child'. If possible, ask someone else to look at the pictures, and compare your impressions with theirs.

1

2

3

4

5

6

COMMENT

When I first looked at these photos, 3 and 4 seemed to me most childlike, showing children in school, and teenagers sitting in a bedroom surrounded by posters of favourite pop stars. Photos 1 and 6 seemed least childlike, because the children seemed to be doing things more appropriate for adults – carrying a young child, and especially working on a building site. I was much less sure about photos 2 and 5. How you judge these pictures depends I think on whether or not you see them as innocent. The boys are playing with guns in 5, but pointing the 'toy' at another child's head looks menacingly similar to television and newspaper images of child soldiers carrying real weapons. I feel the same about photo 2. Is this a child playing at wearing glamorous clothes and make-up, or is there something inappropriately adult-like about the image? I am also aware that my judgements are influenced by the society I've grown up in, and by my experiences as a parent. You may judge things I thought weren't 'childlike' as normal and appropriate for children and young people.

This activity draws attention to different ways of thinking about children – various criteria that can be used to decide what is a child. Physical attributes such as small size are clear markers of childhood, and you may have felt it inappropriate to call the young people in some of these photos 'children', simply because they look too old for that term, especially the teenagers in 4. But the concept of a 'child', as this activity shows, is more complicated than this. It also depends on how children appear or what they are doing. Some of the children portrayed look as though they are 'dressed up as' or 'playing at being' adults. Others are quite definitely taking on adult roles. But think, for a minute, what is meant by the term 'taking on adult roles'. Underlying this phrase are assumptions that some roles and activities – such as doing a job or dressing up to look 'sexy' – are only 'proper' for adults. Children in these roles may be seen as having 'lost' their childhood or even as having had it 'stolen' from them. It is assumptions like these that I will be exploring in this chapter.

However, some aspects of what constitutes a 'child' cannot be seen. They have to do with how children are *treated*, and the assumptions behind the way they are treated.

Allow about 20 minutes

ACTIVITY 2   Don't treat me like a child!

Think about the following situation, and then answer the questions below.

Peter, a youth worker, is arguing with Sara. Peter has been telling Sara off for leaving the computer room unlocked, even though she had promised to leave it secure at the end of the evening. Sara gets very agitated and shouts at Peter, 'Stop treating me like a child! I just forgot, that's all.'

(a) What does 'being treated like a child' mean?

(b) Why do you think Sara objects?

Write notes describing your answers to these two questions.

COMMENT

To be 'treated like a child' (in this context, anyway) tends to mean being viewed as incapable and unreliable – as lacking the ability to act responsibly. When someone treats another person 'like a child' it also often involves taking authority over them – assuming the right (and having the power) to tell them what to do, or to criticize them. Adults usually object to being treated like this. If Sara were Peter's co-worker – say she's eighteen and training in youth work – then she probably found the telling off humiliating and demeaning. But even if she were a younger teenager, she might well experience similar feelings.

You may think that what defines a child is simply a matter of physical size and development. What Activity 2 illustrates is that there is a lot more to childhood than this. Children are treated differently from adults – the norms and rules of appropriate behaviour are not the same.

I can still remember – with great embarrassment – the incident that brought this home to me, even though it happened more than thirty years ago. I was a newly qualified teacher, and that day I had been on duty during break times as well as teaching. So I had spent much of my day supervising pupils while they went from one part of the building to another, lined up for lunch, and when they were in the playground. After school I went shopping, and as I was standing in the queue at the check-out, a woman pushed to the front. Without hesitation I looked her in the eye and said, loudly and firmly, '*Get* to the back of the queue,' pointing my arm in that direction. Then I realized just what I had done. I left my trolley right there and slunk out of the supermarket. My embarrassment was acute because I had treated the woman 'like a child' – just as I had been treating the pupils all day at school. I realized just how authoritarian adults can be – indeed, in some school settings, are *expected* to be – towards children, even when they are teenagers.

The convention sets out basic rights for children. It was drawn up in 1979 and has been ratified by almost every country in the world.

In this book our working definition of childhood is the period from birth to the age of eighteen. This is an internationally agreed definition of childhood as specified in the *United Nations Convention on the Rights of the Child* (UNCRC). As Activity 1 illustrated, this definition encompasses an enormous diversity, from small infants to young people who can be married, fight in armies, be wage earners and, indeed, may have children of their own. What, apart from chronological age, do they have in common that enables them to be called 'children'?

It is not, then, so strange to ask the question, 'What is a child?' It is by no means as obvious as it may appear in modern societies in which childhood is so powerfully taken-for-granted. The affluent parts of the industrialized world are full of commodities specifically designed for children, such as clothes, medicines, equipment (such as playpens, cots, baby-alarms, nappies and car seats), confectionery and food.

There are children's books, comics, theatre, television and films; children's computer games and educational software; children's theme parks and playgrounds. No wonder children are so powerfully real to us.

Many children are surrounded with products designed especially to appeal to them.

This is not just a matter of the commercialization of childhood in the North, where products for children represent a rich market. It also has to do with a society in which newspapers, magazines and TV constantly engage in debates about childhood and children – about child abuse, children's health, children's education; about lost and stolen childhoods, children growing up 'too fast' and so on. If this is the kind of society in which you live, then it is virtually impossible to imagine one in which the idea of a 'child' is not self-evident, and issues around 'childhood' are not matters of common and serious concern.

The argument that childhood is an invention and a relatively recent one has indeed been made by the historian Ariès. He claimed that in the Western Europe of the Middle Ages (c. 500–1500 CE) children were seen as miniature adults, with the same thinking capacities and personal qualities as adults, though, because of their small size, not quite the same physical abilities (such as strength). Equally, others have pointed out that conceptions of childhood and children differ widely between different cultures, societies and communities (see for example, Hill and Tisdall, 1997). You will be exploring these ideas further in later chapters. For now, the main message to take away is that understandings of what a child is are not fixed. They have differed over historical time and they vary from society to society, culture to culture, community to community.

1.1 Children's views of childhood

Children as well as adults are trying to make sense of what it means to be a child and what it means to become an adult. In preparation for this book we interviewed children in the United States, South Africa and Bangladesh. We asked them what being a child means to them:

Brian (8 years, Oakland, US)

'I'm a child because, if I was a baby I would be still small. And, and now I'm a child because I'm not a baby any more. Because I'm, because I'm grown up. And a baby is sort of like, is like almost one year old, two years old or three years old.'

Sophie (12 years, Oakland, US)

'I think I am kind of a child. But I'm kind of more getting out of my child stage and more into my like older stage... I think I'll be an adult when I get my bat mitzvah. I'll feel more grown up.'

Joshua (8 years, Capetown, South Africa)

'A child is like a little person who's learning how to be ... moulded into adult.'

Asanda (15 years, Capetown, South Africa)

'Ever since I joined Molo Songololo [a youth organization] I've kind of changed, in the way that I have – what can I call it? – I have grown into myself, you understand, because now I've been given a chance to express my views: what I think... how I live and how I would express myself as a child.'

Yassir and Yamin (14 years, Chittagong, Bangladesh)

'I think an adult is somebody who has passed school. And we're still young so that's why we are a child... There are less worries being a child. And we would have to be a lot more responsible when we are an adult.'

Maya (about 15 years, Chittagong, Bangladesh)

'There are more responsibilities as a wife and mother but I don't feel like an adult. I feel I'm a young girl. I don't feel like I'm a grown-up.'

1.2 When do children stop being children and become adults?

One way of trying to answer the question, 'What is a child?' is by considering the question, 'When do children stop being children and become adults?' This may, at first, seem a strange place to start. But looking at boundaries can be a valuable way of understanding a concept. Looking at what marks the difference between what something is and what it is not is a good way of gaining insight into what it is.

Earlier I stressed that childhood differs from culture to culture and over historical time. A good example of this is the law on when childhood ends and adulthood begins, which depends on when you were born and where. Legally my childhood did not end until I reached the age of 21, but if I had been born after 1950 my childhood would have ended on my eighteenth birthday. This is because in 1969 the law on the 'age of majority' – the age at which an individual gains adult status – was changed from 21 to 18 in England and Wales. The age of legal majority is a convention – but a useful one, in that it clarifies what an individual can do, and what their entitlements are. But there are many other ways of defining when childhood ends.

Allow about 15 to 20 minutes

ACTIVITY 3 **When does childhood end?**

Begin by writing down a list of at least three *different* ways of defining when a child ceases to be a child and becomes an adult. Think as widely as you can, about all aspects of 'being a child'. Try not to spend more than 10 minutes on this part of the activity.

When you have written your list, look at the grid shown below. Write your answers in the right hand column. Perhaps your answers won't fit these categories – or you think one of them could go into more than one section. Don't worry – there are no right responses. The aim is just to get a general idea of the different ways of defining when childhood ends.

The kind of definition or idea that most informs this answer	Your answers
A definition that focuses on an individual's **developmental status**. Examples include children's bodily maturation, the hormonal changes of puberty and their increasing thinking capacities.	
A definition that views the transition from childhood to adulthood as a matter of the individual's **social status** – for example, gaining the right to participate in certain religious rites.	
Definitions of children that focus on children's **civil status**. In this category would be legal formulations (such as 'age of majority') and social policy provisions (for example a child's entitlement to services such as education).	

COMMENT

In the first category the kinds of definitions you thought about may have included physical aspects of growing up – such as the acquisition of what are called secondary sexual characteristics (like the development of breasts or the start of menstruation for girls). In this category you may also have included other forms of development, such as gaining adult thinking and reasoning capacities.

The sorts of thing you may have included in the second category are passing through religious or cultural rites of passage. These include the Jewish bar and bat mitzvah, Christian ceremonies such as 'confirmation', and in some cultures practices like circumcision which are performed to mark the transition from childhood to adulthood.

In the third category you probably included the legal definition of age of majority that I have already mentioned. Or maybe you listed the right to vote that goes with it. But you probably included other ways in which the law can set age-criteria for doing other things – such as driving a car or getting married. You may also have thought about entitlements to benefits. In some countries, for instance, parents get payments from the state to contribute to the costs of bringing up children, and these are provided for children aged up to a certain age.

1.3 Different approaches

These different ways of answering the question 'When does childhood end?' highlight the wide range of differing understandings of what constitutes children and childhood. They offer three contrasting ways to make sense of childhood, and give a flavour of the main approaches discussed in the rest of this chapter.

- A *scientific approach* seeks to establish the objective facts about children through devising theories and testing them by observation and experiment.

The term 'world view' is used to describe an overall way of looking at and making sense of the world.

- A *social constructionist approach* views different ideas about childhood and understandings of what constitutes a child as the products of different world views.

- An *applied approach* is used by organizations, institutions and people who have responsibilities for children's care and welfare. It is concerned with practical questions about children. How should they be treated? What are their needs and rights? What are the obligations towards them of those responsible for their welfare – such as their parents, professionals and the state?

This three-way classification of approaches to the study of children and childhood is of course an oversimplification. In practice, each approach includes a wide range of perspectives and ways of carrying out research. But it is useful to start from a simple classification in order to convey a sense of the range of standpoints that can be taken when engaging with debates about children and childhood. Each approach 'looks at' children and childhood from different perspectives, focuses on different issues and concerns, and leads to different ways of answering questions about children and childhood. In particular, scientific and social constructionist approaches adopt different stances on what people can 'know' about children, and on how they should go about acquiring this knowledge. An applied approach is slightly different. It is less concerned with what people 'know' and more concerned with what people can 'do' for and about children. But an applied approach frequently draws on knowledge from the other two approaches in trying to answer questions of policy or practice.

In this chapter I will introduce you to the key elements of these three approaches. I will draw on one issue in particular to illustrate the way these approaches can be applied to the study of children and childhood – the issue of when children can be held to be responsible for their actions. In England, in 1993, two ten-year-old boys were prosecuted for the murder of another, much younger boy, James Bulger. This case became the focus for debate about childhood, especially about the age at which children are capable of understanding right from wrong; about how children who commit serious crimes should be treated; and more generally about what it means to be a child.

Section 2 examines a scientific approach that seeks to establish the facts about childhood. I have illustrated this by examining research into how children develop – in particular how they acquire the ability to know right from wrong. Findings from such studies are sometimes used to guide decisions, for example, about when children should be held legally responsible for crimes they commit.

Section 3 introduces a social constructionist approach. It illustrates how this differs from a scientific approach by taking up the theme of Section 2 – children's law breaking – and outlines the different perspectives that can be taken to it. So in this section you will explore how different constructions of what a child is imply different positions on their criminal responsibility and hence different approaches to dealing with children who commit crimes.

Section 4 tackles an applied approach. Again taking up the issue of children's criminal responsibility, it looks at different ways of dealing with children who commit serious crimes such as murder. It explores alternative models of juvenile justice – alternative ways in which the law can respond.

The chapter ends with a short review section, *Section 5*.

SUMMARY OF SECTION 1

- Childhood is not simply defined by the bodily immaturity of being a young human. It is also marked by the way children are dressed, by the way they are treated, and by social and cultural norms about what they should and should not do.

- Concepts of what a child is vary from culture to culture and from one historical time to another. Some definitions relate to children's biological immaturity, some definitions are constituted in laws, but others are more socially and culturally constituted.

- Childhood can also be studied from different points of view. This chapter explores three major viewpoints or approaches: scientific, social constructionist and applied.

2 A SCIENTIFIC APPROACH

In this section I will concentrate on how theories of child development have been constructed and tested using a scientific approach. I have to acknowledge at once that there are different and sometimes competing accounts of 'science', but most of them would agree on some basic features. Science involves:

- devising a *theory* (of how children's thinking capacities develop, for instance);
- from the theory, making *predictions* (such as how children will behave at different stages in their development and in particular circumstances);
- and then *testing* those predictions (by, for example, carrying out experiments).

From the results of such studies information is then gained – for example, about the way children's thinking capacities change as they mature, and at what ages they become competent to undertake particular tasks.

There are other ways in which a scientific approach is used in the study of children. For example, survey methods have been used to compare the numbers of children who die from certain diseases in rich and poor countries. Another scientific approach involves carrying out careful observations, for instance of the interactions between a parent and a young child.

It is important to make clear that a scientific approach builds heavily on systematic research, but not all research into childhood is linked to a traditional view of science. For example, in Chapter 5 you will read about studies of gendered childhoods that use a social constructionist approach to research.

However, in this chapter, you will be introduced to some examples of scientific approaches to researching children's development.

Put simply, science consists of seeking to establish universal laws of cause and effect (whether about physical processes like gravity or psychological and physiological processes like development) through developing theories and testing them by observation and experiment. You can see how these work out in practice in Section 2.1 on Piaget.

2.1 Piaget's theory of cognitive development

Jean Piaget (1896–1980) has been one of the most influential developmental theorists. He began his career as a biologist, but then turned his attention to children's development. For one of his early studies he watched groups of boys playing marbles. He noticed that at different ages they approached the game in different ways. The youngest did not seem to follow any rules at all, they just enjoyed seeing how the marbles rolled, the noises and patterns they made as they knocked against each other. But older boys started playing according to 'the rules of the game', and often had arguments about whether the rules were being followed correctly. And then he noticed that still older boys had started to challenge the rules and to negotiate about how to change them to devise new games (Piaget, 1932).

From observations like this, Piaget built up a theory of how children's thinking capacities typically develop – this is usually referred to as his theory of *cognitive development*. He proposed that children's thinking capacities do not gradually improve as they mature. Children, he argued, do not become more and more cognitively competent, bit by bit, as they grow up. Rather, he claimed that children undergo a series of transformations in *how* they think, passing through a sequence of *stages* of development. The stages Piaget proposed are usually summarized as follows:

- sensori-motor: 0–2 years (approximately)
- pre-operational: 2–6 years (approximately)
- concrete operational: 6–12 years (approximately)
- formal operational: 12 years and over (approximately).

Piaget also devised simple experiments to test his theory. One of his best known experiments is summarized in Box 1.

Box 1 The conservation of liquids task

1 First the child is shown two identical transparent beakers, A and B, each about two-thirds full of water. They are placed side-by-side in front of the child. The experimenter seeks the child's agreement that the amount of water in both is the same, if necessary adding or taking away small amounts until the child is satisfied.

2 Next the experimenter pours all the water from beaker A into another beaker, C, which is taller and narrower than the first one.

3 The experimenter then places the new taller beaker C alongside beaker B and asks the child, 'Is there now more water in the new beaker than in the other beaker or less, or the same amount?'

Typically, up to the age of about six or seven years, the child will assert that the amount of water has changed and is now more than before it was poured. If the child is then asked why this is so, he or she will tend to say something like 'because it's taller' or 'because it's thinner'.

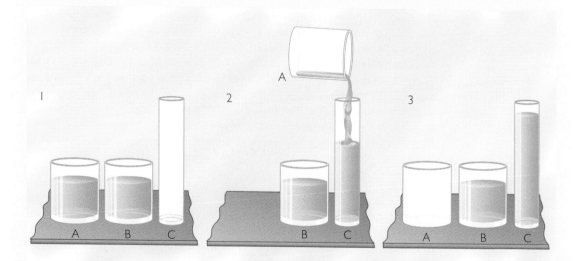

Figure 1 The conservation of liquids task.

Piaget's research group carried out the same basic experiment in lots of different ways. They asked children to compare balls of plasticine after one had been shaped into a sausage. They asked children to compare two identical rows of counters, after one had been stretched out into a longer line. In each case younger children appeared to reason that the change in the appearance meant the quantity of water, plasticine or counters had also changed. (Light and Oates, 1990, pp. 101–106.)

Notice the implications of Piaget's theory. It proposes that young children are not just cognitively less able than adults; rather, they think in fundamentally different ways from adults. Remember that Piaget studied as a biologist. In some ways his theory portrays child development as rather like that of a butterfly, which also undergoes a series of transformations as it develops: first there is an egg, then a caterpillar, then a chrysalis and finally the adult imago.

Piaget's were bold claims and his theory and experiments have subsequently been criticized. Developmental theorists now recognize that children's cognitive development is a lot more complicated than a simple, linear sequence of biologically-based transformations, and you will be learning more about this in Chapter 3. For now, however, Piaget's theory provides a classic illustration of the *scientific approach* to childhood. At its core is the assumption that we can find out about children through establishing objective facts. From observation a theorist can devise hypotheses about the processes going on (in this case the processes of cognitive development). And by testing these hypotheses through conducting experiments, facts can be discovered that add to our understanding of the processes involved. In other words, according to Piaget's approach, answers to the question 'What is a child?' can be found through well conducted scientific research.

An hypothesis is a statement or prediction that can be tested by conducting experiments or carrying out careful observations.

2.2 Knowing 'right' from 'wrong'

I am now going to look at a specific aspect of development – the acquisition of the capacity to tell 'right' from 'wrong'. A few weeks ago I went out to tea with a friend with my granddaughter, Katy, who is just coming up to three. On the way home I looked in my handbag for a tissue, and was mortified to find that Katy must have put my friend's car keys in my handbag at some time in the afternoon. We had to turn round and return them – to a very relieved friend, who had no idea where her keys had gone. Neither of us blamed Katy, of course. We both knew that at almost three she had no understanding of the significance of what she had done. Certainly neither of us saw Katy as having 'stolen' the keys. But it would have been different if Katy had been, say, five or six. Then we would probably have seen her behaviour as mischievous and naughty, for by then we would have expected her to have had a clear understanding of the consequences of taking the keys.

In order to treat children appropriately, adults need to be aware of the extent of children's understanding of the significance and consequences of their actions. When children have this understanding, they are able to make moral judgements about what they do. Indeed, developing this ability is an important goal of child rearing. Young children are taught by, for example, asking them to take the role of the other. Adults say things like, 'Don't snatch the toy from Aslan, how would you feel if he did that to you?'

Piaget's work has been influential in this context. Some of his research was carried out around this question – when does a child gain the capacity to see things from the perspective of another person? He conducted many painstaking experiments to establish how and at what stage children make the shift from seeing the world from just their own perspective, to being able to imagine how another person will see it differently. For one of these experiments Piaget and his collaborators asked children to look at a model of three mountains – see Box 2.

Box 2 The three mountains task

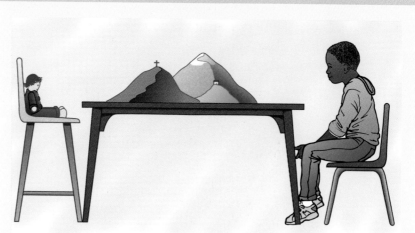

Figure 2 The three mountains viewed from different positions

The three mountains were constructed of papier mâché on a board about one metre square. Each was a different size and colour. The largest was grey and snow-capped, the middle-sized was brown with a red cross on it, and the smallest was green with a house on it.

Children were asked to view the scene. In the basic experiment a small doll was then placed opposite the child, and the child asked what the view of the mountains looked like from the doll's point of view. To assess the child's perspective-taking abilities, the experimenter asked them to arrange three pieces of cardboard shaped like the mountains. The experimenter also asked the child to select the doll's view from a set of ten pictures. Finally the experimenter asked the child to make judgements about what the doll would see when placed in other positions around the scene.

Just as with the experiments on quantity in Box 1, children younger than about seven or eight were very strongly influenced by the appearances of things. In this case they were unable to imagine how the scene would look from another person's point of view. In Piaget's words, they were unable to de-centre, reflecting their egocentric view of the world.

Insights gained from scientific studies of children's egocentricity and perspective-taking abilities can have important implications for the way people think about individual children's actions as well as for policy-making – for example, in terms of devising law and social policy in respect of children who break the law. Until children have gained an understanding of right and wrong you cannot hold them responsible for their wrongdoing. Scientific research helps to inform, for instance, decisions about the age at which a child's misbehaviour might merit legal sanctions, and at what age a child's law-breaking might merit the same sanctions that we impose upon adult criminals. It is obvious that not-quite-three-year-old Katy cannot be seen as having 'stolen' my friend's keys. It would be unthinkable for my friend to have insisted on calling the police, and if we had, the police would have been distinctly unimpressed. But the situation might have been different if Katy had been fifteen and had taken money from my friend's purse.

What does a scientific approach have to offer in these circumstances? You might be shocked by my suggestion that the police could be called to deal with fifteen-year-old Katy's behaviour. Surely that would be something we could deal with privately? All of us have our opinions about when and in what circumstances children should be held responsible for breaking the law. Science cannot tell us what to do in situations like this. But what this approach can do is obtain evidence about typically-developing children's cognitive capacities – about whether, at fifteen, Katy is capable of knowing that what she was doing was wrong and against the law. In this way science can help establish the stage of development that a child needs to attain in order to judge that they have committed a crime rather than having been merely 'naughty'.

2.3 Kohlberg's theory of moral development

Consider the following situation. A woman is in the final stages of a terminal illness. The doctor treating her decides, once the illness becomes very painful and distressing for her, to give her a drug that will accelerate her death. He injects the drug, and she dies some minutes later. Her husband is distraught – he is terribly upset that she has died. The question is – was the doctor morally justified in his actions?

Your response to this question will depend upon your own moral values and judgement. A developmental psychologist, Lawrence Kohlberg, used moral dilemmas like this one to study how children develop the capacity to make moral judgements.

Kohlberg used Piaget's stage-theory of cognitive development (which included the development of moral reasoning) as a starting point for proposing a theory of children's moral development. He believed that this was an appropriate subject for applying a scientific approach because he held that moral judgements are universal – and hence the development of moral reasoning can be understood in terms of 'laws of human behaviour': 'Unlike judgements of prudence or aesthetics, moral judgements tend to be universal, consistent, and based on objective, impersonal, or ideal grounds' (Kohlberg, 1968, p. 490 cited in Thomas, 1996). On this basis, and again (like

Piaget) through a combination of observation and experimentation, Kohlberg devised a stage-theory of moral development. His scheme has three levels, each of which has within it two stages (see Table 1).

Table I Kohlberg's stage-theory of moral development

Levels and stages	Orientation of moral reasoning	Description
Preconventional level		
Stage 1	Punishment and obedience	Wrong things are those that are punished and you obey rules to avoid punishment.
Stage 2	Hedonism	Good and bad are to do with satisfying your own needs. You do what is best for you.
Conventional level		
Stage 3	Interpersonal concordance	Being good is about being loyal, and looking after the interests of those you care about, who show empathy and affection towards you.
Stage 4	Law and order	Being good is about obeying the law and following the rules, which may be statutory or religious.
Principled level		
Stage 5	Social contract	Being good is about fostering the welfare and wellbeing of others.
Stage 6	Universal ethical principles	Being good is defined by your own conscience, in accordance with self-determined ethical principles.

(Adapted from Thomas, 1996, p. 465 [Recast and simplified from Kohlberg, 1967])

Kohlberg proposed that, like other forms of cognitive development, moral development progresses through each of these stages sequentially. To reach Stage 6 a child has to pass through Stages 1 to 5.

Kohlberg used moral dilemmas like the one with which this section began to test his theory and to discover at what age children reach the different levels of cognitive capacity. In his studies, children were given descriptions of moral dilemmas and asked whether the protagonists were 'right' or 'wrong' in the actions they took. Kohlberg and his associates carried out a number of studies using this technique. They began by studying the responses of 75 boys living in the US, and subsequently went on to re-test them as they grew up to adulthood.

To get an impression of how the studies were carried out, compare, for example, these responses to the dilemma about the doctor who practised euthanasia.

13-year-old boy: Maybe it would be good to put her out of her pain, she'd be better off that way. But the husband wouldn't want it, it's not like an animal. If a pet dies you can get along without it – it isn't something you really need. Well, you can get a new wife, but it's not really the same.

16-year-old boy: The doctor wouldn't have the right to take a life, no human has the right. He can't create life, he shouldn't destroy it.

(Kohlberg, 1967, pp. 174–5, cited in Thomas, 1996, pp. 465–6)

The thirteen-year-old boy's response was assessed by Kohlberg and his associates as being at Stage 2, since it focuses on the value of life as instrumental – as serving a purpose. The boy's answer compares the value and function of the woman's life for her, and for her husband. He concludes that the woman should not be killed, because the husband could not simply go out and get a new wife in the way he could go out and get a new pet. The sixteen-year-old boy's response was assessed at being at Stage 4, since it was seen as based upon religious doctrine about the sacredness of life, alluding to the belief that only God can create life so only God can take it away.

In other studies Kohlberg and his colleagues discovered that children's moral development is influenced by their upbringing and their culture. These can affect how rapidly, for example, a child moves through the stages. They found very considerable variation. Some ten year olds, for example, achieve Stage 3 – whereas the majority of children of that age operate at Stage 1 or 2. Some sixteen-year-olds continue to be reasoning at Stage 2 when the majority have at least reached Stage 4. So there is no clear-cut empirical answer to the question of at what age children achieve a Stage 4 of moral development, when they clearly understand the need to follow civil or religious rules and laws.

Kohlberg's attempt to construct a scientific account of children's moral development has been controversial, and some of the criticisms of his research will be summarized in the next section. What is important here is to note the potential power of this kind of knowledge.

Thus what a scientific approach offers here is a means of assessing whether or not an *individual* child has reached a particular level of cognitive competence and moral understanding.

Subsequently, techniques like these have been used by psychiatrists and psychologists when they carry out assessments for courts deciding upon whether a child can be held criminally responsible for their wrongdoing. Such an assessment was made, for example, on the two 10-year-old boys who were prosecuted for the murder of James Bulger, in 1993, in Liverpool, England. The psychiatrist concluded that they did have an understanding that what they had done was wrong, which allowed them to be tried for murder.

SUMMARY OF SECTION 2

- Science seeks to establish objective facts by using rigorous methods. A scientific approach to the study of child development typically consists of three main activities: firstly, constructing theories to explain aspects of child development; secondly, from these theories making predictions; thirdly, testing these predictions, through experiments, observations and surveys.

- Piaget used scientific methods for testing his theory of child development. He hypothesized that children do not gradually get better and better in their thinking capacities, but rather go through a systematic progression of distinct stages. Using observation and experiments, Piaget produced data to test his theory.

- Kohlberg and his colleagues asked children to respond to a series of moral dilemmas. On the basis of their answers, he constructed a theory of stages of moral development through which children pass in their maturation from a child's way of thinking to adult levels of competence.

- The data obtained from such studies can be used to address practical questions such as the ages and stages at which children acquire an understanding of 'right' from 'wrong'.

3 A SOCIAL CONSTRUCTIONIST APPROACH

This approach sees different ideas about children and childhood as products of different world views. A look at the different ways in which children who commit crimes are treated will be used to illustrate the social constructionist approach.

In 2001 a decision was made to release the two boys who had killed two-year-old James Bulger in 1993. At the time of the killing the boys were ten years old. They were prosecuted for murder in a criminal court, convicted, and sentenced to be held in secure units. These are establishments run not by the prison service but by local authorities (the main local government bodies in the UK). Children who have committed serious crimes and are held to be dangerous are kept in them. The primary purpose of such units is not to imprison but to seek to rehabilitate – to offer therapy and intensive social, emotional and educational support. The aim is to try to overcome the problems that are held to have led these children into wrongdoing. They treat the children as in need of *help*, rather than in need of *punishment*.

When the two boys reached the age of eighteen, they could either have been released or transferred to a young offender's institution. These have a much more punitive regime than the secure unit in which they had been held, with the emphasis on imprisonment rather than rehabilitation. The decision was made to release the two eighteen-year-olds – a decision which stirred up very considerable media and public reaction.

A C T I V I T Y 4   Different perspectives on criminal responsibility

Read the different viewpoints set out in the extract from the *Guardian*. This column appears in a weekly section on parenting, and presents a range of viewpoints on a different question each week. Note that the opinions expressed are the respondents' own views, or those of the organization they represent. They are not 'matters of fact' but opinions, although these opinions may be informed by scientific research into children's moral understanding, as described in Section 2.

This column was published in the week that the decision was made to release the two boys who killed James Bulger. For each of the different viewpoints write one or two sentences summarizing the opinion being expressed.

Interviews by **Diane Taylor**

thepanel

The question: The age of criminal responsibility in England is 10, which allowed James Bulger's killers to be prosecuted. Should it be altered?

Dr Ann Hagell
Co-director, Policy Research Bureau
There is no other legal or social arena where we give children complete responsibility at 10, mostly for good reason. The important thing is the consequence of being over the age of criminal responsibility, not the age per se. Other countries with a very low age (10 or less) usually have a period where responsibility is not absolute until mid-to-late teens, or where the response to breaking the law is welfare-oriented rather than retributive. For example, the age in Scotland is eight but the consequences are almost all framed within the welfare system.
Verdict: **Age isn't the issue**

Lyn Costello
Mothers Against Murder and Aggression
Children of 10 know the difference between right and wrong. They know you don't hurt small children. The killing of James Bulger was a planned and covered-up crime. Any parent will tell you there are cases where children play rough and get hurt, but they know it's wrong to kill a child and Thompson and Venables knew that, otherwise they wouldn't have covered it up and lied about it. We have children as young as eight, or even six, terrorizing people on estates such as the one I live on. I also think parents should be held responsible for their children's behaviour.
Verdict: **Yes, to 8**

Carolyn Hamilton
Director, Children's Legal Centre
I would say about 14. I think that at that age children are better able to understand the consequences of what they are doing. A child of 10 who has committed an offence is more appropriately dealt with in the care system than in the criminal justice system. The European court says that a child must be able to participate in their own defence and I think a child of 14 is able to do that. The Committee on the Rights of the Child has said that 10 is too young for criminal responsibility. If our aim is rehabilitation, it is best done under the civil system, not the criminal justice system.
Verdict: **Yes, to 14**

Beate Raedergard
Mother whose child was killed by young boys
My five-year-old daughter, Silje, was killed by two boys near our home in Trondheim, Norway. It was a year after the killing of James Bulger, and the two incidents were compared in the press. In Norway, where the age of criminality is 15, the boys were treated differently. Silje was stripped, stoned and beaten, and left for dead. I do not understand why and I will never recover, but I don't hate the boys. I think they understood what they had done, but not the consequences. The boys went back to school, were helped by psychologists and have had to learn how to treat others to fit back into society.
Verdict: **Yes, to 15**

(*Guardian G2*, 20 June 2001, p. 10)

COMMENT

These opinions cover a very wide range. At one extreme Lyn Costello from the organization 'Mothers Against Murder and Aggression' is arguing for lowering the age of criminal responsibility on the grounds that even young children have a basic understanding of right and wrong. At the other Beate Raedergard is arguing for raising it to fifteen, for forgiveness, and for rehabilitation. Her opinion is all the more striking because her own daughter was killed by young boys. In between there is a range of opinions that vary in their assessment of the age at which a child should be held criminally responsible. However, most take the view that children who commit serious crimes like murder are better dealt with by welfare measures rather than by the criminal justice system.

You will be looking at the comparison between the Raedergard case and the Bulger case in much more detail in Chapter 6. So I won't go any further into the issues it raises here other than to note that whereas James Bulger's killers were tried in a full adult court and convicted of murder, Silje's killers were not subjected to any legal sanctions at all and, as Beate Raedergard mentioned, they returned to school soon after the incident.

Some of these opinions may have been informed by the scientific knowledge about children's moral development in Section 2. But the range of viewpoints suggests more is at stake than whether or not children can understand right from wrong. The purpose of this activity is to illustrate that not only do opinions vary about specific questions – in this case what the age of criminal responsibility should be – they also differ in 'where they are coming from', in terms of the broader views about childhood being expressed.

3.1 Different discourses of childhood

The term 'discourse' is used to mean a self-contained set of interconnected ideas held together by a particular ideology or view of the world.

One way of making sense of what is going on here is to use the concept of discourse, a concept that is extensively used in social constructionist work. The term discourse is taken to mean a whole set of interconnected ideas that work together in a self-contained way, ideas that are held together by a particular ideology or view of the world. People can talk about, for example, a 'children's rights discourse' or a 'liberal-humanistic discourse' – each of which draws upon its own particular knowledge-base, works from its own particular set of assumptions, offers its own explanation of 'how the world works' and incorporates its own set of values and ethics.

The views expressed in the *Guardian* extract go beyond claims about children's capacity for moral understanding. They also express competing discourses about what children 'are' and how they should be treated. Two very different images of the child have been especially powerful. According to one image children are inherently 'innocent and wholesome'. According to another image, children are inherently 'wicked and sinful'. Each leads to a particular 'discourse of childhood'.

The 'innocent and wholesome' viewpoint is based on the assumption that children are inherently good. When they behave badly, this is not from any innate evil or wickedness, but because they either do not understand or because they are acting out in response to mistreatment to which they have been subjected. This viewpoint draws upon a broader discourse of childhood, which sees it as being (or at least that it should be) a time of happiness and innocence, a protected time when children are to be allowed to enjoy their childhood before having to face the trials, tribulations and responsibilities of adulthood. The journalist Nikki Gerrard encapsulates this image very well when she describes a child as 'lispy, thumb-sucking, winsome, adorable, nostalgic and wholesome'. This, she says, is the image of 'a picture-book childhood' (Gerrard, 1997, p. 3). One term that is used for this is the *Romantic discourse of childhood*. Victorian artists and book illustrators frequently represented children this way, as in the picture of the little girl walking with a lamb. Note that the idealized setting, the white dress and the inclusion of the lamb are all potent symbols of the child's innocence and affinity with nature.

A Victorian Romantic view of childhood shown in *Beside the River* by Agnes Gardner King.

The 'wicked and sinful' viewpoint is based upon a discourse framed around the notion of 'original sin'. It assumes that children are inherently lacking in morality and hence children need to be civilized – need to be taught right from wrong and how to overcome their base, animal nature through adult intervention. This is sometimes labelled the *Puritan discourse of childhood*. Another journalist, this time Janet Daley, encapsulates this discourse well, here writing specifically about the two boys who killed two-year-old James Bulger: 'What happened to him [James Bulger] seems to me not an incomprehensible freakish incident but simply the worst possible example of amoral childish viciousness: horrible precisely to the degree that it was childlike – random, aimless and without conscience.' (Daley, 1993, p. 18)

You will be examining these two discourses in much more detail in the next chapter, as well as in Chapter 6. For now you can begin to see how adopting a particular discourse of childhood implies very different ways of thinking about and treating children.

If you adopt a Romantic discourse of childhood this suggests that you should, as far as you can, protect children's innocence. You should take measures to separate them from all the concerns of the adult world – from sex, from violence, from worries about the future. You should do your best to make their childhood happy and carefree. At the same time, you should be forgiving and understanding towards children who do wrong. You should recognize children's inherent goodness, and acknowledge that when they do wrong, this is not because they are evil. Rather it must have happened because they have been mistreated or deprived in some way. When children commit crimes they should be offered the help they need to fit back into society.

By contrast, if you adopt a Puritan discourse of childhood this suggests that children will, if left to their own devices, resort to savagery, and need to be carefully controlled, regulated and disciplined. This image is powerfully portrayed in the story of Cruel Frederick, from a book of moral tales for

Cruel Frederick

Here is cruel Frederick, see!
A horrid wicked boy was he;
He caught the flies, poor little things,
And then tore off their tiny wings,
He killed the birds, and broke the chairs,
And threw the kitten down the stairs;
And oh! far worse than all beside,
He whipped his Mary, till she cried.

An extract from a moral tale in the children's book *Struwwelpeter*.

children. Originally published in Germany around 1900 under the title *Struwwelpeter*, it included graphic images to accompany verses warning children about the dire consequences of indulging in a whole range of childish sins, including children incinerated after playing with matches, and thumb-suckers having their thumbs cut off by the scissor-man.

This discourse implies that adults should have authority over children, and should use this authority to civilize children and punish their wrongdoing, even if this makes the child unhappy or causes them short-term pain and distress. Note that these competing images of childhood as innocent or as wicked are frequently linked to children's gender, a point that will be followed up in Chapters 5 and 6.

3.2 Social constructionism

This consideration of competing discourses of childhood is an example of the second approach to children and childhood that I want to explore with you in this chapter. As you can see, it differs markedly from the scientific approach discussed in Section 2. Whereas science is concerned with establishing the objective facts about children, social constructionism has another goal entirely. Its aim is to describe the alternative ways in which we can answer the questions 'What is a child?' and 'What is childhood?', to explore the origins of these questions, and, crucially, to examine the *consequences* of adopting the different answers.

Thus, as I mentioned earlier, a crucial difference between social constructionist and scientific approaches is that they take fundamentally different stances on the nature of knowledge. Put simply, science views knowledge as objective, value-free and independent from the process of gaining it. Social contructionism, by contrast, views knowledge as always constructed – and hence heavily influenced by whose knowledge it is, how the person went about 'discovering' it, and, crucially, why? For what purpose is the knowledge to be used?

Consequently, there are significant differences in the ways in which research is conducted. Scientific research methods are designed to discover 'facts', using experimentation and conducting surveys in order to *explain* cause and effect. Constructionist research methods are designed to *explicate* (literally, to 'unfold') and explore what may be going on in relation to a particular research question. So a first principle of social constructionism is that there are alternative ways of viewing social phenomena – such as 'childhood' and 'children' – which will influence the actions people take and the value judgements they make. Perceptions and understandings vary between one culture and another, and from one point in history to another.

Whereas scientific approaches seek to discover universal laws of cause and effect that underpin the process of growing up, social constructionism emphasizes the diversity of ways that childhood is constituted and experienced in different situations and circumstances. An example here would be the way beliefs and expectations about childhood vary according to economic and social context. So, in most societies for most periods of human history, a high value has been placed on children's economic contribution – children were expected to work from an early age in the home, in the fields, on the streets or in factories. In modern industrial economies, beliefs about children are very different – shaped by the expectation that much of childhood will be spent learning at school.

Social constructionism, more radically, challenges the status of scientific knowledge itself, as a particular way of understanding childhood. No form of knowledge (even scientific knowledge) is held to be universally 'true' or useful. It is always an *interpretation* that people make, and is always a product of human activity (including conducting scientific research). An example here is the challenge that has been presented to Kohlberg's assumption that 'moral judgements tend to be universal, consistent, and based on objective, impersonal, or ideal grounds' (as described in Section 2.3). From an extreme social constructionist perspective, nothing is 'objective' – all knowledge is a product of human meaning-making.

In fact Kohlberg's assumption has been roundly criticized, even within the scientific approach. The psychologist Carol Gilligan argued that Kohlberg was presenting a specifically masculine world view when he constructed his scale of moral development (Gilligan, 1982). Morality from a masculine perspective, she contended, tends to place the highest value on abstract notions like 'justice'. Hence Kohlberg set this as the most advanced stage (Stage 6) of moral development. But from a feminine perspective the highest value is generally placed on care for others. Thus Gilligan proposed that moral judgements are not universal: they differ between men and women. According to Gilligan, girls develop differently from boys in that the mature, adult end-point they reach is different. Gilligan observed that all of Kohlberg's early studies were based on his sample of boys. When he and his colleagues came on to study girls' moral development they found that girls tended, on average, to score lower than boys. Girls tended to be slower in their progress through the stages, and fewer eventually reached Stage 6. So they concluded that girls are inferior to boys in their moral development. Not so, argued Gilligan. Rather masculine and feminine world views are different. So girls' moral development is not worse, just different.

Gilligan's criticisms illustrate very powerfully how knowledge can be made to *appear* objective when it is so clearly not. Kohlberg left himself open to criticism in the way he went about his research (though studying only males was not at all uncommon in psychological research in the 1960s). He certainly left himself open to the charge of masculine bias. But the stance that extreme social constructionists take is that *all* knowledge is the product of a particular world view. In that sense, they would argue, there is no such thing as 'unbiased knowledge'.

Kohlberg's work has also been criticized – from a more specifically social constructionist stance – as ethnocentric. That is, in assuming that values and moral judgements are not only universal, but also that the Western philosophy of moral values is the benchmark against which a child's moral development can be judged, Kohlberg was operating from the conviction that the Western world view is more advanced.

Kohlberg's critics have pointed out that his stages assume that the Western world view on morality is superior to other perspectives. Kohlberg's Stage 6 – that defines 'being good' as a matter of an individual's own conscience, in accordance with self-determined ethical principles – would not be regarded as the highest form of moral reasoning in many other world views. Religious people of many persuasions view obeying God's will – as revealed in sacred texts – as the highest level of morality. Equally others would regard being law-abiding as the most moral basis for behaviour, and others service and duty to one's family.

Orientalism is a term first coined by Palestininan writer Edward Said. He claimed that historically, Western scholars studied the Orient (and the Middle East in particular) and constructed images of those in the Orient as irrational, depraved and childlike and by contrast with this, images of themselves as civilized, industrious and virtuous.

A key theorist in this context is Edward Said (1994) who has challenged the 'Orientalism' of Western thought. Said argues that the world view that now pervades science – and, more generally, scholarship and public life across the world – tends to regard its own knowledge as 'natural' and 'factual', and to treat all other forms of knowledge as mere dogma, belief, myth or superstition. This, he asserts, is fundamentally racist, embodying an implicit sense of superiority.

Social constructionism, even in its most extreme form, does not deny the practical usefulness of science. In situations like deciding whether a child should stand trial for a crime he or she has committed, for instance, it recognizes the necessity of assessing the child's level of moral reasoning. Rather it cautions us about assuming that there are universal, objective facts – such as any absolute measure of a child's degree of moral reasoning. A constructionist would draw attention to the impact of different ideologies upon how moral reasoning is defined, and hence see attempts to measure it as only being able to arrive at a *working* definition – that is, one that works in a particular set of circumstances. Constructionists acknowledge that such working definitions may be necessary to achieve practical outcomes. But what we must not do, they argue, is to assume that because a particular definition works in a particular situation, that it is therefore objective and unchallengeable.

3.3 The social construction of childhood

Social constructionism asserts that 'children' and 'childhood' are not facts of nature but social constructions. Images of children, attitudes towards them, expectations about them, understandings of who and what they are – like all images, attitudes, expectations, understandings – are socially constructed. The 'realities' that people take for granted – the things they 'know' about their world and how it works – are not what they seem to be: self-evident truths about what the world is *really* like. Rather they are always the products of human meaning-making. In other words, they are constructed through social processes. From this perspective childhood is what a particular group or culture or society defines it as being: 'Childhood is the life-space which our culture limits it to be i.e. its definitions through the courts, the school, the family and also through psychology and philosophy' (Qvortrup, 1994, p. 3).

| READING

Turn now to Reading A, an edited extract from the article 'The social construction of childhood' by Rex Stainton Rogers. As you read it, make notes for yourself about what it suggests are the main elements of social constructionism.

The first point is that what people 'make' of the world depends on context – it is different, for example, in different locations and at different historical times. People who share common circumstances (such as belonging to the same gender or social class) will tend to share a similar world view. But even they will sometimes see the world differently, and even the same person can have different world views (when drunk or sober, for instance).

Secondly, a person's world view tends to become so familiar that they are often beguiled into seeing it as how things really are. One technique social constructionists use is called deconstruction. This involves playing around with taken-for-granted realities in ways that startle us into recognizing them as constructions.

Deconstruction is an analytic technique used to scrutinize ideas in order to expose hidden assumptions and preconceptions.

The 'game' Rex Stainton Rogers played was to draw an analogy between going to school and being conscripted into the army. There are similarities – when children are sent to school, they have virtually no choice in the matter, they are frequently made to wear uniforms and to do things like line up in rows and obey orders. By playing on those similarities he was trying to get you to see going to school as a lot less normal and natural than it might seem, and, in this way, to begin to raise questions about how some children and teenagers may view school. He highlights a significant benefit that social constructionism offers us: the potential for achieving better childhoods. To press this point home, consider that in February 1814 at the Old Bailey court in London, five children were condemned to death. Two boys aged twelve were convicted of burglary, and three boys aged eight, nine and eleven of stealing. All five were hanged. Such a thing is unthinkable in the UK today.

This is not to say that British society has necessarily become better in its treatment of children. It is more complex than that. It can be argued, for example, that while children in the UK are no longer condemned by law to execution, very large numbers of children are now killed in traffic accidents – far more than were ever hanged. And yet British society tolerates this, and almost sees it as inevitable – these deaths are called 'accidents', after all.

Even so, it remains true that the construction of children in the UK has changed sufficiently to establish a legal system in which children's crimes are generally dealt with by attempts to rehabilitate them rather than punish them. Nonetheless, ideas about children and crime are still very confused, as the following fictitious example illustrates.

Allow about 20 minutes

ACTIVITY 5   The paradoxical child

Consider the following paradox:

A fourteen-year-old boy is convicted of raping a woman in her thirties, a teacher who accompanied him on a school trip. There was a bit of a party one night in the hotel where they were staying and although she should, strictly, not have been drinking on duty, she got very drunk. He went up to her room with her – he offered to help her up the stairs. They talked for a while. They then had sex. He says that she consented, but she claims that he took advantage of her drunkenness. She was barely conscious, and certainly gave no consent.

A fourteen-year-old boy visits the house of his teacher, a woman in her thirties. They watch TV together and get rather drunk. She takes him to the bedroom and encourages him to have sex with her. When his parents find out what has happened, they call the police. The woman is subsequently prosecuted and convicted of having sexual intercourse with a minor.

Think about what makes the difference – between the boy being regarded as a victim, and being regarded as a criminal. Spend about ten minutes listing the assumptions and beliefs about what a child is that underpin these two divergent attributions.

COMMENT

The situation here is a strange one. In both cases a fourteen-year-old boy has sex with a thirty-year-old woman who is in a position of authority over him. But in England, in strictly *legal terms*, what he does and what he 'is' are dependent on *her* consent. Where she gives no consent, he is a criminal and she is a victim. Where she gives consent, she is the criminal and he is the victim. The first is treated as a case of juvenile crime, the second as an example of child abuse.

The more you examine this situation, the more complex it becomes. This illustration demonstrates another facet of social constructionism: that people's opinions and actions are often inconsistent because people do not have a single, coherent understanding of the world. While (as you saw in the *Guardian* extract in Activity 4) different standpoints tend to lead to different opinions, people and institutions can and do operate from contradictory standpoints. If you look at the images of children presented by the media you will find *both* Romanticized images of wholesome childhood innocence *and* Puritanical images of children as uncivilized beasts. Equally the law, as the last activity demonstrates, treats children *both* as innocents in need of protection, *and* as criminals in need of punishment.

Social constructionism does not try to establish 'facts' – it sees this as impossible. Rather it concentrates on taking a critical stance towards knowledge. In the case of the boy in Activity 5, a social constructionist approach would point to how the different interpretations of his actions and his status arise from different contexts – the effects that historical time, society and culture have upon the judgements made. It also points to how these answers are created and sustained by social processes – the law, cultural attitudes to children committing crimes, the impact of theories like child development. And it highlights the ways in which different answers imply different actions – punishing the woman for child abuse or punishing the boy for rape, for example.

By drawing your attention to the way knowledge is socially *constructed*, social constructionism encourages you to be vigilant and critical – to continually ask yourself questions like: Who made this knowledge? Whose interests does it serve? Who is likely to benefit and who is likely to be harmed? In particular, in relation to children, it warns against expecting that there can ever be any easy answers or solutions:

...[H]eroic 'child saving' or 'child protection' and villainous 'child mistreatment' are not two different kinds of action, with opposing mandates (to work for the good or for the bad of children). They are two alternative facets, or readings, of virtually *any* kind of conduct towards children. Similarly, children themselves are not either innocent victims of adult mistreatment, or culpable delinquents whose anti-social behaviour must be controlled. Rather these (and many more in between) are alternative placements that the adult world creates for children, into which individual children are located at different times, in different circumstances, according to the adult gaze adopted...

(Stainton Rogers and Stainton Rogers, 1992, p. 191)

Children are not passive in this. Children can, for instance, locate themselves, for example, as 'survivors' of abuse rather than 'victims'. They do not have to accept the identities that adults seek to impose upon them, they can and do resist them. But it remains important to recognize that they are generally in a relatively powerless position in relation to adults, and often have only limited choices. The issue of power is an important but complex issue for any consideration of children – you will be meeting it in later chapters.

SUMMARY OF SECTION 3

- Social constructionism draws attention to the influences of culture, history and social processes on the way people make sense of the world and, in consequence, the way people act.
- The concepts of a 'child' and 'childhood' are socially constructed – they exist only because people have brought them into being as meaningful categories.
- Social constructionism is not just about there being different 'realities' created by the way people think and make sense of children, for example. It is concerned with the practical and moral consequences of these alternative 'realities' – what they allow and encourage people to do, and what they cover up from view and prevent people doing.
- Social constructionism challenges the assumption that things like moral values can be objectively defined and measured.
- Using a social constructionist approach allows people to recognize that children who commit serious crimes like murder can be seen through two different discourses. The *Romantic discourse of childhood* sees children as inherently good, doing terrible things only if they have been damaged in some way. Consequently, child murderers should be treated by therapy. The *Puritan discourse of childhood* sees children as inherently evil and amoral. If they do terrible things, this is because of their innate wickedness and they should be punished.

4 AN APPLIED APPROACH

So far we have examined two different approaches to studying childhood: scientific and social constructionist. In this section I will look at a third – the applied approach. This is where concern is focused on practical issues and questions, such as: how children should be brought up and cared for; what should be done to foster their development; what support and services should be provided for them; and what should be done when they cause trouble.

There are two rather different aspects to studying the applied approach. The first is to explore the influences on applied areas such as social policy, professional practice and law. An example here is examining shifts in the strategies adopted to protect children from abuse (see, for example, Stainton Rogers, 1992). The second is to explore the ways in which theory and research have been used to inform practical issues of how children should be treated. The law, social policy and professional practice towards children all draw on assumptions of what constitutes a child, and how actions towards them need to take account of them being children.

In this section I will focus on just one aspect: the way in which the law takes account of the transition from child to adult in respect of children who commit crimes. In the previous section you considered this in terms of the age of criminal responsibility. In this section I am going to open up this issue further by examining two models of how the law can deal with young offenders – the *welfare* model and the *justice* model. I will argue that these draw on the two discourses of childhood that I introduced in Section 3 – the *Romantic* and *Puritan* discourses. When they respond to questions like, 'What are children like?', 'What do children need?', 'How should we treat children?', these discourses each come up with a different answer. Hence they each offer different conclusions about how to deal with children who have committed crimes.

In recent historical times in the UK, child criminals were usually treated no differently from adults. In England in the nineteenth century children as young as eight were executed for theft. Today it is more usual to assume that there is a difference between an adult and a child criminal, and so they need to be treated differently. Children are seen to need – and to be amenable to, in ways that adults are not – measures to help them deal with and overcome the effects of the troubles they faced in their early life. Ann Hagell, co-director of the Policy Research Bureau (whose answer was included in the *Guardian* extract you read for Activity 4), puts this cogently:

> The important thing is the consequences of being over the age of criminal responsibility, not the age per se. Other countries with a very low age (10 or less) usually have a period where responsibility is not absolute until mid-to-late teens, or where the response to breaking the law is welfare-oriented rather than retributive.

(Hagell, 2001, p. 10)

So even in legal systems that specify a low age at which children can be held, in law, responsible for committing a serious crime like murder, it is usual to deal with them differently from adults if they are convicted.

Rather than being sent to prison (where the primary focus is on punishment) they will be placed in an establishment where the primary concern is for their welfare. In other words, even when the law regards a child as being 'criminally responsible' for the crime they have committed, it may still regard them as a child, and hence in need of and entitled to different treatment from an adult.

4.1 Punishment or rehabilitation?

Social constructionism can help us gain insight into what is going on in disputes about whether children who commit crimes should be punished or rehabilitated. But a scientific approach also has a place in the debate.

> READING
>
> Turn now to Reading B, an extract from Stuart Asquith's article 'When children kill children: the search for justice'. Make notes on the two models he describes for dealing with children who commit crimes – the 'welfare' and the 'justice' models. Also, note where Asquith is drawing on scientific approaches and where he draws on social constructionism.

The 'welfare' and 'justice' models discussed by Asquith have links with the discourses on childhood that you have considered already. The *Romantic discourse of childhood* implies that since children are 'naturally' good, children who commit crimes should not be punished, but rather rehabilitated. The *Puritan* discourse, by contrast, sees children as 'naturally' wicked, and hence regards children who commit crimes as in need of 'being taught a lesson' – of being punished in ways that bring home to them the wrong they have done. Of course, it is not that straightforward. There are, for example, other discourses in play (such as a discourse which focuses on children's citizenship and rights). But in broad, simple terms you can recognize that the two discourses each imply a different model of the way to deal with young offenders – a *welfare* model or a *justice* model.

The welfare model

In general terms it is the welfare model that primarily informs current UK social policy towards children (especially very young children) and the law about children's care and upbringing. For example, the Children Act 1989 covering England and Wales, has as its core principle that: 'When a court determines any question with respect to ... the upbringing of a child ... the child's welfare shall be the court's paramount consideration.' [section 1, paragraph (1)].

More particularly, the welfare model views children who do wrong as doing so because they have themselves been mistreated and/or deprived, and hence as needing nurture and care to help them to overcome the disadvantages to which they have been exposed. For example, within a welfare model for dealing with children who commit crimes, therapy may be offered alongside opportunities to re-build their self-esteem and self-confidence.

An art therapy session aimed at helping adolescents to work together and to overcome their hostilities to one another.

The justice model

The justice model rests on the assumption that children, once they can be held at least partially responsible for their misdoings, should be treated as criminals and subjected to punishment.

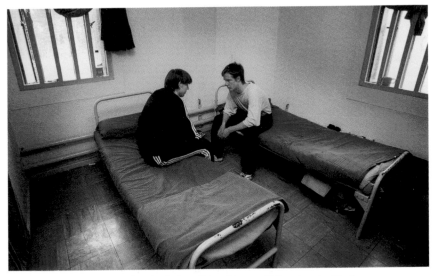

Two remand prisoners chat in their cell in a Young Offenders Institution.

In Reading B, Asquith's applied approach draws on both scientific and social constructionist approaches to childhood. An example of a scientific approach is where he notes that 'recognition is made of the developmental aspect of childhood in the formulation of policies on the incarceration of children'. In other words, he is building his analysis in part on developmental theorizing and the results obtained from scientific studies of children's capacities at different stages in their development.

At the same time Asquith (as he makes clear in Reading B) is also drawing upon social constructionism in his analysis of how children who kill are treated by the law. He says there are two fundamentally different models of how to deal with children who commit crimes – a welfare model and a justice model – each of which has its basis in a different construction of the child.

As I argued earlier, the welfare model can be seen as implied by the *Romantic discourse of childhood*, and the justice model as implied by the *Puritan discourse*. Both discourses have a long history in Western thought (you will be exploring these in the later chapters). In this sense you can think of these discourses as 'historically sedimented' (the analogy is geological – like the gradual laying down of layers of soil or rock).

In the present day *both* are still 'active', in that they inform and mould the images and understandings that people have of children and childhood. People can see them, Asquith proposes, brought into sharp focus when they try to make sense of children who kill. They can see child murderers either – and, indeed, both – as innocents-in-need-of-compassion, and/or as sinners-deserving-of-retribution.

What policy and law makers are trying to do, Asquith contends, is to decide how to revise juvenile justice systems in ways that accommodate both. They are attempting to steer a path between meeting the calls of public opinion for retribution, and what is known (from scientific research) about the causes of child criminality and the ways in which child criminals can be rehabilitated.

To conclude my examination of the question, 'What is a child?', the first point to note is that any attempt to answer it opens up not only all manner of other questions about what children are, but also all sorts of practical questions about how children should be treated. In order to try to answer these questions people can draw upon a scientific approach – since it is the most effective means of providing us with 'the facts about children'. But science alone cannot tell people what to *do* with and about children. As I mentioned earlier, while scientific research may be able to demonstrate that the average fifteen-year-old is perfectly capable of understanding that stealing from someone's purse is both wrong and a crime, it cannot tell me what to do if I find out my granddaughter has stolen money from my friend's purse. Nor can it tell people what to do if a fourteen-year-old boy has sex with an older woman, even though he too knows this is against the law.

To make those kinds of decisions people need to take account of the circumstances and of the variety of ways in which children and childhood are constructed. They have to acknowledge that there are different – and, indeed, conflicting – standpoints on the nature and status of childhood that create (and are created by) the social, cultural and institutional conditions in which action towards children can be taken. An applied approach can use both science and social constructionism to gain insight into children and childhood. Both are necessary and both are useful, and in almost every circumstance people's understanding will be better if they apply both of them to the particular topic or issue being addressed. In some chapters of this book you will find one or other taking more prominence. But mainly you will see that in the various chapters, authors are drawing on both approaches, especially when they are seeking to answer applied questions about how children should be treated.

SUMMARY OF SECTION 4

- An applied approach can draw on both scientific and social constructionist approaches when applying theory and research to social policy, professional practice and the law.

- A scientific approach – particularly that provided by developmental theory and research – has produced information about children's capacities at different stages in their maturation. This information has been used, for example, to inform policy about ways in which children who commit crimes can be reformed.

- A social constructionist approach provides insight into why there is so much controversy about what to do with children who commit serious crimes. Identifying the historical, social and cultural roots of two antagonistic models of treatment – the welfare and justice models – helps us to make sense of current moves to change systems of juvenile justice.

5 CONCLUSION

The overall purpose of this chapter has been to introduce you to three different approaches to the study of children and childhood that can be adopted: a scientific approach, a social constructionist approach and an applied approach. I stressed that they are not so much in competition as complementary. They offer different ways of thinking about children and childhood, and alternative approaches to considering how children should be treated. But by now you should also be aware that there are some complex interplays between the three approaches.

Social constructionism offers many challenges to the scientific approach. In particular it cautions people not to be too triumphant about the 'progress' that scientific research can bring. While not denying its pragmatic uses, it warns us against the dangers of complacency and elitism – of believing that science offers a morally as well as experimentally superior knowledge-base and ideology.

I mentioned Said's criticism of the assumption of the superiority of 'Western' thought. His criticism is highly relevant to the study of childhood, given that the majority of its scholars (or, at least, those who are well-known) are white, rich and from the West. It tends to be assumed by such scholars that they have the capacity and knowledge to present a fully global and international overview of childhood. It is all too easy for them to slip into Orientalism, and offer portrayals of children and childhood in *their* culture as the 'norm', contrasted with images of children from other locations and cultures as colourfully and quaintly exotic.

As I have noted, however, a scientific approach is crucial when we want to decide how to treat children – for example, whether to submit young criminals to punitive or rehabilitative programmes. A scientific approach is able to generate data, for example, that tell us what kinds of reformatory regimes work best at preventing young criminals from re-offending. Without such information all people can do is fall back on basing their actions on subjective opinions and preconceptions. Even though it is crucial to retain a level of reflexivity – to recognize the impossibility of true objectivity – a scientific approach offers clarity and practical guidance to people's actions.

In the chapters that follow you will be given opportunities to explore these three approaches in much more detail.

REFERENCES

ALDERSON, P. (2000) *Young Children's Rights: exploring beliefs, principles and practice,* London, Jessica Kingsley.

ASQUITH, S. (1996) 'When children kill children: the search for justice', *Childhood,* **3**(1), pp. 99–116.

DALEY, J. (1993) 'Janet Daley column', *The Times,* 25 November, p18.

GERRARD, N. (1997) 'Little girls lost', *The Observer,* Review Section, 31 August, p. 3.

GILLIGAN, C. (1982) *In a Different Voice: Psychological Theory and Women's Development,* Cambridge (Mass.), Harvard University Press.

GOLDING, W. (1959) *Lord of the Flies,* New York, Capricorn.

HAGELL, A. (2001) *Guardian G2,* 20 June, p. 10.

HILL, M. AND TISDALL, K. (1997) *Children and Society,* London, Longman.

JAMES, A., JENKS, C. AND PROUT, A. (1988) *Theorizing Childhood,* Cambridge, Polity.

JOHN, M. (1996) *Children in Charge: the child's right to a fair hearing,* London, Jessica Kingsley.

KOHLBERG, L. (1958) *The Development of Modes of Moral Thinking and Choice in the Years 10 to 16,* Chicago, University of Chicago Press.

KOHLBERG, L. (1967) 'Moral and religious education in the public schools: a developmental view' in SIZER, T. R. (ed.) *Religion and Public Education,* Boston, Houghton Mifflin.

KOHLBERG, L. (1968) 'Moral development', *International Encyclopedia of the Social Sciences,* New York, Macmillan.

LANSDOWN, G. (2001) 'Children's welfare and children's rights' in FOLEY, P., ROCHE, J. and TUCKER, S. (eds) *Children in Society: contemporary theory, policy and practice,* Basingstoke, Palgrave.

LIGHT, P. AND OATES, J. (1990) 'The development of children's understanding' in ROTH, I. (ed.) *Introduction to Psychology,* London, Erlbaum/The Open University.

MARSHALL, K. (1997) *Children's Rights in the Balance: the participation-protection divide,* London, HMSO.

PIAGET, J. (1932) *The Moral Judgement of the Child*, London, Routledge and Kegan Paul.

QVORTRUP, J. (1994) 'Childhood matters: an introduction', in QVORTRUP, J., BARDY, M., SGRITTA, G., and WINTERSBERGER, H. (eds) *Childhood Matters: social theory, practice and politics*, Aldershot, Avebury.

SAID, E. (1994) *Orientalism: Western conceptions of the Orient*, Harmondsworth, Penguin.

STAINTON ROGERS, R. and STAINTON ROGERS, W. (1992) *Stories of Childhood: shifting agendas of child concern*, Hemel Hempstead, Harvester Wheatsheaf.

STAINTON ROGERS, W. (1992) 'Introduction' in STAINTON ROGERS, W., HEVEY, D., ROCHE, J. and ASH, E. (eds) *Child Abuse and Neglect: facing the challenge*, London, Batsford.

THOMAS, R. M. (1996) *Comparing Theories of Child Development*, Pacific Grove (Calif.), Brooks/Cole.

WOODHEAD, M., FAULKNER, D. M. and LITTLETON, K. (1998) *Cultural Worlds of Early Childhood*, London, Routledge/The Open University.

READING A

The social construction of childhood

Rex Stainton Rogers [edited by Wendy Stainton Rogers]

'We live in a socially constructed world.' In this chapter I want to introduce you to the power of that idea and what it can do for our understanding of childhood.

A socially constructed world

If you accept the idea that childhood experiences mark us for life, you could trace my development as a social constructionist back to a holiday in Italy when I was about 11. It was my first time abroad and in 1953 holidays abroad were something few young people of my background experienced. In the bath I reached up to pull [what I thought was the light-switch cord to turn] on the light and – you've guessed it – called the maid instead! The knowledge I took for granted – that cords in bathrooms invariably switch on lights – proved wrong. But it wasn't only things that weren't the same in Italy, people weren't either, and that difference made me different. Finding out it was my eleventh birthday, an Italian family invited me to dinner. They generated a sense of occasion which made it quite unlike any birthday I'd experienced in England, 'killing the fatted calf' (looking back, I suspect literally) and plying me with champagne and liqueur. Needless to say, I also found out how mind-altering drugs change reality and I still have a vivid visual memory of their dog seeming to be walking up the wall!

Nowadays, like most adults, I seldom undergo such a dramatic sense of surprise. Experience has taught me to be a lot more cautious about what I 'know' and how matters 'must be'. My only certainty is that the world of things and people can be constructed in many alternative ways. I'm also pretty wise by now to the alternative ways in which I construct the world – I know it when sober and drunk, happy and sad, when I'm well and when I'm ill. Unless I'm very mistaken you could tell similar stories – you are that much of a social constructionist already. And, although you might not use my words, I don't think you would argue that this article, the word processor it was written upon, the language I wrote it in, are all socially constructed; that is, made through human activities and actions.

But what about childhood? ... For example, the children of Long Wittenham have come to understand that they 'have to go to school', that the human-made 'thing' down the road *is* a school, that certain activities belong in the classroom and others in the playground, and so on. The social world works because we share common understandings.

Indeed, so real can the socially constructed world seem that it often just gets taken for granted. It appears so normal, so right, so reasonable for children to go to school that they (and perhaps we sometimes) fail to imagine anything else.

To demonstrate the alternatives, social constructionists use a technique of challenge (or to use the jargon term, 'deconstruction'). What if I now call the school 'a camp', refer to the children as 'being conscripted', [and] to schooling as '11 years of National Service' [– drawing a parallel with compulsory military service]? Are you tempted to say I am being deliberately 'unrealistic' because I am not following the usual taken-for-granted rules for seeing the world? My answer would be that whether or not my reinterpretation is realistic can only be answered by posing a further question – 'in what reality?'. Different social realities (or world views as they are often called) imply different taken-for-granted ground rules.

There are no hard-and-fast principles for defining when disagreements about how things are seen become significant enough to talk about them as different social realities. However, it is usually assumed that the more distant people are from one another (in terms of historical time, geographical location, culture or class) the more likely they are to have different world views. It is also generally accepted that ideologies imply social realities ... [Communists] and capitalists see the world differently... Contrasted social realities can co-exist within a complex society and even battle 'inside our own heads' ...

When social constructionists look at childhood, it is to these different social realities that they turn. The interest is not just in learning about the constructions of childhood in history or in different cultures – it is also a technique that throws light on why we construct childhood as we do in our own time and society ...

The social construction of better childhoods

As Hoyles points out, the concept of a socially constructed childhood is, amongst other things, a political theory, one concerned with social actions and outcomes. It *can* be taken very radically. The feminist Shulamith Firestone (1971), for example, sees the condition of children and women as very similar. To become 'fully human' children need to be liberated from childhood as women need to be liberated from femininity.

This is an interesting argument and one which is attracting increasing attention. Being socially constructed by those in power as 'child-like' (naïve, emotional, easily led, living for the moment) has been a significant taken-for-granted truth in the oppression of, and denial of human rights to, slaves, women and colonial peoples. If such groups can reconstruct themselves and be reconstructed as 'fully human' could not the same liberation come to children?

But other politicized writers see children's human rights as better thought about in terms of a right to protection than liberation:

> The child's capacity for acting upon the world, and changing it, will always be less than that of an adult. This cannot be 'equal*ized*' by social transformation: even by *socialist* transformation ... The child's right is thus not to a formal *equality* ... but to a *relatively* protected space in which childhood can take place.

(Fuller, 1979, p. 102)

What separates these two utopian visions are unanswered questions about whether what our society construes as the inevitable physical and psychological weaknesses and vulnerabilities of the young *are* inevitable or are just more social constructions. Don't forget that social constructions are not just ideas. They are also what we make and do, so the liberationists have on their side arguments drawn from the experience of physically challenged people who can be disabled or enabled according to how we construct the physical world and the aids we do or do not manufacture. On the other hand, the protectionists see the vulnerability of the young in a rather different way: to lower a gas hob so that someone in a wheel-chair can cook a meal is enabling, to lower a gas hob in a family with young children runs the risk of being horrifically disabling!

However, I think I'd argue that the real power of social constructionism to point to better childhoods lies not in its ability to deconstruct our present world as a less than perfect one to grow up in, nor in any specific utopia it may open up to examination, but in the *idea of multiple realities itself*. In other words, we do not need to opt *either* for the uplifting of children to a 'fully adult' status (arguably hardly an enviable state anyway) *or* for the creation of a 'protected species' status from which children can subsequently become 'better' adults (with all the patronizing potential this view has). We do not need to do so because both constructions (and many others) already exist in our culture as viewpoints or 'discourses' about children.

Once frameworks for better childhoods come into being through political debate and argument they become part of the 'moral menu' potentially on offer to *all* in a society (including the young). Young people can construct their worlds around notions of their rights when, and only when, such concepts (and alternatives) are available both to them and the not so young with whom they must negotiate. If any truth exists in the notion that in our dealings with children we revisit our own childhood – with the roles reversed – then those children who are *au fait* with being seen as persons with rights will, in turn, become themselves adults who respect children's rights.

In opting for a menu of constructions of better childhoods (each containing its own utopia), we respect what we already have – a plural society in which ideas are allowed to argue with each other – and what we know of the people in this society – that they themselves can negotiate across realities (e.g. as parents or caregivers negotiating both 'freedom' and 'protected space' with young people). Many things, of course, can curtail or threaten such negotiation. These can encompass both individually enacted cruelties and neglects and corporatively enacted ones (like poverty and ignorance), as well as a dogmatic adherence to any singular view of 'their needs' or 'their rights' – arrived at without consultation and imposed without consent.

To negotiate with a less powerful person (whether a child or not) is not merely a liberal action of recognizing their humanity, it is to involve them in the very core of the human endeavour – the construction, deconstruction and reconstruction of the social world. *All* inputs change the potential future. That we no longer hang children, burn them as witches or brand them as vagrants is not the victory of a few reformers, it is the victory of a whole society which has overcome the constructions that made such actions possible. The killings and maimings of children that our society still generates can also be consigned to the history book – by the same processes which have made possible the worlds in which we now live...

References

ARIÈS, P., *Centuries of Childhood*, Penguin, Harmondsworth (1973).

BERGER, P. L. and LUCKMAN, T., *The Social Construction of Reality*, Penguin, Harmondsworth (1967).

FIRESTONE, S., *The Dialectic of Sex*, Cape, London (1971).

FULLER, P., 'Uncovering Childhood' in HOYLES, M. (ed.) (1979).

HOYLES, M. (ed.), *Changing Childhood*, Writers and Readers, London (1979).

ILLICH, I., *Deschooling Society*, Penguin, Harmondsworth (1973).

POLLOCK, L. A., *Forgotten Children*, Cambridge University Press (1983).

Source

STAINTON ROGERS, R., (1992) 'The social construction of childhood' in STAINTON ROGERS, W., HEVEY, D., ROCHE, J. and ASH, E. (eds) *Child Abuse and Neglect: facing the challenge*, London, Batsford/The Open University, pp. 23–29.

When children kill children: the search for justice

Stuart Asquith

Children who commit offences

Any system of justice for children has to be seen in the context of the social, political and economic climate in which it is located. Over the past two decades there have been important shifts in political ideology (some of which do not fit easily with a system of justice for children based on welfare principles); there have been significant changes in social work thinking about how to deal with children; the economic situation has changed considerably; there have been a number of dramatic occurrences involving the deaths of children, some of whom have actually been in care; child and sexual abuse have been 'discovered' (see Qvortrup 1994); and, with the ratification of the United Nations Convention on the Rights of the Child by a number of countries, the very citizenship status of children and their rights are now firmly located on the political agenda. The Bulger case is remarkable in the way in which it touches on almost all of these areas, prompting a consideration not just of criminal policy as it relates to the young but also of other areas more traditionally associated with broader social policy concerns – parenting, childcare, poverty, social injustice and so on.

In referring to the alleged failure of welfare approaches to dealing with offenders, and suggesting that we should 'condemn more and understand less' the British Prime Minister, John Major, was implying that too much attention had been paid to identifying the factors which are used to account for criminal behaviour, whether by children or adults, and that more effort should be devoted to sanctioning offenders for what they have done. In this respect, what he had to say reflects a clear divergence between two basic ideologies of delinquency and crime control.

One might simply be called the 'justice' model in which offenders are seen to be responsible for what they have done, should be dealt with in a court of criminal law and can rightly be considered worthy of punishment. The other, again put rather simply, is the 'welfare' model in which offenders are not necessarily viewed as responsible for what they have done (their behaviour explicable by individual or social factors), need not be dealt with in a court of criminal law, and should be dealt with by measures designed to promote their welfare or interests.

The James Bulger case had a considerable impact on discussions about future developments in delinquency control throughout Europe, including Eastern Europe. In particular, it gets to the very heart of the issue of just how to deal with those very young offenders who commit serious offences and tends to polarize 'welfare' and 'justice' philosophies and the conception of children as vulnerable and in need of care or as responsible and appropriate subjects of punishment ...

That this is not just a matter of purely academic concern is clear as illustrated by a reading of developments in the United Kingdom and throughout Europe, where most countries are currently reviewing their systems of justice for children along the dimension of the 'justice' and 'welfare' models (Dunkel, 1991). In relation to the United Kingdom, it has to be remembered that there are great institutional differences between Scotland and England, where juvenile justice, education and law are based on very different principles. With specific reference to crime and delinquency, most children in Scotland are dealt with by what is known as the Children's Hearings system (see Asquith, 1998) based on a philosophy of welfare where the decision as to how to deal with children who commit offences is made in reference not to the offence but, rather, to the child's need for compulsory measures of care. The comments made by the Prime Minister challenged the basic philosophy of the Scottish Children's Hearings system, and reinforced the obligation on analysts to locate any understanding of how children are conceived of and, in the case of children who offend, dealt with in a social, cultural and historical context.

But even in Scotland, children who commit serious offences may be dealt with in the criminal courts. And, throughout Europe, the general trend in relation to children who commit offences is best characterized as the 'twin track approach'. By this is meant that for the majority of children, punishment and judicial proceedings are seen to be inappropriate. For the minority of serious or persistent offenders, judicial intervention and punitive measures may be imposed ...

Criminal responsibility

... Where differences are most obvious in relation to juvenile justice is in the age limits set both for criminal responsibility and for the application of penal measures. For example, Scotland is not the only country to have a low age of criminal responsibility. In Switzerland and the Republic of Ireland, the age of criminal responsibility is set at 7, and it is of course in England and Wales set at 10. This has to be compared with France, where it is 13, the Scandinavian countries, where the age is uniformly set at 15, and other European countries such as Belgium, Romania, Lithuania and others, where it is 18.

The two boys who murdered James Bulger were 10 and therefore, in terms of the English legal system, just above the age of criminal responsibility. The issue that has to be considered is the extent to which we are willing to maintain that children as young as 10, or even younger in Scotland, Ireland and Switzerland, can be said to be capable of the appropriate mental capacity for criminal responsibility to be ascribed. The wider issue at stake is of course the whole issue of the competence and responsibility adults are prepared to ascribe to children generally and whether adulthood and childhood can be clearly differentiated on such dimensions. There is evidence, for example, to suggest that very young children may be just as capable as adults at making rational and responsible decisions in a number of areas of their lives (Weithorn and Scherer, 1994).

Even if that is the case, children who are technically criminally responsible may nevertheless not be subjected to the rigours of the penal system. For example, in many European countries where there is a low age of criminal responsibility, children and young people may not be subjected to custodial sanctions until they are near the age of penal majority. And, more generally, in Switzerland, though the age of criminal responsibility may have been set at 7, up to the age of 14 only educational measures can be employed. In Scotland, where the age of criminal responsibility remains technically at 8, the majority of children who commit offences are dealt with through the welfare and care measures supported by the Children's Hearings system. But again illustrating the tension experienced in all systems of juvenile justice across the world, even in Scotland the child who commits a serious offence will be dealt with in court. Again, recognition is made of the developmental aspect of childhood in the formulation of policies on the incarceration of children.

... Cases such as that of James Bulger may well demand, for a number of reasons, criminal justice intervention, but they cannot be used as the basis for the development of policy for the majority of children who offend. The pursuit of justice for children must surely be based as much on a concern with the effects of social and economic inequalities and injustice as on the rules and standards set by the criminal law. That is, not only do they provoke questioning of the justice of the process by which children in such cases are dealt with, they also demand fundamental examination of the contribution of social inequalities and social injustice to the growth and development of children. And this is certainly the trend throughout Europe, where there is generally increasing recognition of the need, in relation to young offenders, to integrate a social policy perspective with more traditional criminal policy approaches. But even in relation to the two young boys who murdered James Bulger (and to other children who commit particularly serious offences) it is clear that dealing with them in the criminal justice system itself allows justice at least in part to be seen to be done and may assuage public reaction to what they did. The real problem, though, is in identifying how best to deal with such children and to prepare them for eventual release. On that there is less certainty.

On a more theoretical level, current debates and discussions about what philosophers call 'hard cases' have important implications for our understanding of childhood, children and the philosophies on which our social institutions are based. As notions of childhood alter so too the patterns of control imposed on the behaviour of children change. In many respects, changing notions of childhood may also be a measure of the extent to which society is itself undergoing change. It is for such reasons that the United Nations Convention on the Rights of the Child has to be viewed, if it is ever implemented fully and meaningfully, as a document with the potential for radical social change. The change in the social, political, and economic status of children on which it is premised is inextricably linked to the need for change in the social and political structure of the situations children find themselves in around the world. The ready acceptance of an ideology of the child as a rational, responsible being and evil, wicked being and of childhood as essentially different from adulthood, in the light of some of the reactions to the murderers of James Bulger, is easily understood since it demands no radical change in our conception of children. More importantly for adults, it also thereby demands no change either in the structure of their social and political world or in the power relations between children and adults. Changing conceptions of childhood and associated expectations challenge cherished notions of adulthood and the rights of adults to control the behaviour of children ...

References

ASQUITH, S. (1998) 'Scotland', in J. MEHLBYE and L. WALGRAVE (eds) *Confronting Youth in Europe: Juvenile Crime and Juvenile Justice.* Copenhagen: AKF forlaget.

DUNKEL, F. (1991) 'Legal differences in juvenile criminology in Europe', in T. BOOTH (ed.) *Juvenile Justice in the New Europe,* Social Services Monograph: Research in Practice. Sheffield: University of Sheffield.

QVORTRUP, J. (1994) 'Childhood Matters: An Introduction', in J. QVORTRUP, M. BARDY, G. SGRITTA AND H. WINTERSBERGER (eds) *Childhood Matters: Social Theory, Practice and Politics.* Aldershot: Avebury.

WEITHORN, L. and D. SCHERER (1994) 'Children's Involvement in Research Participation Decisions: Psychological Considerations', in M. GRODIN and L. GLANTZ (eds) *Children as Research Subjects: Science, Ethics and the Law.* Oxford: Oxford University Press.

Source

ASQUITH, S. (1996) 'When children kill children: the search for justice', *Childhood,* **3**(1), pp. 99–116.

Chapter 2

Childhood in time and place

Heather Montgomery

CONTENTS

When you have studied this chapter, you should be able to:

1   Illustrate the social construction of childhood by reference both to historical changes and to cultural differences in the way that childhood has been, and is, understood.

2   Analyse the theories of Philipe Ariès and the arguments of his critics.

3   Give examples of two non-Western constructions of childhood.

4   Outline some of the main themes in Western constructions of childhood.

5   Give examples of the different ways people talk about childhood and the different discourses they draw on to do so.

6   Understand the ways in which Western constructions of the child have been exported and globalized.

I CONSTRUCTIONS OF CHILDHOOD

This chapter explores the idea that childhood is a social construct – an idea introduced in Chapter 1. I will ask you to examine various constructions of childhood in Europe and, briefly, elsewhere. I will question the idea that childhood is a universal state and will instead look at childhood as an idea which is a product of particular times, places and cultures. Social constructionism is concerned with *ideas* about children, not *facts* about them. Indeed, many social constructionists would deny the existence of any universal facts about children. For example, it is impossible today to consider childhood in Britain or America or Singapore (or anywhere else) as a single thing or to contrast British and American views of childhood because it becomes immediately apparent that there are too many differences that need to be taken into account – for example, variations in ethnicity, income, gender, disability and age. All of these affect the ways that people think about childhood.

Social constructionists look at how categories are constructed, how bodies of knowledge are built up and how childhood and adulthood are seen and understood in any given society. Ideas about children change because they are dependent on their social, cultural and historical context. Furthermore, these ideas have consequences and the way in which a category is constructed affects how members of that category will be treated. For example, there was a saying common among some social classes in Britain as late as the 1950s that 'children should be seen and not heard'; that is that adults were not interested in what children had to say and that children should aspire to deference and quietness in the presence of adults. In contemporary Britain this idea seems old fashioned and unnecessarily authoritarian; children have a different place in the family and ideas of equality are much more common.

As Wendy Stainton Rogers explained in the last chapter, a basic principle of social constructionism is that there are different ways of viewing social phenomena such as childhood. This chapter draws on anthropology and European history and philosophy to look at some of the ways in which children have been socially constructed. From anthropology, I give examples of non-Western constructions of childhood. One chapter of this length cannot be comprehensive – I have not represented the great religions of Islam, Hinduism and Buddhism and have selected only a few examples from non-Western culture. However, the examples do illustrate the variety of different ways in which ideas about childhood have been constructed and should encourage you to think about other ways of conceptualizing or imagining childhood. After this look at childhood in different cultures, I then move on to childhood in European history. Section 3 explores the major philosophical ideas that have informed European constructions of childhood. Again, there is not space here to go into the important issues around class, gender or disability as they affect children. There are enormous differences in the ways that childhood is constructed which depend on social, cultural, economic and other factors. This chapter can only introduce a critical framework that can help you to evaluate these variances.

1.1 What is a discourse?

Even within a Western tradition, there is no single set of beliefs about childhood. Social constructionism, therefore, looks at the *discourses* around childhood. The concept of a discourse was introduced and defined briefly in the previous chapter but it recurs so frequently in discussions of social constructionism that it is worth repeating that definition.

> This concept is extensively used in social constructionist work to mean a whole set of interconnected ideas that work together in a self-contained way, ideas that are held together by a particular ideology or view of the world. We can talk about, for example, a 'children's rights discourse' or a 'liberal-humanistic discourse' – each of which draws upon its own particular knowledge-base, works from its own particular set of assumptions, offers its own explanation of 'how the world works' and incorporates its own set of values and ethics.

Discourses are not simply statements, but are sets of ideas which are rooted in a historical, social and political context. People make sense of the world differently according to their social and political position in that world. The rulers of any society have different discourses from those of the poor and marginalized (although those in power often succeed by various means in getting those whom they rule to accept beliefs that are in the rulers' interest rather than their own). Men have different discourses to women, adults to children. The final point to note about discourses is that they do not simply reflect reality, they also create it. The way people speak and think about things has effects on their lives and those of other people.

Discourses about childhood reflect, among other things, how any particular culture interprets the biological immaturity of children and how it places children in relation to other age groups. Discourses about the nature of childhood are produced from religion, philosophy, law and medicine (among others). Each of these produces ways of understanding children and consequently ways in which they are treated. The important thing to note here is that discourses co-exist with and challenge each other. Often views of childhood are very contradictory.

Allow about 20 minutes

A C T I V I T Y I   Parents talk about childhood

In preparing this book, we interviewed parents and children in different parts of the world about their childhoods compared to those of their children. The three short quotations below are taken from these interviews. Read these through and for each write a note on the differences that you can see between the ways that they think about their own childhoods and the ways they think about their children's. Then think about your own childhood. How would you say that your childhood was different, either from that of your parents, your children or the children you see around you? How were your parents' ideas about childhood different from your own? Make brief notes.

Rubin and Brenda, anti-apartheid activists, from Cape Town, South Africa, talking about their son, Joshua (eight).

[In our childhood], as a child you were supposed to be quiet, you were supposed to be seen and not heard and in Joshua's case that's very different because Joshua speaks a lot, he speaks openly, I think he's much more confident and I think he's much happier as a child.

We always had that subservient mode, you know which is a silent thing, we were not allowed to question. When it comes to authority we wouldn't approach our parents and ask questions, whereas Joshua would ask questions, very pertinent questions often, because we had reared him in that way. The subservience is not in Joshua's case, Joshua questions everything which is very good.

Shafia, a woman living in a poor district of Chittagong, Bangladesh, talking about her daughter Maya (fifteen).

When I was a child our parents didn't have to discipline us that much. We listened to our parents and when they told us to do something we did it. But nowadays they don't listen to you, so you

have to discipline them a little bit. So I had to discipline Maya in a way that my parents didn't have to with me. When Maya started going to school at about seven or eight, I tried to discipline her a little bit. I would smack her when she did something wrong, but I was also very affectionate towards her.

Oscar is a first-generation El Salvadoran migrant to California, talking about his children, Brian (eight) and Karen (ten).

I began working before I was twelve years old. I wasn't allowed to study ... However, I want something different for my children. I want to support them in anything they want to do. I won't let them work while they're still very young. I want [them] to take full advantage while they're little, I want [them] to enjoy their childhood.

COMMENT

Rubin and Brenda are aware of the power inequalities in their relationships with their son, and try to construct a childhood where there is greater equality in the family than they experienced. The childhood they construct for Joshua is based on ideas of freedom – where he is free to ask questions, he is not scared of authority and where children and adults are of equal importance in the family. As anti-apartheid activists, the wider political battles of their generation, and their struggles for freedom and equality in their society, affect the discourses they use about childhood. Shafia, however, is arguing that she tries to give her daughter more freedom than she had as child but consequently she also has to discipline and even punish her more. She is attempting to find a balance between freedom and discipline. In contrast, her own childhood did not have this balance. It was more hierarchical, she had little freedom, her parents expected and received total obedience and she did not have to be punished. Oscar wants his children to have a very different childhood from his. He missed out on education and is determined that his children will get a better start. He is strict with his children, but not as strict as his own parents.

These quotations are, of course, examples from individuals. I am not presenting them as typical of all parents in these places. However, they do illustrate the discourses that some parents draw on when thinking about their children's childhoods. The point here is not that the previous generation were right or wrong or that some societies bring up children better than others but that as societies and cultures change, discourses and ideas about childhood change with them. The parents quoted above have thought about the sort of childhood that they want for their children and are trying to provide it. Often their discourses about what they wish for their children are formed in relation to their own experiences of childhood. Everyone is influenced by their own background and inevitably people do make value judgements about which sort of childhood is better (or more appropriate) for the children that they know. Although these views of childhood can be analysed as social constructs, they do have consequences. Parents hold views on what is appropriate for their children to do, experience or know. They bring up their own children and they support particular social, educational or health policies which are relevant to children's welfare. Parents are not morally neutral bystanders.

Allow about 15 minutes

A C T I V I T Y 2   **Children talk about childhood**

The following statements were made by the children of the parents quoted in the previous activity. Read through them and consider whether these children view childhood differently from their parents.

Joshua

Maya

Brian

> *Joshua*: A child is like a little person who's learning how to be moulded into an adult. The good things about being a child are getting toys and playing with friends. The bad thing about being a child is that you don't know right from wrong.
>
> *Maya*: When I was young I had happy times. I stayed with my parents so that I didn't have to worry about anything. I'd play, I'd go to school and I didn't have to do any work.
>
> *Brian*: What's really good about being a child is to be bad – to chase sisters!! What's bad about is that you sometimes, your mum or your dad, they spank you.

C O M M E N T

These quotations show that children, not surprisingly, think about and interpret childhood. Their views do not always coincide with their parents' views (again not surprisingly). The discrepancies show that social constructions of childhood are not simply an abstract philosophical debate among adults but that children construct their own meanings. People who study childhood are increasingly seeing children as capable of creating their own cultural constructions, including that of childhood (Qvortrup, 1994; James and Prout, 1990). Children's voices are sometimes difficult to find in analyses of constructions of childhood but books such as Anne Frank's diary, where she discussed both the personal and political situation of her life as she grew from a young girl into a young woman, show that childhood is not something passively experienced by children. They interpret and re-interpret the world around them and play an active part in what they see as childhood.

Who else but me is ever going to read these letters? Who else but me can I turn to for comfort? I'm frequently in need of consolation, I often feel weak, and more often than not, I fail to meet expectations. I know this, and every day I resolve to do better.

[My parents] aren't consistent in their treatment of me. One day, they say that Anne's a sensible girl and entitled to know everything, and the next that Anne's a silly noodle who doesn't know a thing and yet imagines she's learned all she needs to know from books! I'm no longer the baby and spoiled little darling whose every deed can be laughed at. I have my own ideas, plans and ideals, but am unable to articulate them yet.

(from the diary of Anne Frank; Frank, 1997, p. 64)

Having looked at several individuals' responses to questions about childhood, I am now going to look at some of the different discourses concerning childhood. Drawing on examples from anthropology, philosophy and Christian theology, I will examine the widely different discourses about childhood and look at the ways that social constructionism can help to make sense of them.

SUMMARY OF SECTION I

- Ideas and beliefs about children are not fixed but are a product of the particular social and cultural setting.
- Ideas about childhood also change over time and depend both on individual experience and wider socio-cultural beliefs.
- Many social constructionists use the term 'discourse' to refer to the set of interconnected ideas which people draw upon when discussing childhood (or any other social construct).
- Both adults and children use discourses to make sense of their experiences of childhood.

2 STUDYING CONSTRUCTIONS OF CHILDHOOD

2.1 Childhood in place

This chapter has emphasized that childhood is a cultural construct. In this section, I will be arguing that ideas about childhood depend on the culture into which a child is born, and culture varies across place and time. The previous chapter used the question 'when does childhood end?' as a vehicle to explore different constructions of childhood using legal, sociological and psychological discourses. In this section, I am going to look at how people answer the question of where childhood *begins*. This is an important question because it deals with very fundamental ideas about when life itself begins and when a child becomes fully human. The beginning of a child's life is one of the clearest examples of the vast differences in cultural constructions of childhood in different places. Looking at the cross-cultural record shows even greater diversity. For Catholics and some other groups of Christians, life begins at conception; at this moment a child is fully human and a complete person. In some sectors of Islam, life begins when the soul enters the body at 40 days' gestation, while in other variations of Islam it enters earlier. Under UK law, a child is not considered to be living until he or she is born and until 1994, if a child was stillborn, it could not be officially named on a birth certificate. Until recently, if a child was born dead or died before baptism, it could not be buried in sanctified ground in many Christian churches. In other communities, such as parts of China or Vietnam, children have to be named and welcomed before their life truly begins. In some societies in West Africa, stillborn babies are thrown angrily onto the rubbish dump, not because they are worthless, but because their community is angry that they are in such a hurry to join their ancestors that they cannot be bothered to join this difficult life (Judith Ennew, personal communication).

Allow about 10 minutes

ACTIVITY 3   Two views on when life begins

Read the short extract below concerning the Waiwai and the Trio (small, neighbouring, Amerindian groups in Surinam, a country in northern South America). Make short notes on how they conceptualize the beginning of life and the nature of childhood. Note down one strength of taking a social constructionist approach to this material and one possible limitation.

Trio and Waiwai beliefs on infants

In Trio cosmology there is a reservoir of soul matter at the end of the world. The soul of each individual is drawn from this reservoir at birth and returns there on his death. To begin with this soul matter is not properly fixed in the newborn child, nor has he enough of it to make him an independent being. Indeed the short-lived infant is regarded as someone who has not made a proper and complete entry into the world; he fails to become an individual in his own right. The soul flows into the child by way of the parents, whose duties therefore are not simply concerned with the physical growth and care of the child but also with his spiritual nurturing. Although the father is thought to be as much involved in this as the mother, the Trio represent the mother/child relationship more positively. They depict the existence of a spiritual umbilical cord which is the counterpart of the physical one. The spiritual cord survives long after birth has taken place, and it gradually disappears as the child becomes stronger and more independent. It is through this cord that the soul matter flows to feed the child ...

... the Waiwai seem to express some doubt about the nature of the young child's proper being since the term used for such a person is *okopuchi*, which literally means 'little corpse' ... After three years the child's soul is thought to have become large and independent enough no longer to follow the parents but to go its own way in the child's body. Presumably, from then on the child is an individual in his own right, being completely formed with his own body and soul.

(Rivière, 1974, p. 429)

Young Trio girl carrying an infant.

COMMENT

From this material, you can see that what a person is and when life begins are not questions which have absolute answers but are concepts which are dependent on socially constructed categories of life or personhood. Some people might find this approach to this material problematic, for instance, Christians who believe that life begins at conception and that at this moment, a human being is formed who is divinely created. Such Christians might describe a person as a being with a soul who is of God's creation and see that as a divine fact, a universal truth, not a social construct. Similarly of course, the Waiwai might see these Christians as equally misguided, and with equal conviction. As a social constructionist, I am not looking to find out which of these beliefs is true, but am interested in the discourses around these beliefs.

Taking a social constructionist view certainly does not solve the emotive issue on where childhood, and indeed life, begins. However, it does enable these issues to be put in their particular contexts, within their own cultural and moral settings. People can argue on the basis of their own faiths, but by taking a social constructionist approach, it becomes feasible to look at *why* people hold the views they do and consequently why they treat children as they do.

Another much quoted example is the issue of twins. Several societies across the world, including the Yanomamö of Brazil, the Dobe !Kung of the Kalahari and the Kikuyu of Kenya, have practised selective infanticide on twins (Ball and Hill, 1996, p. 861). Within their own societies, people do not consider that this practice is wicked or evil because they do not consider twins to be human. For them, human beings have one child at a time; only animals have more than one. Twins are animals and must be killed. This may horrify people who do not share these beliefs and some people may condemn them rather than try to understand. The Trio and Waiwai practise infanticide for reasons of birth control. This may appear brutal unless you know that they do not consider newborn babies to be fully human or even properly alive. Social constructionism allows an analysis of the belief systems behind practices such as these, arguing that they must be put in their contexts before any judgements about right and wrong can, or should, be made.

The case of oyako shinjū

The following case study offers a different example of the way that children are socially constructed. Moving away from the issue of where childhood begins, it nevertheless deals with similar questions to those raised before – of when a child becomes fully human in the eyes of their community. The extract describes the reaction of the American legal system to the Japanese practice of double suicide committed out of love, known as *oyako shinjū*. In Japan mothers of young children who commit suicide often kill their children first. This is known as family suicide rather than child murder, and mothers who have committed suicide without first having killed their children are often severely criticized. In Japan, children are often considered extensions of their mothers and are not seen as having an independent life from them. The anthropologist Roger Goodman writes: 'In Japan the child is often described as a *mono* (object) which is an extension of, rather than separate from, the parent' (Goodman, 2000, p. 165).

Indeed there is a strong argument that Japanese culture and language generally do not have the notions common in the modern North of separate, autonomous and individual 'selves'. The life of a motherless child is therefore considered an incomplete life and a woman is very wrong to inflict that on her children. The story below describes how a failed attempt at *oyako shinju* by a Japanese mother, living in the United States, was interpreted by other Americans.

> In 1985 a Japanese mother in her mid-thirties, on discovering her husband's infidelity and with one failed marriage behind her already, decided to commit suicide and took her two children (aged 4 years and 6 months) to the beach with her. She managed to drown the children in the Pacific Ocean, but was herself rescued by others who were on the beach at the time, and she subsequently found herself facing prosecution for the double murder of her children. The Japanese-American community, with support from Japan, managed to collect a 25,000-name petition on her behalf appealing that the case should be viewed as an example not of child murder but of *oyako shinjū*. Her supporters argued that there had been no malice towards the children in what she had done; indeed she had done it out of her love for them and hence she should be given a lenient, probationary sentence … Her American lawyer was unwilling to pursue this cultural defence, not least because in arguing that she knew what she was doing when killing the children she would be seriously prejudicing her own position in terms of American law. Instead, he found a number of American psychologists who were able to diagnose her mental state at the time of the incident as one of 'introjection' – the inability to distinguish her own life from those of her children which in American cultural terms could be termed a form of temporary insanity – and therefore neatly turned a cultural practice (*oyako shinjū*) into a psychological pathology.
>
> (Goodman, 2000, p. 165).

ACTIVITY 4   **Conflicting discourses of childhood**

What does this example tell you about how

(a) the Japanese-American community and

(b) the American legal system construct childhood?

Write notes on what these imply about childhood and for children in these contexts.

COMMENT

The *oyako shinju* example points to the vast differences that exist between cultures about the nature of childhood. This case shows what happens when such different discourses come into conflict with each other. In this case, the Americans and the Japanese-Americans placed different moral weights on different principles. For the Japanese-Americans, children are not constructed as individual beings separate from their parents but are seen as an extension of them. They are not viewed as individual, autonomous beings but as 'objects' who cannot exist separately from their parents. They are tied physically and spiritually to their mothers and are incomplete without them. In this context, therefore, a child is not regarded as entitled to the full protection of the law against being killed, because the child is not a complete individual. While those in the Japanese-American community may not have approved of what this mother did, nevertheless, killing a child through *oyako shinju* is not seen as murder by this community. In contrast, in the US legal discourse, a child exists as an independent, individual being and is entitled to the full protection of the law in all situations.

2.2 Childhood in time

Philipe Ariès: childhood is a modern idea

So far this section has explored what it means to say 'childhood is socially constructed' by drawing on examples from anthropologists' descriptions of cultures around the world. I am now turning to social constructions of childhood within Europe but across time, using the work of Philippe Ariès.

The French historian Philippe Ariès pioneered the idea that childhood is a social construction in his book *Centuries of Childhood* (Ariès, 1962). Ariès claimed that the view that childhood is a distinct human condition started to emerge after the Middle Ages, around the end of the fifteenth century. Ideas that childhood is special and different from adulthood gained ground during the seventeenth century, and culminated in what Ariès saw as the sentimentalization of childhood and the 'child-centred family' in the nineteenth and twentieth centuries. Ariès' thesis relied mostly on an analysis of European art of the Middle Ages, in which, he claimed, children were depicted as small adults. He used this evidence to suggest that childhood, as a separate state from adulthood, did not exist in medieval Europe and that the people of this time had no conception of childhood. Medieval art represented the infant Jesus as a scaled-down adult, with the posture and muscles of an adult. It was not until the sixteenth century that artists began to represent real children in portraiture. By this time specialized clothing, literature and toys for children were also developing alongside new ideas about the importance of education. Furthermore, demographic patterns were changing and mortality crises such as the Black Death, which depleted the population of Europe in the fourteenth century, were on the wane.

Ariès claimed that because of the uncertainty of infants' survival in the Middle Ages, parents and carers were indifferent to babies. It was only after children's survival was assured (at around the age of seven) that people began to invest much emotional energy in children. He further argued that children had to work and to contribute economically to the family. There was no room for sentimentality in parent–child relationships. Children were economically useful, not sentimentally worthwhile. Another characteristic feature of the time was the precocious entry into the adult world by those who survived infancy. As soon as children ceased to be infants, they were regarded as independent individuals. Poor children were also financially independent as they had to engage in productive work.

Allow about 20 minutes

ACTIVITY 5   **Paintings and children**

The following paintings are similar to those that interested Ariès. Examine them carefully and note the extent to which these pictures support or challenge Ariès' thesis.

Painting 1: Giotto di Bondone, *Ognissanti Madonna (Madonna in Maestà)*, c. 1310, © Uffizi Gallery Florence/Archive Alinari/Giraudon.

Painting 2: Federico Barocci, *The Madonna and Child with Saint Joseph and the Infant Baptist*, c. 1575, © The National Gallery.

Painting 3:
Cornelius Johnson, *Sir Thomas Lucy and his Family, c.* 1630, © National Trust Photo Library/Derrick E. Witty.

Painting 4:
William Powell Frith, *Many Happy Returns of the Day*, 1856, © National Trust PhotoLibrary/Derrick E. Witty – Harrogate Museum & Art Gallery/ Bridgeman Art Library.

COMMENT

These pictures represent children very differently. They are also representative of the prevailing styles of their times. Ariès' thesis would hold that in the first one, the child is not based on a real child but is a stylized representation of Jesus. It is clearly Jesus and a religious painting but the face is that of an adult, the size of the head relative to the body shows adult, not child, proportions and the body has muscle tone that a young child's would not have. In the second painting, although the theme is still religious, the children could have been modelled on actual children.

By the third picture, the differences between adults and children are very clearly marked in dress, in the way the latter play with the dog and their position at the feet of the adults. The final picture shows a Victorian tea party, where the tone of the picture is much more sentimental. The children in this picture are playing, being brought gifts and obviously separated from adult life. These pictures seem to support Ariès' theory that there has been a change in the way that children have been depicted in portraiture between the twelfth and nineteenth centuries. His interpretation of that difference, however, remains more controversial.

Ariès claimed that ideas about childhood have changed over time. He further argued that attitudes to child-rearing have also changed, as has the experience of being a child. In medieval Europe, childhood was not a distinct stage, separate from adulthood, and this remained the case until the fifteenth and sixteenth century. At this time, children's clothing, literature and games became different from adults' and the idea of a distinct stage of life called childhood emerged. Ariès suggested that the modern concept of childhood was introduced because it was the wish of the 'moral' elite (i.e. the Church and the royal court) to impose order on what they regarded as the undisciplined medieval population. These 'champions of moral order',

> taught parents that they were spiritual guardians, that they were responsible before God for the souls, and indeed the bodies too, of their children. Henceforth it was recognized that the child was not ready for life, and that he had to be subjected to a special treatment, a sort of quarantine, before he was allowed to join the adults.

(Ariès, 1962, p. 412)

So, relying mainly on pictorial sources, Ariès claimed that childhood, as a separate state from adulthood, was an invention of the sixteenth and seventeenth century and did not exist beforehand. This view has since been heavily criticized but few social scientists now question the idea that childhood is a socially constructed notion and that ideas about childhood change depending on historical and cultural setting. Despite criticisms of the notion that childhood as a state in its own right did not exist in the European Middle Ages, Ariès is still the starting point for studying childhood as a social construction which is why I have covered his thesis in such detail here.

Criticisms of Ariès

Why have Ariès' views of medieval childhood been criticised? His reliance on paintings led to several problems (he did take other factors into account such as the absence of childcare manuals, but his overwhelming evidence comes from paintings). First, paintings are not produced in a social and political vacuum. They are usually commissioned by a particular person or institution for a specific purpose. Paintings in the Middle Ages were almost exclusively connected with, and painted for, religious purposes. They illustrated religious themes and used symbolism to represent religious ideas and narratives. They were in no way concerned with the lives of ordinary, real, embodied children, but rather, with what the infant Jesus and child saints represented: innocence, purity and the soul. The growing wealth of the merchant classes in the fifteenth and sixteenth centuries resulted in them commissioning artists to paint portraits of themselves and of their children in a secular rather than religious way. But such paintings still employed symbolism. Particular animals, fruit and flowers carried wide symbolic meanings and were used in portraits of children to convey certain ideas relating to the social and economic position of the child and its family. But not all children were represented. Poor children were rarely portrayed and boys were much more frequently represented than girls. Consequently critics have argued that Ariès' thesis does not take into account issues of class, gender or historical period.

Secondly, Ariès' reliance on paintings means that he ignores other sources of information about children. For example, there were several scientific and medical books on children's illnesses which recognized childhood as a different stage from adulthood, a stage with specific needs and attributes. The legal system of this period set ages for criminal responsibility (the age at which children could be held responsible for their crimes), implying that children were seen as being different from adults, and not as morally aware. Finally, there were the teachings of the Church on the role and duties of children (see Section 3 for further details).

Another point for which Ariès has been heavily criticized is his idea that children were treated with indifference in the Middle Ages and beyond. Ariès thought that parents viewed children under seven as being of no importance and until that age more or less ignored them. His critics, however, using firsthand accounts from that period, have argued that children were much loved, even from infancy (Pollock, 1983). Child mortality meant parents were only too aware of the fragility of their children and a great deal of emphasis was placed on nurturing and protecting them (Hugget, 1996). There are few firsthand accounts from parents in the earlier medieval period, although in the 1490s, an Oxford schoolboy wrote 'A great while after my brother died, my mother was wont to sit weeping every day. I trow that there is nobody which would not be sorry if he had seen her' (quoted in Morrison, 2001, p. 10).

However, Ariès claimed that attitudes of indifference survived as late as the seventeenth century; up to this point, children under the age of seven simply 'did not count' (Ariès, 1962, p. 128). Firsthand accounts from parents in the early seventeenth century dispute this; for them their children obviously did count. Pollock quotes three diarists who were grieved by the deaths of their children. William Brownlow (1594–1675) lost many children but was far from indifferent. He wrote upon the death of his first son, 'O Lord thou has dealt bitterlie with mee and broken me with breach upon breach, when wilt though comfort mee.' On the death of his second, he wrote, 'I was at ease but Thou O God has broken mee a sunder and shaken mee to peeces'.

The shopkeeper Nehemiah Wallington (1598–1658) wrote about his grief over his four-year-old daughter's death, 'The grief for this child was so great that I forgot myself so much that I did offend God in it; for I broke all my purposes, promises, and convenants with my God, for I was much distracted in my mind, and could not be comforted' (quoted in Pollock, 1983, pp. 135–6).

The poet and playwright Ben Jonson's seven-year-old son died of plague in 1603. He wrote a poem, *On My First Son*, expressing his pain.

Farewell, thou child of my right hand, and joy;
My sin was too much hope of thee, loved boy.
Seven years thou wert lent to me, and I thee pay,
Exacted by thy fate, on the just day.
Oh!, could I lose all father now! For why
Will man lament the state he should envy?
To have so soon 'scaped the world's and flesh's rage,
And, if no other misery, yet age?
Rest in soft peace, and, asked, say here doth lie
Ben Jonson his best piece of poetry;
For whose sake, henceforth, all his vows be such,
As what he loves may never like too much.

SUMMARY OF SECTION 2

- Ideas of what a person is and when life begins vary widely among and across societies.
- Social constructionism enables the study of these ideas, these discourses, as part of the whole system of beliefs within any society.
- Such discourses have real consequences for the treatment of children and adults, and when they come into conflict may cause great difficulties.
- Ariès was one of the first historians to point out that childhood was a social construction not a biological given. He claimed that the idea of childhood did not exist in medieval Europe and that children during this period 'did not count'.
- For students of the evolution of childhood as a social construction, Ariès' thesis remains an important starting point in beginning to understand ideas about childhood in European history.

3 MAJOR THEMES IN WESTERN CONSTRUCTIONS OF CHILDHOOD

Philippe Ariès argued that European childhood is a specific, modern construction dependent on the particular social and historical factors in Europe. However, the criticisms levelled at his argument show that his is not the only theory surrounding ideas of childhood. Other writers have argued for different constructions, emphasizing different ideas and pointing out that ideas about childhood are intercut with ideas about gender, class, religion and ethnicity. More recent theorists have emphasized the multiple, competing discourses. The sociologist Chris Jenks has aptly described the complex Western discourses around childhood:

> Whether to regard children as pure, bestial, innocent, corrupt, charged with potential, *tabula rasa* [a blank slate], or even as we view our adult selves; whether they think and reason as we do, are immersed in a receding tide of inadequacy, or are possessors of a clarity of vision which we have through experience lost; whether their forms of language, games and conventions are alternatives to our own, imitations or crude precursors of our own now outgrown, or simply transitory impenetrable trivia which are amusing to witness and recollect; whether they are constrained and we have achieved freedom, or we have assumed constraint and they are truly free – all these considerations, and more, continue to exercise our theorizing about the child in social life.

(Jenks, 1996, p. 2)

As Jenks comments, ideas about children are so contradictory that it is possible to take one adjective to describe childhood and believe it to be true, and then take its opposite and also believe this. It is possible to hold several of these constructions to be true at the same time, or about different stages of childhood, or even about the same child. Some of these complex Western contemporary ideas about children and childhood in the West are inherited from past philosophical, artistic and scientific discourses, three of which I will outline in this section.

Allow about 10 minutes | ACTIVITY 6   **Good or bad children**

Jot down briefly two lists, one of the good qualities that you think children possess, one of the bad qualities.

COMMENT

In my list of characteristics, I have written down words like spontaneous, loveable, affectionate, happy, natural and trusting as good characteristics. On the negative side, I wrote down words such as thoughtless, demanding and unwittingly cruel. How are two such contradictory views of childhood possible? Given that both children and adults can act badly, why do I think of the stereotypical image of a child pulling the wings off a fly and imagine this is a feature of childhood? Other people's lists will have very different ideas from the ones I have come up with. The goodness or badness of particular characteristics can never be taken for granted: they are always socially constructed and open to challenge. I mentioned 'trusting' in my list of positives yet this can be seen in two ways. Suppose that children are ready to believe what adults tell them – do we call this 'trust' (a good thing) or 'gullibility' (a bad thing)?

I am now going to outline the philosophical basis for some of these contradictory notions. I will begin with two discourses that have already been mentioned in Chapter 1: the Puritan discourse and the Romantic discourse. There are many different and varied discourses throughout the world on childhood and I do not have the space to discuss all of them. I am therefore returning to two that have been mentioned briefly in the previous chapter and introducing a third one – the child as a blank slate.

3.1 The Puritan discourse – childhood as a time of evil and wildness

Children as potentially evil or wicked is a prevalent image in European Christian cultures. An important source of this view is the Christian belief that since the fall of Adam and Eve all humans are born sinful. St Augustine of Hippo (354–430 CE), believed that the child was a creature of will, a sinner even while in the womb, a view which persisted well into the seventeenth century and beyond. Some writers in the medieval period thought that persistent crying or failure to thrive in a child were manifestations of the Devil himself. According to historian Lloyd deMause, 'Baptism used to include actual exorcism of the Devil, and the belief that the child who cried at his christening was letting out the Devil long survived the formal omission of exorcism in the Reformation' (deMause, 1976, p.10).

The newborn child was particularly vulnerable to the Devil and therefore a constant watch had to be kept on the child for signs of the Devil to come out. However, although this notion was particularly relevant to children, it was not only children who had to beware of the constant temptations of the Devil. All people were born into sin and stayed sinners throughout their lives. Sin could not be cured by adulthood.

In the sixteenth century, the Protestant churches split from Roman Catholicism, a move called the Reformation. In the post-Reformation period, the innate wickedness of children was constantly emphasized, especially among the Puritans, fervent Protestants who believed that children were born both ignorant and sinful. In 1653, Richard Allestree wrote: 'The new borne babe is full of the stains and pollutions of sin which it inherits from our first parents [Adam and Eve] through our loins' (quoted in Plumb, 1975, p. 65).

However, Puritans also believed that children could be enlightened through discipline and education. Cotton Mather (1663–1728) expressed attitudes typical of contemporary American Puritanism. He believed his role as a parent was to correct the 'sinful and woeful condition' of his children's nature. He believed in total paternal control over his children, mirroring God's authority in Heaven with a father's on earth.

I first begett in them a high Opinion of their Father's Love to them, and of his being best able to judge, what shall be good for them.

Then I make them sensible, it is a Folly for them to pretend unto any Witt and Will of their own; they must resign all to me, who will be sure to do what is best; my word must be their Law.

(quoted in Pollock, 1983, p. 153)

Thomas Hobbes

Thomas Hobbes
(1588–1679)

Similarly, the English philosopher Thomas Hobbes (1588–1679) is known for his belief that children (and indeed people in general) are innately evil. He believed, like the Puritans, that children were born unruly and anarchistic, and that it was the parents' responsibility to constrain these traits through discipline (this point will be returned to later in this section). Again, like earlier writers, his views applied to people in general, not just children. It was not just children that needed strict control. The central proposition of his philosophy was the need for authoritarian rule by an unconstrained sovereign, otherwise life, in his famous phrase, would be 'nasty, brutish and short'. Susanna Wesley, the mother of John Wesley, the founder of Methodism, reflected this view in her own child-rearing practices. She saw children as creatures of will and sin. In a letter to her son in 1732, she wrote:

Break their will betimes: begin this great work before they can run alone, before they can speak plain, or perhaps speak at all ... make him do as he is bid, if you whip him ten times running to effect it ... Break his will now and his soul will live, and he will probably bless you to all eternity'.

(quoted in Jobling, 1978, p. 24)

This view has echoes in contemporary culture, famously in William Golding's 1954 book, *Lord of the Flies*. In this fictional story, a group of school boys are stranded on a remote island after a plane crash and gradually descend into savagery, losing all the attributes of civilization (represented by adulthood) until they run totally wild and commit murder.

Ralph moaned faintly. Tired as he was, he could not relax and fall into a well of sleep for fear of the tribe. Might it not be possible to walk boldly into the fort, say – 'I've got pax,' laugh lightly and sleep among the other? Pretend they were still boys, schoolboys who had said 'Sir, yes, Sir' – and worn caps? Daylight might have answered yes; but darkness and the horrors of death said no. Lying there in the darkness, he knew he was an outcast ...

There were sounds coming from behind the Castle Rock. Listening carefully, detaching his mind from the swing of the sea, Ralph could make out a familiar rhythm.

Kill the beast! Cut his throat! Spill his blood!

(Golding, 1954, p. 205)

3.2 The 'tabula rasa' discourse – childhood as a time of becoming

John Locke

John Locke (1632–1704)

In contrast to Hobbes, the philosopher John Locke (1632–1704) rejected all notions of 'innate ideas', i.e. that children were born with any qualities such as evil or goodness. Instead, he believed that children arrived as a *tabula rasa* (Latin for 'blank slate'). In 1690, he published his *Essay Concerning Human Understanding*, in which he set out his thesis that the child was an inadequate precursor to the real state of a human being, which was adulthood. However, the child was born with a potential which, through the right guidance and the right sort of experience, could develop into reason. According to Locke, experience shapes the child, and given the right kind of environment and education, the child will become rational, self-controlled and a responsible citizen. Locke recognized that children are not only in the process of becoming adults, but have certain needs and interests which are specific to them and which should be recognized. Locke believed that developing a rational and reasoning mind was the purpose of education. He thought it pointless to beat children when they were too young to understand what they were doing but once they did know, he felt that the rod should put 'fear and awe' into them. Locke saw children as neither intrinsically good or bad but as a product of their environment which had to be shaped by adults for the children's own good.

The modern commentators who, when children behave badly or evilly, do not blame their innate wickedness but the failure of their moral teaching are reflecting Locke's views. Indeed the book *Lord of the Flies* mentioned earlier can be seen as representing both the innate savagery of the child and the need for adult control and moral teaching. In the North today, alongside beliefs about children being wild creatures who need to be civilized by adults, the belief is also widespread that children who behave badly have been corrupted by adults. For example, children's murderous shooting sprees at American high schools are often held up in the British media as the result of America's adult gun culture and its violent films, television and video-games. In an opinion piece in a British Sunday newspaper, columnist Melanie Phillips discussed the rise in violent crime committed by children. Under a headline, 'A new strain of cruelty possesses the young', she blamed not the children themselves but their parents' and community's lack of a firm moral code:

> What are the causes of this terrible, violent anger among so many children? There are many. First and most important is the growing dismemberment of the family and the catastrophic failure of parenting, which between them are leaving children in emotional chaos and tearing up their moral maps ...

> Lack of parental presence, love, interest, care and supervision destroy children's sense of identity and can create a literally murderous rage.

> Parents in all types of family seem increasingly unable or unwilling to set the boundaries that civilise and socialise children ...

> The adult world has made a fetish of youth and no longer grasps what parental responsibility entails. It smokes and gets drunk in front of the young ... It gives its children no discipline, puts its own freedom first and blames everything but itself for the abandonment of the young. Is it any wonder then that savagery among them is on the inexorable rise?
>
> (Phillips, 2001, p. 17)

Phillips's sentiments might be seen as typical of the kind of commentary which bemoans the breakdown of traditional structures of authority and responsibility. To her, this breakdown leaves children without supervision and guidance, and leads to an increase in alienated, violent children. Yet what she presents as fact is not an undisputed truth but a particular discourse about children. The language she uses in this article is very emotive. Also is it very generalized: she talks about 'so many children' when she is only referring to a minority. This article is shot through with causal assumptions about children, about society, and about parental attitudes, with which many people will profoundly disagree. It is however, a good example of one discourse of childhood, a discourse that constructs children as needing adult control, without which they will turn violent and threatening.

3.3 The Romantic discourse – childhood as a time of innocence

In contrast to the image of childhood as evil, dangerous or wild, or to the idea that it is a blank, neutral state, the image of childhood as a time of innocence also features strongly in Western minds. One of the commonest words used to describe children in modern Western contexts is 'innocent'. What this word means will be unpacked in more detail in Chapter 6, but it is worth taking a brief look now at the idea of children's innocence and goodness. This idea contradicts that of a child's inherent wickedness but both ways of seeing childhood can co-exist.

The most obvious example of this is in the teachings of the Christian Church. As stated above, many theologians have said negative things about children, seeing them as innately sinful and wicked. Yet the image of the innocent child is central to New Testament teachings. Jesus is often portrayed with children and as being their special protector. At several times in the Bible, children are referred to explicitly as the inheritors of Heaven, for example:

> At the same time came the disciples unto Jesus, saying, Who is the greatest in the kingdom of Heaven? And Jesus called a little child unto him, and set him in the midst of them, And said, Verily I say unto you, Except ye be converted, and become as little children, ye shall not enter into the kingdom of heaven. Whosoever therefore shall humble himself as this little child, the same is greatest in the kingdom of heaven.
>
> (Matthew 18: 1–4, King James Version)

The Church did not always recommend beatings or harshness of treatment for children. St Anselm, for example, asked: 'Are they [children] not human? Are they not flesh and blood like you?' (quoted in deMause, 1975, p. 42).

Jean-Jacques Rousseau

Jean-Jacques Rousseau
(1712–78)

The discourse of the innocent child found its most influential exponent in eighteenth-century French philosopher, Jean-Jacques Rousseau (1712–78). He believed that children were born innocent and were naturally good, and that it is through experience that humans learn evil. A child's heart was angelic and pure at the outset, but this was corrupted by society. In 1762, he published *Emile, or On Education* in which he set out the principles by which he believed that children should be educated. He argued that children should be allowed to develop at their own rate in natural surroundings, shielded from civilization and oppressive adult authority which corrupted them and turned good into bad. In the opening paragraph of *Emile*, he wrote 'Everything is good as it leaves the hands of the Author of things; everything degenerates in the hands of man' (Rousseau, 1762, p. 37 of the 1979 edition).

For Rousseau, happiness was the highest ideal of childhood. This happiness was related to the child's natural goodness which needed protection from the misery and constraints of the adult world. Rousseau was one of the first to construct the child as a special kind of being who passes through distinct developmental phases, most importantly the 'Age of Nature', which lasts from birth to twelve years of age. This is a period of idyllic innocence when the child should be free 'to jump, play and run all day' (p. 107 of the 1979 edition). One of the key ideas in Rousseau's work is the understanding that children have a particular nature which should be valued in itself. Contrary to Hobbes's idea that children should be controlled and disciplined, Rousseau thought adults should worship the intrinsic good that children bring to the world. Children should be granted freedom to be who they are and education should take account of their particular development and progression.

In this construction of childhood, children are regarded as naturally innocent. If their innocence is corrupted in some way, because they are abused or because they are violent or uncontrollable they are viewed as having 'lost their childhood', having had their innocence 'stolen' or their childhood taken away. Childhood becomes synonymous with innocence, although this is a deeply problematic term which will be explored in greater detail in Chapter 6. Related to this particular notion of children's innocence are ideas about their perceived 'worth'. According to Viviana Zelizer in her book, *Pricing the Priceless Child*, the child in contemporary North America (and by extension Western Europe) is economically 'worthless' but emotionally 'priceless' (Zelizer, 1985). In communities where children do not work, they have became expensive to keep because they contribute nothing materially to their families. Their one contribution to the family is to the emotional satisfaction of their parents. Zelizer contends that the modern North American child is viewed as 'a privileged guest who is thanked and praised for "helping out", rather than a collaborator who at a certain age is expected to assume his or her fair share of household duties' (Zelizer, 1985, 209).

A child's perceived innocence is part of their high emotional value and the currency that they bring to an adult–child relationship. In other contexts, of course, people regard this way of treating children as untenable. There, children have to work and must be economically active. Children's innocence is seen very differently.

READING

Reading A is by sociologist Jane Ribbens in which she examines everyday discourses of childhood. While examining daily patterns of child-rearing, she asked parents how they conceptualized their children. She uses the word 'typification' rather than discourses in this extract, although the meaning is much the same. When reading it, note down resemblances between these parents' discourses about children and the three discourses that have been outline above (Puritan, *tabula rasa*, Romantic). How far you agree with each discourse about the nature of children.

COMMENT

Like the parents quoted in Activity 1, many of the parents interviewed for this piece of research have probably never heard of Hobbes, Locke or Rousseau. Yet the discourses that they use to describe their children are directly related to the ideas of these seventeenth and eighteenth-century philosophers. The contrasting views of children as wicked or innocent are directly related to Hobbes and Rousseau and to the Puritan and the Romantic discourses. The interaction between parents and children is, of course, complicated, and these parents, like many, veer between anger and fondness with their children. Parents use several different discourses about their children – a child might be a 'devil' but 'he also has a way about him'. These discourses are not consistent and certainly no parents in this article states the formal position of Hobbes or Rousseau. However, the constructions of children as angelic, corrupt, devilish or innocent have a history in Western thought, and their influence can still be seen today. It is interesting to consider whether these philosophical discourses will continue to exist or whether the final discourse that Ribbens mentions – children as small people – will become more important in parents' lives. It is noticeable that neither the parents quoted here nor those quoted in Activity 1 talk about children as incomplete beings becoming adults. Thinking about children in terms of their rights is the subject of Chapter 4.

SUMMARY OF SECTION 3

- In the North, there are multiple, contradictory discourses that surround children.
- Three such discourses can be found in the work of Hobbes, Locke and Rousseau.
- Hobbes saw children as inherently evil (the Puritan discourse);
- Locke saw children as neither inherently good or evil but as blank slates to be shaped by their upbringing (the *tabula rasa* discourse).
- Rousseau saw children as inherently good (the Romantic discourse);
- These ideas are still debated today (Chapter 6 will have a fuller discussion of contemporary views of innocence and evil) and still affect the ways that children are thought about and treated.
- Discourses of childhood change. For example, children are increasingly being talked about as small people with rights.

4 THE GLOBALIZATION OF CHILDHOOD

In the last section, I looked at a particular set of Western discourses about childhood, particularly those based on seventeenth and eighteenth-century British and French philosophy. In Section 2 I used examples of other societies which have very different views on who is a child and how children should be treated. I chose extreme examples to show the vast differences between people's constructions of childhood. However, Western constructions of childhood, especially childhood as a time of innocence where children must play and be protected from the adult world, have been exported to other countries, raising the question of whether there is now such a thing as a 'global child'.

Chapter 1 mentioned applied approaches to childhood – ways of seeing children through a legal or policy perspective, and in discussing the globalization of childhood, these need to be taken into account. The ways in which childhood is socially constructed affects the way that they are treated and different polices reflect different notions of what a child should be. Anthropologists and sociologists have long understood that different cultures have different ways of raising children and have different ways of constructing what they mean by childhood. It is clear that if childhood is a social construct, then it must differ from society to society. Yet the contemporary world is often said to be going through a period of globalization, defined by sociologist Anthony Giddens as 'the increasing interdependence of world society' (Giddens, 1997, p. 64). In this world the balance of power is shifting between individual cultures and governments and multinational corporations or international bodies such as the World Bank or the International Monetary Fund. Companies like McDonald's, Coca-Cola or CNN have global markets where very few people are untouched by their advertising. Globalization has meant that increasingly people across the world are subject to the same influences in advertising, the media and through the products available to them. Through the United Nations, the World Bank and aid projects which demand that recipient governments adopt particular policies, a certain form of political philosophy, based on the language of human rights and the values of liberalism, is also being exported. The intellectual basis of these notions is a Western one and is now influencing children's lives across the world in a variety of ways.

Some argue that globalization is simply a new version of an older phenomenon and had its precursors in Christian missionaries or colonial rulers trying to 'civilize' natives (see, for example, Edward Said's *Orientalism*, 1994). However, there are features of globalization that do make it unique. Institutions such as the United Nations, the World Bank and the International Monetary Fund emerged relatively recently. They are often seen as dominated by the richer countries of the North and, as such, are responsible for pushing a particular agenda on the rest of the world. 'Structural adjustment programmes', good governance initiatives (where countries will only receive aid if they structure their society along Northern lines, featuring democracy, press freedom and the rule of law as well as particular monetary and trade policies) and international treaties all make it easier to talk of a 'New World Order' (see Giddens, 1990, for a fuller discussion of these processes).

Beliefs and values about childhood are also becoming globalized. To give one example, every country in the world except the US and Somalia has signed and ratified the United Nations Convention on the Rights of the Child, agreeing with the Convention that 'a child means every human being below the age of eighteen years'. Yet this is clearly problematic. As the previous chapter explained, children do not suddenly become adults at eighteen in all societies, nor are they necessarily treated as children up to that age. In many societies, there is a gradual process of attaining rights and a complex series of rituals and rites of passage. Nevertheless, there is a compelling argument that variations in cultures are becoming fewer and fewer as globalization spreads. Notions of childhood inevitably become part of this process. For example, in 1997 the World Bank published a report on early child development called *Early Child Development: investing in the future.* The report aimed to have world-wide significance and be applicable to all children. It divided children under eight into four categories: infants (birth to age one), toddlers (age one to three), pre-schoolers (age three to six) and young school age children (age six to eight). It then listed the expected developmental stages that every child, regardless of whereabouts in the world, should be expected to reach. Although its recommendations were meant to be universal and based on scientific fact, its division of children into these categories and developmental stages shows a bias towards Western notions of what childhood is and what children should be. For example, calling children 'pre-schoolers' is only relevant in societies where most children go to school. But the report goes further and spells out the standards that these children, wherever they live, should meet:

> *Pre-schoolers (age three to six).* Active learning for pre-schoolers entails engaging in simple problem-solving tasks; developing such self-care skills as dressing and eating; developing the social skills needed to interact with adults and other children; and developing such cognitive skills as telling stories, associating the written word with spoken language, drawing pictures on their own about their play, and listening and moving to music.

(Young, 1997)

Many of the attributes described here might sound very ethnocentric to the peoples of the world whose children do not go to school, who do not wear clothes, or certainly not the complicated clothes with the zips and buttons of Western children. Many cultures are non-literate and others do not have pictorial traditions. Yet these developmental standards have been laid down as universal, applicable and relevant to all children (these ideas will be discussed at greater length in the next chapter).

In 1946, Dr Benjamin Spock published *The Common Sense Book of Baby and Child Care*. Radical for its times, this book encouraged parents to do away with rigid feeding schedules, to be flexible and see the child as an individual. It started with the famous phrase; 'Trust yourself. You know

Dr Spock (1903–98)

more than you think you do'. During his lifetime this book was translated into 39 languages and sold more than 50 million copies. Only the Bible has sold more copies. Developmental standards and child-rearing practices from the North are thus set for children in many other communities, as are immunization programmes and minimum standards of law and provision to which all governments should aspire. Models of dealing with 'problem' children have sometimes been imported from the North, often to little effect. In Nigeria, for instance, imported methods based on Northern models of dealing with child delinquents have proved unworkable. Juvenile courts, probation services, approved schools and reformatories have had no impact on the levels of juvenile crime in Nigeria (Boyden, 1990). As childhood becomes more scientific, with child development experts on hand to assess physical, physiological and moral development, the idea of a universal child with universal needs gains ground. For parents, influential authors such as Dr Spock wrote about children without reference to cultural background as if a child in America was the same as one in Europe, Africa or Amazonia. Ideas that children should not work because, in Rousseau's words, children should be free 'to jump, play and run all day' have now been exported to countries in the South without always taking into account the local conditions there where children work through necessity and through tradition. Societies in the North have constructed the idea that childhood and work are incompatible and that school is the most appropriate place for children. These notions have been exported through the media, through inter-governmental organizations like the United Nations, through aid agencies and sometimes through direct government pressure. For example in 1992 in the USA, Senator Harkin proposed a bill after concern was raised about child labourers in the Bangladeshi garment industry. His bill proposed a ban on the import to the US of all Bangladeshi products, especially clothes, made with child labour. Similar boycotts have been instigated by consumers in the US, such as the Don't Buy Thai! Campaign which ran from 1996 to 2000 in protest at the Thai government's failure to end the sexual exploitation of children. In the 1990s, certain aid agencies gave aid to Guatemala only on condition that the street children in the cities were not harassed by the authorities (Boyden, 1990).

On one level this is wholly admirable. Few people would argue against equality of opportunity for all children or their protection from hazardous labour, oppression or harassment. Many children's lives have been saved through interventions such as smallpox vaccinations and emergency food programmes in times of famines. The UN Convention on the Rights of the Child has forced governments to focus on children and to give more resources to the children of their countries. However, there is also another aspect of globalization. Interventions do not always work and indeed, they can be harmful to children. A follow-up survey of some of the children sacked from garment factories in Bangladesh showed that many went into *more* hazardous occupations such as brick chipping and rickshaw pulling (Boyden, 1990). In the quotation below, Erica Burman identifies further problems. She argues that the globalization of Western notions of childhood actually penalizes poorer children in the South as 'the global child' represents an ideal that children in the poorer parts of the world cannot and never will be able to fulfil:

Childhood is celebrated as a universal stage or period of life which is characterized by protection and freedom from responsibilities. But although it purports to be universal, this representation of childhood turns out to be specific and geographically distributed. In this view, childhood becomes an entity the deprivation of which constitutes a violation of human rights. The polarities set up between this supposedly universal stage and those deemed to lack it map, of course, onto the North–South divide: in the North children develop, and in the South they merely survive, if they're lucky. While we in the North are exhorted to encourage 'development through play' (as the toy manufacturers, Duplo, put it), the dilemma we are invited to resolve for children in the South is 'starvation or survival' (Ethiopiaid, 18 November 1992). For us in the North, development is equated with consumption, as in the 1992 Children's World advertisement, 'she's got the whole world before her' … We identify more modest goals for children in the South; we hear only of appeals for food and water, to make the difference between life and death. This life stage that all have a right to enjoy is in fact an idealized representation of Northern models of childhood. It achieves a globalized status through its inscription within international aid and development policies and legislation.

(Burman, 1994, p. 32)

READING

In Reading B, Patricia Holland discusses the ways in which aid agencies represent children in their advertising campaigns and the ways in which viewers respond to this and what this says about the social constructions of the global child. Patricia Holland looks at how images of children in distress in the South have been used to bolster Northern stereotypes of African and Asian peoples being incompetent and unable to look after themselves and needing civilization in the form of aid from the North to survive. In this instance the child is constructed not only as individually powerless and helpless but also as a symbol of the powerlessness of the whole of Africa or Asia.

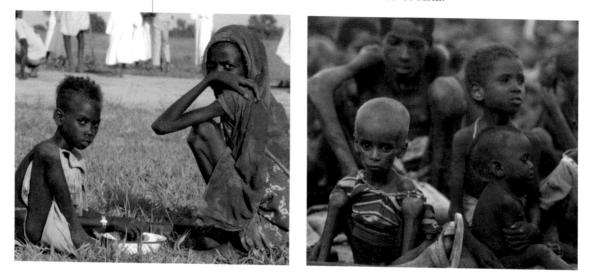

COMMENT

Like Erica Burman, Patricia Holland argues that people in the North have expectations of how children in countries of the South should be. These expectations are reinforced at many levels, photographers shoot certain pictures which they feel are the most powerful, picture editors choose images that the public will respond to and viewers of these pictures are distressed most by pictures of children which show their helplessness and vulnerability. Patricia Holland argues therefore that the imagery of newspapers and advertising has three functions. Firstly, it appeals to the idea that there is a global ideal of childhood that children in the South fail to meet. The children represented are set up in contrast to white children in the North. Secondly these images play on the racist stereotypes that people in the South are poor and helpless because they are incompetent; they cannot look after their children and are passive in the face of disaster. Thirdly, it reinforces the notion that because of this, the only way to help these people is through Northern intervention, giving money and saving the innocent children who are the victims of their county's failure to ensure a childhood based on the Northern model. In this view of childhoods in the South, however, Holland sees children as essentially passive. There is no room in her analysis for children's active participation and the children she writes about are simply adult constructions.

Allow about 10 minutes

ACTIVITY 7   **Children of the South**

Look through a recent newspaper and find a picture of a non-white child from the South. How far does this picture support Patricia Holland's analysis?

SUMMARY OF SECTION 4

- Discourses of childhood are changing under the new social and economic conditions caused by globalization.
- Images of the ideal childhood have been standardized and exported globally so that now all countries are judged by a single set of standards.
- International legislation, direct financial pressure and advertising, have all contributed to impose a Western notion of childhood on countries which have previously constructed childhood and children's roles very differently.
- The globalization of childhood has also had several unforeseen effects which have penalized poorer countries, stigmatising them and reinforcing power differentials between them and richer nations.

5 CONCLUSION

This chapter has extended the discussion of childhood as a social construct begun in Chapter 1. I have attempted to show that there are many different childhoods, which are affected by their historical, social and cultural context. Consequently discourses of childhood may be contradictory. Ideas about childhood are being constructed on every level by children themselves and their parents, based in lived experience and daily contact, as well as exposure to historical writers such as Hobbes, Locke and Rousseau who dealt with idealized, philosophical notions of abstract childhoods. To talk about one childhood is impossible as the ways in which children experience it and adults view it vary depending on their own background and expectations. Nevertheless we can talk about the discourses surrounding childhood and look at how these have both shaped and changed and been shaped and changed by the cultural setting. This chapter has looked at ways of understanding children, topics which will be picked up again in the next chapter which deals with the issues that developmental psychology raises about children and looks at how this discipline views childhood.

REFERENCES

ARIÈS, P. (1962) *Centuries of Childhood*, translated by Robert Baldock, New York, Knopf.

BALL, H. and HILL, C. (1996). 'Re-evaluating "twin infanticide"?', *Current Anthropology*, **37**(5), pp. 856–63.

BOYDEN, J. (1990) 'Childhood and the policy makers: a comparative perspective on the globalisation of childhood' in JAMES, A. and PROUT, A. (eds) *Constructing and Re-constructing Childhood: contemporary issues in the sociological study of childhood*, Brighton, Falmer Press.

BURMAN, E. (1994) 'Poor children: charity appeals and ideologies of childhood', *Changes*, **12**(1), pp. 29–36.

DEMAUSE, L. (1991) 'The evolution of childhood' in deMause, L. (ed.) *The History of Childhood*, London, Bellew Publishing.

Frank, A. (1997) *The Diary of a Young Girl*, edited by Otto H. Frank and Mirjam Pressler and translated by Susan Massotty, London, Viking.

GIDDENS, A. (1997) *Sociology*, Cambridge, Polity Press.

GIDDENS, A. (1990) *The Consequences of Modernity*, Cambridge, Polity Press.

GOODMAN, R. (2000) *Children of the Japanese State*, Oxford, Oxford University Press.

GOLDING, W. (1954) *Lord of the Flies*, London, Faber and Faber.

HOLLAND, P. (1992) *What is a Child?*, London, Virago.

HUGGET, J. (1996) *The Book of Children, 1480–1680*, Bristol, Stuart Press.

JAMES, A. and PROUT, A. (1990) *Constructing and Re-constructing Childhood: contemporary issues in the sociological study of childhood*, Brighton, Falmer Press.

JENKS, C. (1996) *Childhood*, London, Routledge.

JOBLING, M. (1978) 'Child abuse: the historical and sociological context' in CARVER, V (ed.) *Child Abuse: a study text*, Milton Keynes, The Open University Press/The Open University and Newcastle upon Tyne Polytechnic.

JONSON, B. (1985) *Ben Jonson – The Oxford Authors*, edited by Ian Donaldson, Oxford, Oxford University Press.

LA FONTAINE, J. S. (1986) 'An anthropological perspective on children' in RICHARDS, M. and LIGHT, P. (eds) *Children of Social Worlds* , Cambridge, Polity Press.

MORRISON, B. (2001) 'The child in time', *Guardian*, 15 September 2001, p. 10.

PHILLIPS, M. (2001) 'A new strain of cruelty possesses the young', *Sunday Times,* London, 13 June 2001, p. 17.

PLUMB, J. H. (1975) 'The new world of children in eighteenth-century England', *Past and Present*, 67, pp. 64–95.

POLLOCK, L. A. (1983) *Forgotten Children: parent–child relations from 1500–1900*, Cambridge, Cambridge University Press.

QVORTRUP, J. (1994) 'Childhood matters: an introduction', IN QVORTRUP, J., BARDY, M., SGRITTA, G., and WINTERSBERGER, H. (eds) *Childhood Matters: social theory, practice and politics*, Aldershot, Avebury.

RIVIÈRE, P. (1974) 'The couvade: a problem reborn', *Man*, **9**(3), pp. 423–35.

ROUSSEAU, J.-J. (1979) *Emile, or On Education,* translated by Allan Bloom, New York, Basic Books (first published 1762).

SAID, E. (1994) *Orientalism*, New York, Vintage.

YOUNG, M. E. (1997) *Early Child Development: investing in the future*, Human Development Department, World Bank, on line, www.worldbank.org/children/ecd/book/ (last accessed 17 October 2001)

ZELIZER. V. (1985) *Pricing the Priceless Child*, Princeton, Yale University Press.

Mothers' images of children and their implications for maternal responses

Jane Ribbens

Introduction

... In a study carried out in the late 1980s, I interviewed 24 women about their experiences and views of bringing up their children, using minimally structured, quasi-life history interviews. All the women had an eldest child aged seven and lived in a home-owning, middle-income household in south-east England.

When I first began to analyse the women's accounts, I started from the nitty gritty details of everyday child rearing issues, such as food, sleep, clothing and cleanliness. However, it became apparent that there were considerable difficulties in this procedure, and I realised that I needed to change my approach around. It was not that the everyday details were not important as elements of the child rearing accounts – they were indeed profoundly important:

> ... that's, I think, how you really show children that you love them, by all the little ways, all the little things (Christine).

> ... by examining the most boring details of domestic and child rearing practices, we are ...uncovering the most fundamental political questions about the production of democracy, about freedom and about women's oppression. (Walkerdine and Lucey, 1989:33).

I came to realise that the significance of the everyday details for my analysis concerned what they revealed about the *underlying* frameworks of meaning and images which shaped how women dealt with any particular issue. These implicit understandings and images were intricately interlaced by the women to create particular frameworks of meaning to make sense of their concerns in bringing up their children. Women might appear to adopt the same position on any particular substantive issue but for quite different reasons. Conversely, they might appear to be doing different things, but the underlying rationales might be very similar. Thus, to understand what was being said it was crucial to include a *consideration of the meanings* that particular actions held for the women themselves.

Conceptions of children

[...] The notion of child as a particular category defines children as individuals who are not-adults, who have their needs recognised and met by others who are adults. George Kelly (1955) discusses how we may understand and identify a construct by defining how it is different from something else – a process of construing through the perception of difference. Jenks (1982) suggests that adulthood is only recognisable through being contrasted with childhood. Children are construed as

'Other' than adult, from the adult perspective, children are defined as 'Not-me'. 'Children are all foreigners. We treat them as such' (R. W. Emerson 1803–1882). In the present study, the view of children as different from adults was very widely assumed, and referred to in passing – 'children will be children' (Kay).

Nevertheless, there may be great variability in the perceived content or *nature of children's needs,* closely associated with variations in the underlying images of what it means to be a child. Schutz (1979) suggests that social life is possible through the use of typifications, which are available in the socio-cultural world to be drawn upon to make sense of other individuals' behaviour ...

The typifications identified in these women's child rearing accounts I have labelled as:

> children as natural innocents,
> children as little devils, and
> children as small people.

The last typification minimises the view of children as not-adults. The first two typifications are alike in sharing a perception of *children as different-from-adults,* although this difference is construed in quite opposite ways:

a) Children as natural innocents

This typification defines children as different from adults in that they have a natural innocence, which adults have lost. Furthermore, this innocence is something that is 'given', in the sense that it is something that children are born with and that they will retain if allowed to develop without distortion from society:

> Children are different, they're loveable little beings ... you just think they're the most wonderful things that's come on earth (Amy).

This view can extend to a construction of childhood as a very special almost magical – phase of life (Peter Pan).

> It is important to respect and protect the child's childhood, it will never come back again, when it's gone it's gone and they can never catch up (Ellen).

> I think children have the reality – we strive all our lives to recapture what we have as a child I think (Christine).

Such childhood innocence may be lost as children become more aware of social life and more 'knowing':

> ... she's getting a bit more knowing now, and she may know she's been naughty and she'll give you a sort of defiant look (Sally).

> ... one little girl in particular is just so adult ... this little girl turned round and looked at me with such a knowing look ... I felt absolutely squashed into the floor (Christine).

The magical specialness of childhood is perceived in various ways, notably the idea of childhood as a special carefree time for play, fun, 'mess' and creativity. Although some educational theories regard play as part of the serious business of learning adult skills, this was not very apparent as a perspective in these parents' accounts. Indeed it is the view of play-as-fun, and therefore not-work, that underlies criticisms that children 'play too much' in the early years of school life.

Some accounts clearly made consistent use of this typification, while others also used such imagery even if only fleetingly. Kay and Angela both used this typification in the context of something which had been lost through the disruption of 'family life' resulting from divorce. Angela thus discussed the possibility that the 'break-up of the family' had reduced the time available for their son to enjoy 'being a child', a view of childhood which his father promoted.

> I say, 'He shouldn't be doing that, he ought to be reading', and (his father) will say, 'Let him be a child, don't expect too much of him at this age', and maybe I am a little bit over the top. He says. 'Don't be so serious with him all the time'... It's always a lot of fun and laughter when they are at Dad's ...

Kay also suggested that her son's childhood might have been left unprotected because his father was not part of the household, so that the child showed signs of becoming an adult before time. Kay defined childhood at times as innocent and also silly, while adults are rational and sensible. Descriptions of children's activities as 'silly' carry some ambiguity. If children are silly they are not part of the adult world of rationality and responsibility, yet this silliness is not necessarily seen in such a destructive light as the potential for anarchy, and parents may allow themselves to join in children's silly games – 'We play quite a lot of silly games...I suppose that's quite fun' (Margaret).

However, it is also important to note within this typification, that images of innocence do not just view the child as 'all sweetness and light' but may *encompass a variety of emotions* in the child, including 'anger':

> I sometimes find with (my daughter) that I'm about to correct some aggression, and then I think, no, you're going to need that (Amy).

Such emotions are regarded as needing expression as well, but such expression expels the anger which will then be 'spent', without unleashing unlimited forces as the next typification suggests. There is thus a sense of *natural self-regulation* underlying this typification.

b) Children as little devils

This typification also sees childhood as a particular phase in life, because children are viewed as very different from adults. However the nature of this difference is regarded as potentially destructive – 'she's on the fiendish side' (mother quoted in Newson and Newson, 1965:184). This imagery refers to the possibilities of children disrupting life with asocial tendencies, with hints of the possible unleashing of latent uncontrollable forces unless the child is shaped to fit into social order. However, there may also be some ambivalence in how this is evaluated:

> 'He's such a little devil that I think you can laugh about him and enjoy him completely all the time ... Even when he's being a devil, 'cause he's got such a way about him you know'

> (mother, quoted by Newson and Newson 1978, p. 283).

If children's anarchy is left unrestrained, anything might happen. Lindsay described children as potentially infinitely disruptive:

> (If) you just give in to them all the time ... as soon as you start doing that they just push you, and push you, and push you, until they're doing the most awful outrageous things, and you're not able to control them at all ...

Marty also suggested that an absence of restriction on children might unleash almost limitless and unknowable lawlessness:

> ... it's the trend nowadays isn't it, not to be too strict. Free-thinking, and let them do what they like. Let children rule. You wonder what's going to happen don't you?

In Stephen's account, this typification of children led to a careful consideration at times of children's real 'needs', since 'attention-seeking' children might 'play on' their needs to obtain unjustified concessions from their parents, leading to almost unlimited possibilities:

> ... once they start (coming into the parents' bed) I think that's the thin edge of the wedge – probably there until they're about nineteen or twenty!

Again, some accounts repeatedly used this typification, while other accounts drew on such imagery at times.

c) Children as small people

This typification did not appear in the accounts as frequently as either of the previous two, and no-one drew exclusively on this sort of imagery. This typification minimises the notion of childhood as a special phase. From babyhood dependency, the child becomes an *individual*, a *person* like any other – albeit rather small in size – '... she's an individual ... she can argue, she's got a mind of her own already' (mother of seven-year-old, quoted by Newson and Newson, 1978:280, original emphasis). Such a perspective links with mothers' construction of their children as individuals, with age status being minimised. There is less tendency to identify children and adults as separate categories, and less of an implicit hierarchy based on age. While dependency needs are minimised, independence is valued.

In Margaret's account, individuality – being your 'own person' – was something that could potentially be hindered and stopped and it therefore required some nurturing from the more powerful adult. In Janet's account, there was more of a sense of her son being his own person here and now, having an individuality which he expressed vigorously and which she did not have the power as an adult to stop, even if she wanted to.

This typification also appeared occasionally in other accounts, particularly in the belief that children should be respected. Children might thus be defined as having rights as well as needs. Tom's account used imagery of children as small people, although there was also, as for Margaret, the suggestion that adults are in fact more powerful and may choose whether or not to recognise the child's perspective.

I wouldn't say they have equal voting rights to us, there's not quite a democracy, we do tend to have the casting vote if it comes to a tie, but we certainly do listen to them and you just don't see that with other people. The great majority, the children are under the thumb ...

Children may thus also be construed as different-from-adults, not because their needs are different, but because they occupy a less powerful position ...

References

JENKS. C. (1982) 'Constituting the child'. In Jenks. C. (ed.) *The Sociology of Childhood.* London: Batsford.

KELLY. G. (1955) *The Psychology of personal Constructs.* New York: W.W. Norton.

NEWSON, J. and NEWSON, E. (1965) *Patterns of Infant Care in an Urban Community.* Harmondsworth Middlesex: Pelican.

NEWSON. J. and NEWSON, E. (1978) *Seven Years Old in the Home Environment.* Harmondsworth Middlesex: Pelican.

RIBBENS, J. (1990) 'Accounting for our children: Differing perspectives on "Family Life" in middle income households'. Unpublished PhD thesis, CNAA/South Bank Polytechnic.

RIBBENS, J. (1994) *Mothers and Their Children: a feminist Sociology of Childrearing.* London: Sage.

SCHUTZ. A. (1979) Concept and theory formation in the social sciences IN BYNNER. J. and STRIBLEY, K. (eds.) *Social Research: Principles and Processors.* London: Longman/Open University Press.

WALKERDINE, V. and LUCEY, H. (1989) *Democracy in the Kitchen: Regulating Mothers and Socialising Daughters.* London: Virago.

Source

Ribbens, J. 'Mothers' images of children and their implications for maternal response' in Brannen, J. and O'Brien, M. (eds) *Childhood and Parenthood: proceedings of ISA Committee for Family Research Conference on Children and Families, 1994*, London, University of London Institute of Education, pp. 60–78.

READING B

What is a child?

Patricia Holland

Crybabies and damaged children

Save the children?

Without the image of the unhappy child, our contemporary concept of childhood would be incomplete. Real children suffer in many different ways and for many different reasons, but pictures of sorrowing children recall those defining characteristics of childhood: dependence and powerlessness.

Children living in poverty, children suffering from neglect or disadvantage, children who are the victims of wars or natural disasters – they figure in imagery as the most vulnerable, the most pathetic, the most deserving of all of our sympathy and aid. They are on the receiving end of an oppression in which they can only acquiesce. Children are seen as archetypal victims; childhood is seen as weakness itself. As the children in the image reveal their vulnerability, we long to protect them and provide for their needs. Paradoxically, while we are moved by the image of a sorrowful child, we also welcome it, for is can arouse pleasurable emotions of tenderness, which in themselves confirm adult power.

As with children, so with all those other groups who bear the characteristics of childhood – women, Black people and the whole of the Third World are among those who stand in a childish relation to the exercise of power. The non-white nations are regularly presented as if in themselves they lack potency, and it is among the children of the developing countries – in stark contrast to the well-fed, well-equipped mini-consumers of the domestic image that we find the most frequent pictures of childhood suffering.

The one area where the British image industry regularly and predictably produces pictures of Black and other non-white children is in press reports of wars, famine and natural disasters and in the appeals for aid which accompany such reports. The wide eyes of the needy dark-skinned child look reproachfully out from news pages and from those advertisements that solicit rather than seduce. The ragged child who is not ashamed to plead so dominates the available imagery of Africa, Latin America and the Indian subcontinent that the whole of that vast area beyond Western culture seems in itself to be a place of distress and childish subservience. Third World suffering acts to secure our sense of First World comfort by assuring us that we have the power to help. That power is confirmed by the gaze of an appealing child, carefully selected so that it in no way undermines our complacent certainty of our own position. These pictured children are not refugees challenging our borders; they are not armed guerrillas causing international disruption; they are without the stench of disease which might make their physical presence repellent. Their humble and submissive appeal protects our compassion and enables us to give.

In the act of looking at these presentations, viewers recognise themselves as both adult and Western, as individuals with the ability to change a child's life for the better without changing their own for the worse. The only possible relationship for this pictured child is with the putative viewer. The Black child is seeking a white benefactor, a surrogate parent who will be more effective than his own absent Black parent. The appeal is to the competence of Western civilisation, seen not as the controlling father, imposing the harsh disciplines of international finance, but as the nurturing mother, the Mother Countries. He looks to the First World as his only source of help and succour: Be my postal parent! Help me!

Over the last twenty years the increased accessibility of information in words and pictures in the press and on television has made war, famine, drought and disasters of cataclysmic proportions familiar parts of our everyday consciousness. From the worsening famine in the Sahel region of Northern Africa and the increasingly serious floods and cyclones in the Indian subcontinent, to the wars which have devastated Lebanon, Cambodia, East Timor, Iraq and many other parts of the globe, pictures which document natural disasters have formed a continuum with those which show the results of human atrocity. In the filtering and selection processes which lead to a decision about which picture will make the front page, and which photographer will become photographer of the year, attention is consistently directed towards those whose hardship is greatest. Children have remained at the centre of the image.

As familiarity has blunted their effectiveness, pictures of suffering have become less restrained. If they are not sufficiently shocking, photographs will not break through the news barrier and on to the front pages. 'It's an unfortunate truism of famines, that by the times the pictures are horrific enough to move people, it's almost too late', wrote journalists and film-maker Paul Harrison. The Western public has become familiar with an imagery of extremity at the expense of context, and the wrenching emotion at the expense of understanding.

The implicit question that runs through the imagery of distress which has echoed between aid advertisements and the news pages is: Who can take responsibility for the child?

The pictures can be read as a series of reflections on that problem. A frequent image is that of mother and child together, the weakness of the mother serving only to intensify the plight of the child. Her breasts are drained dry, she cannot fulfil the only role that justifies her presence ...

Men are rarely visible in the iconography of disaster. It is they who signify culture, and whose presence tends to locate a picture in its geographical context. They are more likely to be fully clothed or to be engaged in some task. As the strongest group they are least likely to conform to the expected image of the victim and the most likely to be involved in attempts at reconstruction or resistance, confusing the clarity of the story, complicating a reaction of pity alone. Thus the community to which the suffering child belongs is visually bypassed, and the extent to which it is caring for its own children is rarely explored ...

But the use of a child both in the press and in advertisements refers to a value that claims to be beyond explanation and outside politics. Children may express emotions that are universal while remaining separate from those other qualities that make humanity so diverse. Not yet fully participant in diversions of language, nationality, culture or even race, the child is presented as uncontaminated by their antagonistic forms. As the symbol of common humanity, a child may be the bearer of suffering with no responsibility for its causes. This view is in stark contrast to the practice of the starving nations, where the child is the most expendable. 'If a parent dies the family is doomed. The father eats first and dies last; the children eat last and die first', wrote Richard Dowden of the aid camps in Ethiopia. The irony of the aid imagery, then, is that however accurate the picture, an appeal on behalf of the children may necessarily be *against* the community of which they are a part, rather than on that community's behalf. Since their community has failed them, the children need to be saved. They may be given a Western education, removed, adopted or even airlifted out. Children 'rescued' from the perceived disorder of the Third World are seen in the imagery with a symbol of the 'civilisation' they have reached – they clutch a teddy bear or stroke a dog. ...

The child who appeals to the viewer, humbly requesting help, has remained the mainstay of aid imagery. But children's actual response to conditions of deprivation may well refuse qualities of childhood which give them their pathos. It is less easy to deal with the image of children who have become fighters, workers or brutalised dwellers on the streets. In 1990 the United Nations estimated that 200,000 children under fifteen are bearing arms around the world, most of them in rebel armies. The image of a child with a gun has carried the ambivalent meanings of resistance to oppression by children fighting alongside their elders, as well as the exploitation and corruption of children by those elders. It moves from the extreme of the violent child out of control to that of the disciplined young person playing their part in an organised force.

Although the practice is common in many parts of the world, pictures of children at work under conditions of forced labour and with minimal wages have rarely found a place in available imagery despite the efforts of organisations like the Anti-Slavery Society to expose such scandals as the carpet industry in India. By contrast, the image of the street urchin has an uneasy presence within travel imagery. The packaging of the people of the nations for the Western tourist has long included an element of sexual tourism. Tour guides have sections on red light districts, and certain parts of the world – for example, Sri Lanka and Thailand – are known to be places where child prostitutes operate. The engaging impudence of the street urchin image carries overtones of both sexuality and children's contribution to the tourist economy of those states. But it needs only a slight shift of perspective to see the child on the streets as an undesirable vagrant.

For many years the Western media have made spasmodic reports on the street children of Latin America. They attracted mild international scandal, but seen from the distance of a continent could easily be made light of. But to many 'respectable' inhabitants of Rio and Bogota such children are like garbage, spoiling the attractiveness of the city, as they pester tourists and rob respectable citizens. By 1990 there were reports that street children were being routinely murdered by semi-official death squads. In Rio such killings were said to be 'socially acceptable'. 'When you talk about Brazilian children you must understand that they are not the same as European children. They really are savages here. Most of the time they are killing *each other*', a Brazilian businessman told Zoë Heller of the *Independent on Sunday*. The high-circulation Rio daily *O Povo* is filled with photographs of mutilated corpses. Sometimes these are the only record of the deaths of children who have no parents, no birth certificates, no official existence. But that most shocking of images is by no means confined to Third World children.

'The victimisation of children is nowhere forbidden', wrote Alice Miller in *Thou Shall Not be Aware*. 'What is forbidden is to write about it'. Imagery, sometimes the most extreme imagery, can put together meanings that words hesitate to admit. Childhood is about impotence and weakness. Acceptable victimisation is part of the visual repertoire with which the concept of childhood crosses and influences the concepts of race and class. Starving child from the Third World or helpless child from the domestic imagery of poverty, the image of the child as victim prepares the way for an open expression of adult hatred and cruelty.

References

HARRISON, P. and PALMER. R., (1986). *News out of Africa,* Hilary Shipman. p. 97.

DOWDEN, R. (1991). *Dying by Darwinian logic.*

STANLEY, A. (1990). UN estimates of children bearing arms in 'Child Warriors', *Time International.*

ENNEW, J. (1986) (For an account of sexual tourism), *The Sexual Exploitation of Children,* Polity Press p. 97.

GUARDIAN. (1991) Socially acceptable. *Guardian*

HELLER, Z. (1991) *Independent on Sunday*, 5 May 1991.

MILLER, A. (1985) *Thou shall not be aware,* Pluto p.192

Source

Holland, P. (1992) 'Crybabies and damaged children' in Holland, P. *What is a Child? Popular images of childhood*, London, Virago, pp. 148–63.

Chapter 3

The child in development

Martin Woodhead

CONTENTS

When you have studied this chapter, you should be able to:

1   Describe features of a developmental approach to childhood, explain its historical roots and its global influence.

2   Explain key concepts and methods used in the study of development, illustrated through examples of observational and experimental studies.

3   Illustrate the way researchers test the adequacy of developmental theories by devising new experiments or carrying out new observations.

4   Analyse debates about how far child development is a universal, staged process and how far it is a social and cultural process.

5   Evaluate the claim that developmental research and theories are a social construction of childhood.

I INTRODUCTION

During the winter of 1799, people living in a rural community in Aveyron, France, noticed a dirty, naked boy in nearby woods. He was behaving strangely and apparently surviving alone on a diet of acorns and roots. Nobody knew where he had come from, how long he had been living wild, or how he had managed to survive. He was reluctant to wear clothes, didn't speak and didn't seem to have the abilities of other village children of his age (about twelve years old). Many people thought he must have been abandoned during infancy and survived on his own ever since. The 'wild boy' was brought to Paris where he became the subject of widespread debate about how far his 'wildness' was due to the deprivations of his childhood. Some argued that capacities for mature rational thinking and cultured behaviour amongst adults are the product of society – transmitted to children through nurture, teaching and training – of which the boy had clearly been deprived. Others argued that human civilization is an expression of human nature – based on inborn human qualities that grow naturally through maturation – so the boy had probably been born 'mentally defective'. These competing beliefs about childhood will already be familiar to you from Chapter 2. Recall the writings of John Locke, especially the emphasis placed on the importance of children learning through experience and through good teaching. By contrast, Jean-Jacques Rousseau believed childhood is a natural state, and that children should be given freedom to grow and learn in natural surroundings, according to nature's plan.

A young doctor called Jean-Marc Itard heard about the 'wild boy'. He was more inclined to follow the theories of Locke than of Rousseau, believing that the child's strange and immature behaviour was the result of years of deprivation and social isolation. Itard decided to put these theories to the test, by demonstrating the possibility of reversing the effects of social deprivation. He named the boy Victor, made a careful assessment of his capacities for speaking and thinking and then set about to introduce basic skills. While Victor made some progress, Itard was disappointed that the child never came close to his expectations for normal development. A brief extract from Itard's report indicates the systematic way he approached the task. He began by training Victor to discriminate shapes and then sounds:

> The aim of my first efforts was to make him distinguish the sound of a bell from that of a drum. Just as I had previously led him from the larger comparison of two pieces of cardboard, differently shaped and colored, to the distinction between letters and words, I had every reason to believe that the ear, following the same progression of attention as the sense of sight, would soon distinguish the most similar and the most different tones of the vocal organ. Consequently, I set myself to render the sounds progressively more alike, more complicated, and nearer together. Later I was not content with requiring him to merely distinguish the sound of the bell from that of a drum, but introduced the differences of sound produced by striking with a rod upon the skin, the hoop or body of a drum, or upon the bell of a clock, or a fire shovel, making a ringing noise.
>
> (Itard, 1962 (first published in 1806), p. 56)

I start with the wild boy of Aveyron for two reasons: firstly, because his case illustrates the way competing theories about childhood have informed the way children are understood and treated; and secondly, because the young doctor tried to resolve these debates through the application of systematic scientific principles. Itard's experiment was one of the earliest attempts to bring childhood within the domain of scientific enquiry – applying principles of observation, measurement and experimentation originating from the natural sciences.

As we shall see, during the nineteenth and twentieth centuries, interest in the scientific study of childhood grew from strength to strength. Child development was established as a field of academic research, as well as being applied to educational, clinical, health and social welfare policies and practices affecting children.

You have already been introduced to one major topic of child development research and theory in Chapter 1 – to children's emerging capacities for thinking, reasoning and making moral judgements, especially associated with Piaget and Kohlberg. This chapter builds on that, and has two major aims. The first is to introduce developmental studies of childhood, with some examples of major research debates, including a discussion of the way Piaget's theories about children's competence at various stages of development have been challenged by more recent research. The second aim is to reflect on the significance of this way of studying children, in terms of what it tells us about the social construction of childhood. We will be asking about some of the ways developmental psychology constructs the child, through the questions asked, theories formulated, research methods employed and practical implications proposed.

1.1 Science or social construction?

This second aim may strike you as puzzling at first. Chapter 2 was all about the way childhood has been socially constructed in philosophical and religious teachings, paintings, literature etc. By contrast, the focus of this chapter is on *scientific* knowledge about children. One of the goals of scientific research has been to evaluate competing theories, beliefs and claims about childhood, in order to find out what children are really like – the basic principle of a scientific approach. This is certainly what Itard hoped to do when he embarked on research with young Victor and his faith in the power of science is echoed in textbooks to this day. For example:

> Developmental psychology today is a truly objective science ... Today a developmentalist determines the adequacy of a theory by deriving hypotheses and conducting research to see whether the theory can predict and explain the new observations that he or she has made. There is no room for subjective bias in evaluating ideas: theories of human development are only as good as their ability to account for the important aspects of children's growth and development.

(Shaffer, 1993, p. 38)

Science can and does shed a great deal of light on many important issues. Academic libraries are filled with volumes of journals and books reporting what children know and are capable of at different ages, how their growth and adjustment is shaped by their circumstances, what are the most effective approaches to teaching and learning, and so on. But I will argue that developmental research isn't a straightforward enterprise of establishing the truth about the way children really are in a once-for-all way. The storehouse of knowledge may be much greater than in Itard's day, but many of the underlying debates live on, especially where scientific theories link to beliefs about how children should develop and how they should be treated.

'George! What are you doing with the baby?'

Gahan Wilson

Besides informing the treatment of children at home, in hospitals, child-care centres, schools etc., developmental concepts have become part of everyday language.

Allow about 30 minutes

ACTIVITY I   **Childhood as development**

Spend a few minutes making a list of some of the ways that you think children develop. On a sheet of paper, mark ages from 0 to 18 down one side, and then make a note of some of the major milestones against these ages. If it helps, you could organize your list under headings such as physical growth, social relationships, knowledge and understanding. Start by thinking about babies and small children, then think about school-age children and adolescents. What do you think are the major changes? While children are different in lots of ways, how far do you think it is possible to generalize about stages of development?

COMMENT

You may have found yourself wanting to make a very long list! There are so many changes that happen between 0 and 18 years, it is hard to know where to start. You may have noted rapid physical growth during infancy as babies learn to coordinate muscle systems, grasp objects, sit, crawl, stand and walk. You may have thought about the importance of a baby's first relationships, how they learn to talk, and develop a sense of their own identity. For slightly older children, you may have been reminded of the theories about children's intellectual and moral understanding in Chapter 1. You may have noted the changes that take place around puberty, in terms of physical growth and changing relationships, the increasing importance of friendships and peer culture etc.

In making a generalized list, you were probably aware of the differences between children, such as those related to temperament, gender and ability. Much developmental research has concentrated on describing and explaining general patterns of growth and change, as well as accounting for differences between individuals and groups of children. But developmental concepts aren't just used in research. They are also widely applied in everyday talk about children. For example, new parents share experiences about 'milestones' in their babies' development, about what's 'normal' for this or that age, about which kinds of experience might 'harm' and which 'promote' healthy development, and later on they may discuss whether adolescent rebellion is a 'natural' stage of growing up, and so on. Expectations of normal development also inform the assessments made by professionals concerned with children, notably health visitors, doctors, teachers, and psychologists.

The cultural significance of thinking about childhood in terms of development is indicated by the importance attached to knowing a child's age. One of the questions adults in the UK often ask when they meet a child for the first time is 'How old are you?' – or if the child is too young to answer for themselves, they ask the parent about the baby's age. Knowing a young person's age is an important way to position them, linking their appearance and behaviour to knowledge and expectations about competences and social experiences. It opens the way to such questions as whether they've started talking yet, whether they go to playgroup, what class they are in at school, whether they have learned to read, how well they are getting on compared with others their age and so on. In other words, knowing a child's age is a clue to knowing how to place them within the life-phase childhood. The very familiarity of developmental ways of thinking and organizing children's lives means it is easy to overlook how powerful age/stage thinking has become in contemporary Western constructions of childhood, as well as the ways in which these expectations of childhood may be culture-specific.

In many societies, birthdays have not traditionally been recorded or celebrated. Expectations of children have not been so strongly linked to their age. One anthropologist with extensive knowledge of Bangladesh observed:

> When children are asked about their age, they are likely to reply, 'How do I know? Ask my mother,' as if this information did not concern their individual self ... As for mothers, when pressed to give the age of their children, they commonly reply by giving a range. For example, my son is 8 to 9, my daughter is 11 to 12 years old.

(Blanchet, 1996, p. 41)

She goes on to explain that, in Bangladesh, expectations of children are linked to their life circumstances as much as to their age. Expectations hinge around when children are seen as having achieved understanding, or competence appropriate to their situation:

> A child who is orphaned, for example, is expected to develop rapidly a state of 'understanding'. A poor child placed as a domestic servant, a pre-pubertal girl given in marriage are under similar pressures. They are excused for behaving as small irresponsible children, but not for long. Middle class children on the other hand are expected to show an early maturity about school work, but in other aspects of their development, for example sexuality, they are expected to remain innocent and act as though they did not understand.

(Blanchet, 1996, p. 48)

Another example comes from a study of beliefs about development amongst Navajo of North America. In Navajo thinking development isn't seen as applying only to children, but continues well into adulthood (see Box 1 opposite).

While all societies recognize that children are growing, learning and acquiring culturally valued competences, there is considerable variation in how far expectations are strongly linked to their age, and how far other factors come into play, notably gender and social class or caste.

Despite these cultural variations in the way children's development is understood, Western beliefs and expectations play an increasingly important role worldwide. Globalization processes have spread these beliefs and expectations, especially through schooling systems, as well as through the influence of expert knowledge, and the interventions of

Box 1 An outline of the Navajo model of development

Stage 1 'One becomes aware' (2–4 years)
A child's awareness is said to begin when he or she no longer has to be restrained from touching a hot stove or from wandering away and getting lost. These are seen as the first indicators of self discipline.

Stage 2 'One becomes self aware' (4–6 years)
Children are said to become aware of their own thoughts, perceptions, and intentions to do things. Children of this age are thought to be able to begin learning the importance of kinship relations and to show 'respect' for others.

Stage 3 'One begins to think' (6–9 years)
Now that the child has begun to learn the importance of kinship relations, he or she must begin at least to initiate, if not always fully carry out, action that embodies this 'respect'. For example, children at this stage are expected to offer morning prayers (respect for the Holy People) and to begin to care for lambs or kids (respect for the means of making a living).

Stage 4 'One's thought begins to exist' (10–15 years)
This is the transitional stage to adulthood, in which children are expected to carry out all activities without help or supervision. During this stage the girl's puberty ceremony is also performed. The key at this stage is knowing not only what one's responsibilities are, but 'how they came to be'. This includes knowledge of the complete versions of certain legends and thus full understanding of the hierarchy of Navajo clans, one's place within this scheme, and the basis in kinship for one's responsibilities to all others.

Stage 5 'One begins to think for oneself' (15–18 years)
At this stage parents say to young people, 'You are on your own now; I cannot think for you.' Except for marriage, they are considered fully adult, and expected to manage all their affairs on their own – except that they are still responsible for helping with the duties of their parents' household.

Stage 6 'One begins thinking for all things' (17–22 years)
The young person has now mastered every aspect of the responsibilities of the adult life, including raising and trading in livestock. The training of the past culminates in marriage.

Stage 7 'One begins to think ahead for oneself' (22–30 years)
In this stage, the successes of one's life are manifested in one's own children. 'Success' here means not only jewelry, nice clothes, and a good appearance, but increasing herds, a good marriage, and evidence of 'good thought' in one's children.

Stage 8 'One begins to think ahead for all things' (30+ years)
The qualities of the previous stage are further developed, and one begins to acquire recognition as 'one who has the knowledge and ability to speak and plan ahead for both his children and neighbors'.

(adapted from Chisholm, 1996, pp. 172–3)

UNICEF and other non-governmental organizations concerned with children. The Geneva Declaration of the Rights of the Child (1924) and the UN Declaration of the Rights of the Child (1959) were both framed in terms of promoting children's 'normal development'. The UN Convention on the Rights of the Child (UNCRC) (1989) also draws heavily on child development concepts, especially Article 6: 'States Parties shall ensure to the maximum extent possible the survival and development of the child'. Another example is Article 32 of the UNCRC, about child labour, which is expressed in terms of protecting children from work that is likely to be harmful to 'physical, mental, spiritual, moral or social development'. Similarly, Article 12 states children's views must be 'given due weight in accordance with the age and maturity of the child'. Note that the UNCRC will be discussed in detail in the next chapter.

The global influence of developmental approaches can be seen as a positive indicator of the value attached to scientific knowledge about children. But dissemination of scientific knowledge is not straightforward. 'Development' is neither a precise concept, nor a neutral one. With some notable exceptions, most research into children's development has been based on the lives, experiences and expectations of children growing up in Western societies, according to the theories and methodologies adopted by researchers living within those societies, especially in Europe and North America. But they have been applied much more widely, to the lives of children growing up in very different circumstances (Boyden, 1997).

Much of my university teaching and research has been in the field of child development, but I have increasingly felt it is important to acknowledge the way in which developmental research constructs particular versions of the child in the theories proposed and textbook accounts written. I became especially aware of this issue when I started working on a project looking at the place of work in children's lives, in a global context. Work is a major feature of growing up for most of the world's children – everything from carrying out simple domestic chores, caring for younger siblings, working in fields and plantations, fetching water and firewood, and fishing, to trading in the streets and markets, right through to the most harmful and exploitative child labour in backstreet workshops and bonded labour. But most child development textbooks have very little if anything to say about the place of work in children's development and this reflects the shortage of research on this aspect of growing up. For the most part, textbook childhoods are constructed as a time for nurture, care, play and learning in the family and at school, consistent with modern Western settings and ideals (Woodhead, 1999). This example draws attention to the ways in which accounts of child development may express particular constructions of the child, despite the aspiration for objectivity and universal truth.

In this chapter I will introduce you to some examples of developmental research and theory, including some major debates about how best to understand the child. But I also want to convey a sense of the distinctiveness of these ways of thinking, debating and researching childhood and the sense that developmental research (and indeed all scientific research) is historically and culturally located.

Most research is carried out in societies where school is a major feature of growing up.

Work is still a normal part of childhood for most of the world's children.

1.2 What is development?

Before going any further, let us establish what researchers mean when they talk about studying children's development.

Allow about 20 minutes

ACTIVITY 2   **What is development?**

Read the explanation below, taken from a widely-used introductory child development textbook.

> The term 'development' refers to the process by which a child, or foetus and more generally an organism (human or animal), grows and changes through its life-span. In humans the most dramatic developmental changes occur in prenatal development, infancy and childhood, as the newborn develops into a young adult capable of becoming a parent himself or herself ...
>
> Generally, developmental processes have been related to age. A typical 3-year-old has, for example, a particular mastery of spoken language ... and a 4-year-old has typically progressed further. A developmental psychologist may then wish to find out, and theorize about, the processes involved in this progression. What experiences, rewards, interactions, feedback, have helped the child develop in this way?
>
> (Smith, Cowie and Blades, 1998, pp. 6–7)

Make a note of the key ideas and concepts within a developmental approach, using these questions as a guide:

1   What is development about – what kinds of change are being described?

2   Who or what is developing – how broad is the scope of developmental research?

3   What age range is covered by a developmental approach – how far does it extend beyond childhood?

4   How far is developmental research about describing development, and how far about explaining what causes growth and change?

COMMENT

1   In answer to the first question, I underlined the following words:

age   grows   changes   progression   mastery   typical

Charting growth and change, most often linked to chronological age, is one of the most distinctive features of a developmental approach to childhood. But the emphasis on progression and mastery signals that development is about change in a particular direction, towards more mature 'adult' ways of functioning, about becoming more competent, more autonomous, and so on. Another distinctive feature is the emphasis on normal, universal processes of growth and change, signalled by the reference to 'a typical three-year-old'. Differences are recognized, for example related to gender or social class, but overall the emphasis is on what's shared by children at a certain age rather than on what is unique to an individual.

2   The authors make clear that they view children's development in a very broad context. Reference to 'an organism (human or animal)' draws attention to the scientific interest in understanding how human development relates to that in other species, and specifically the evolutionary significance of human immaturity, as will become clear in Section 2 of this chapter.

3   Development isn't just about childhood. The authors also refer to 'prenatal development' and they talk about growth throughout the human 'lifespan'. Legal definitions and cultural practices may formally define when childhood begins and ends (as discussed in Chapters 1 and 2), but in developmental terms, the foundations of the child's nervous system are established during the foetal stage, and the processes of learning and development continue throughout adult life.

4   Describing children's development is only one goal of developmental research. Explaining development is another goal, as is understanding the processes driving development. For example, how far is development about growth and how far about 'experiences, rewards, interactions, feedback'? Recall that theoretical questions about what factors promote development, as well as how deprivations can be overcome, were what prompted Itard to try to help Victor. These questions continue to inspire much research, especially applied studies in education and childcare.

One other thing to note is that some phases of development receive more research attention than others. Major theories do cover the full age range from infancy to maturity (e.g. Piaget's and Kohlberg's stages of moral reasoning in Chapter 1). But as a general rule, there are many more studies of younger children than older children – perhaps because growth and change appears so rapid on so many fronts. As confirmation of the point, one of the introductory textbooks on my bookshelf devotes more than 350 pages to infancy and early childhood (up to about 6 years old), but less than 200 pages to the rest of childhood and adolescence (Sroufe *et al.*, 1996). Studies of adolescent change are an exception to this general rule, again because this appears to be a major period for personal change in Western societies (see Barnes, 1995; Morrow, 2002). You will find a similar emphasis in this chapter – on research and theory related to early childhood.

It isn't possible to convey the diversity of approaches to studying childhood within the field of developmental research in one chapter. This chapter concentrates mainly on the development of children's intellectual and social understanding, and introduces examples of both observational and experimental research. Section 2 includes a short extract from one of the earliest observational studies of infant development and considers the impact of the emerging field of child research on social and educational issues in the late nineteenth and early twentieth centuries. Then in Sections 3 and 4, I turn to two major theoretical approaches to studying children's development. Section 3 considers the work of Jean Piaget (introduced in Chapter 1), who is best known for his emphasis on identifying universal stages of development. Then, in Section 4, I introduce a contrasting approach, linked especially to the theories of Lev Vygotsky, who placed much greater emphasis on the way cultural context and social processes shape children's development.

Inevitably, in the space of one chapter, there is not room to cover other major traditions of child research. For example, I refer only briefly to psychoanalytic approaches originating from the work of Sigmund Freud (in Section 2), and I give no attention to behaviourist approaches, for example linked to the work of B. F. Skinner (see Das Gupta, 1994).

SUMMARY OF SECTION 1

- The story of the Wild Boy of Aveyron illustrates the origins of scientific studies of childhood as well as the link with wider cultural ideas about childhood.
- Developmental research has been the dominant academic framework for studying childhood. It has been very influential on the treatment of children, as well as on everyday ways of talking about young people.
- Developmental research is founded on scientific principles, but it also constructs particular images of the growing child.

2 A NEW SCIENCE OF CHILD STUDY

In this section I will continue to trace the early history of developmental research, and consider the impact of the new science on social issues during the twentieth century.

I began Section 1 with Itard's account of the Wild Boy of Aveyron. Another landmark piece of child research was written by a young parent living in London during the 1840s. He kept a detailed diary of his son William (affectionately nicknamed Doddy). This account was especially influential because the parent was Charles Darwin – who went on to write the *Origin of Species* (1859). Towards the end of his life, Darwin returned to the diary and wrote it up in an article for the journal *Mind* (published in 1877).

Charles Darwin made a scientific study of his son's early development.

2.1 The impact of Darwin

READING

Now read the short extracts from Darwin's 'A biographical sketch of an infant' in Reading A. Note the way he approaches the task of recording his son's 'biography' – within a scientific frame of mind, which aims for objectivity, achieved through precise observation and description. Notice how he makes these observations within a time framework linked to the baby's age. Note also the simple experiments employed to try to find out what his son feels and understands. As you will see, Darwin wasn't content to describe what he saw each day. He was searching for patterns of growth – evidence of progress from immaturity to competence. Also note the questions that seem to be guiding Darwin's enquiry, especially about how far observed behaviours are the expression of 'instinct' or shaped by experience and learning, about how his son's development compares with his daughter's, and how this human child's development compares with other species.

When I first read this account, I was struck by the way Darwin set about recording his son's 'biography' as well as by the topics he focused on, many of which connect with research traditions continuing to this day. Darwin was one of the first, and certainly one of the most influential to offer an evidence-based account of early development, in keeping with traditions of the physical and biological sciences. Darwin's approach is cool and unsentimental. At the same time he isn't judgemental about his young son's immaturity, but concentrates on trying to understand what makes him behave the way he does. He frames his observations in terms of a series of categories – reflex actions, vision, movement, affection, reason, moral sense – and charts each category in relation to age. As well as making precise observations Darwin carried out experiments to test hypotheses about his son's capacities. For example, he tested Doddy's reflex reactions when he touched on the sole of his foot, and his empathy towards his nurse when she pretended to cry. Several of these experiments anticipate major research traditions. For example, children's reactions to seeing their mirror image have been studied as an indicator of self-recognition (Lewis and Brooks-Gunn, 1979).

Darwin's observation that Doddy first showed clear preferences for his nurse's affection at five months hints at the emergence of emotional attachment (which will be discussed in Section 2.3). The boy's sympathy towards his nurse's distress, his sensitivity to ridicule, and his attempts to deceive his father resonate with recent debates about young children's capacities for social understanding (which are elaborated in Section 4 and Reading B).

Another important feature of Darwin's scientific approach is that he acknowledges the gaps in his understanding, such as how to explain Doddy's early recognition of his mother's breast. At the same time, Darwin doesn't always hesitate in making judgements, which perhaps reflect his cultural values as much as his observations. For example, Darwin compares Doddy's development as a boy with that of his daughter at the

When do babies first recognize their image in a mirror?

same age, judging that his daughter was 'not nearly so acute' when faced with an image in a mirror. (Gender issues are followed up in Chapter 5.)

Most significantly, Darwin makes comparisons between human children and other species (such as when he compares his son's reactions to seeing himself in a mirror with the reactions of 'higher apes' to the same procedure). Darwin's approach to studying children made a big impact on the research community and on society at large. From now on children came to be viewed as scientifically interesting, especially because their development was seen as related to that of other species, which reinforced the interest in studying children as part of 'nature' that had been kindled by Rousseau's writings.

Following Darwin, the study of human childhoods became firmly established as a respected subject for scientific scrutiny, detailed description, theorization and experimentation. Pioneers of the science of childhood include James Sully (who established a laboratory for psychological research into children at London University during the 1880s), Wilhelm Preyer (a German biologist who wrote an influential book on *The Mind of the Child* in 1882) and G. Stanley Hall (who became an advocate for basing child-rearing on scientific principles in the United States and wrote one of the first books on the psychology of *Adolescence* in 1908). Another advocate of the new scientific approach was Arnold Gesell (see Box 2 opposite).

Box 2 Early studies of child development

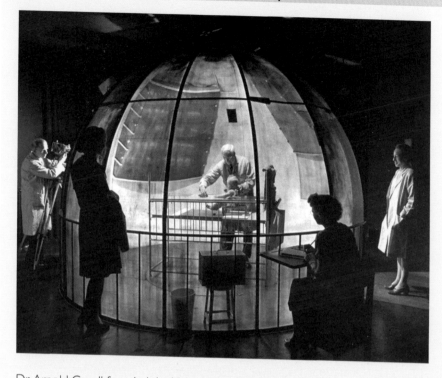

Bringing the child into the laboratory: Arnold Gesell's observation dome.

Dr Arnold Gesell founded the Yale Clinic of Child Development in the USA in 1911. Gesell's approach emulated the science laboratory. It was based on observing children's natural behaviour unobtrusively, devising simple tests, and recording their behaviour in minute detail, following a standard procedure. The photograph shows white-coated Gesell working with a child in a large glass observation dome he had specially constructed. He took advantage of the new technologies of the day (photography and movie cameras) to assemble a massive data bank of young children's behaviour at various ages. For example, in his major work on the first five years of life, he organized his observations under a list of categories broadly grouped into motor, language, adaptive behaviour, and personal and social behaviour. He distilled this research into what he called 'normative summaries', charts representing the milestones of normal development for each age group. An example at four months old is given below.

Motor characteristics
Prefers to lie on back
Tries to raise self, lifting head and shoulders
Can roll from side to side (or back to side)
Holds head erect when carried
Lifts head when prone
Pushes with feet against floor when held

Language
Coos
Smiles
Laughs aloud
Makes several vocalizations

Adaptive behavior
Notices large objects
May notice spoon on table
Hands react to table

Personal-social behavior
Shows selective interest in animated face
Makes anticipatory postural adjustment on being lifted
Not much affected by strange persons, new scenes or solicitude
Turns head to voice
Plays with hands

(Gesell, 1925, cited by Beekman, 1977, pp. 156–7)

2.2 Developmental science and social issues

Valerie Walkerdine (1984) summed up the new enthusiasm for studying children during the early years of the twentieth century:

> Children's bodies were weighed and measured. The effects of fatigue were studied, as were children's interests, imaginings, religious ideas, fetishes, attitudes to weather, to adults, drawings, dolls, lies, ideas and, most importantly for us, their stages of growth. (All this is a full twenty years before Piaget began to study children.) What is important is that children as a category were being singled out for scientific study for the first time ...
>
> (Walkerdine, 1984, p. 171)

In Britain, seeds of knowledge from systematic studies of children's development fell on fertile ground. The social climate was sympathetic to the application of scientific method to social issues associated with industrialization and urbanization, especially where generalizations could be made about large numbers of children. Making generalizations became especially important at a time when health, education and welfare services were being established for all children – not just for elite groups (Hendrick, 1997).

Interest in scientific studies can be detected even during the early decades of the nineteenth century. Social reformers looked for evidence to support their claim that the employment of children in mines, mills and factories was harmful to growing bodies, minds and morals. Child study offered the research tools to monitor how far early deprivations might be stunting their growth.

Defining the stages in children's normal development became even more salient with the establishment of mass education, culminating in the Education Acts of 1870 and 1880, which laid the framework for a compulsory school system. Confronted with a group of children all aged around 6 or 8 or 11, teachers needed to know what it was reasonable to expect of a child this age. What standard should be set in relation to the range of abilities in a class of 30 or 40 children?

Evidence of what is 'normal' or 'typical' became a standard to judge which children were 'subnormal' or 'retarded', not just in physical and motor development, but also in intellectual development. The first intelligence tests were devised by Binet and Simon in Paris in 1905, as a direct response to a French Ministry of Public Instruction Commission enquiring into the problems of 'low ability' children within the public school system. In due course a new profession would emerge, able to apply these new techniques to sort and classify children according to their aptitudes and abilities – one of the skills of the educational psychologist.

By the early twentieth century monitoring children's health and growth was becoming normal practice in Britain with the establishment of infant welfare centres and school medical inspections. For example, by 1917 seventeen infant welfare centres had been set up in Birmingham where babies were weighed and checked over, and advice given on feeding and so on.

With the growth of mass schooling, teachers needed to know what standards to expect.

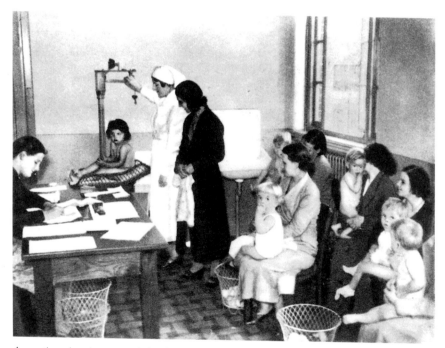

A routine developmental check-up at a health centre in Leeds, 1942. Health professionals needed to set standards for weight and height.

Thinking about children in terms of ages and stages, normality and abnormality wasn't restricted to professionals. Parents shared the new knowledge, as an increasingly literate society was receptive to the earliest child-rearing manuals (Hardyment, 1984).

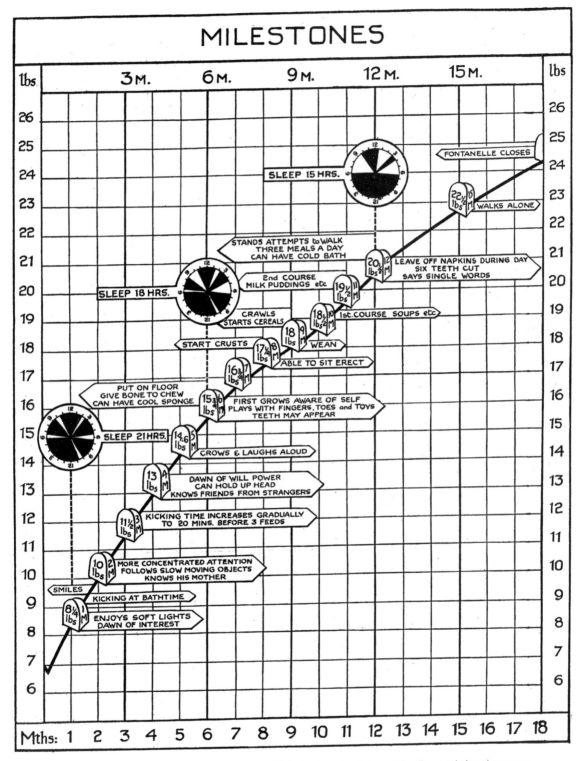

MILESTONES

A chart for parents from the *Mothercraft Manual* (1923). Strict schedules of feeding and sleeping were advocated, following the principles of child-care expert Truby King.

Writing in the 1970s, Newson and Newson reflected on the growth of interest in the development of children, especially the increasing attention paid to children's psychological development:

> Seen in historical and anthropological perspective, perhaps the most interesting aspect of the contemporary preoccupation with childrearing is that today we are self-consciously concerned with the possible *psychological* consequences of the methods which we use in bringing up our children. This attention to the total psychological development of the child is indeed a new phenomenon, in that earlier generations of parents have been chiefly preoccupied by the related themes of physical survival and moral growth, rather than with concepts of mental health or social and emotional adjustment.
>
> (Newson and Newson, 1974, pp. 53–54)

Newson and Newson draw attention to the growing interest during the twentieth century in children's mental health and social and emotional adjustment. The rest of this section focuses on this topic, because it very clearly illustrates the way scientific theories connect with wider discourses about children's needs, especially when research is closely tied to applied issues.

2.3 Natural needs?

Babies and young children often get upset if they are separated from their parents, or from the people who most often care for them. What's less well known is that babies' tendency to get upset follows a developmental pattern. *Separation protest* (as psychologists call this kind of crying) begins to happen more often when babies are around seven to eight months of age. Younger babies are less sensitive to being separated – or at least they don't protest so loudly. *Separation protest* typically reaches a peak around twelve months and

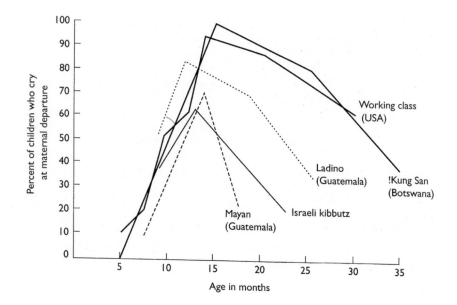

Figure 1
Separation protest shown by babies from five different groups around the world.

Source: Adapted from Kagan, 1976, pp. 186–96.

then gradually becomes less frequent as most babies become better able to cope with brief separation. Cross-cultural research has also found the same developmental patterns in very varying cultural contexts (see Figure 1, previous page). These are generalizations of course, and there can be marked individual as well as cultural differences in the ways separations are managed. Also, a change of care arrangements (such as starting nursery) can cause renewed upset in much older children.

You may recall that Darwin included the development of affection in his study of his son Doddy, noting that Doddy was several months old before he seemed to show a clear preference for his nurse's affections. The onset of separation protest during the second half of the first year is now recognized as an indicator that the young child has formed close emotional *attachments* to a parent or other care-giver. This line of research originated with studies carried out by John Bowlby in the 1930s, exploring the effects on children of being deprived of maternal care. Bowlby wanted to explain why children brought up in baby homes, orphanages and other institutions common in England at that time so often had relationship difficulties and behavioural problems later on. He was also concerned about the emotional distress

Children from a babies' home in the 1930s.

experienced by young children in hospital who were deprived of contact with their parents (also common practice in England at the time). Notice the parallels between Bowlby's interest in the effects of social deprivation, and Itard's interest in the deprivations suffered by the Wild Boy of Aveyron.

Ethology is the study of the behaviour of animals in their natural habitat.

Imprinting is the process by which baby birds learn to follow their mother, soon after hatching.

Bowlby's background was in medicine and he was trained in psychoanalysis. He was also very interested in the study of evolution, especially the lessons from ethological research into animal behaviour. Ethological studies of baby geese seemed to show that young goslings *imprint* on their mother (or indeed the first moving thing with which they come into contact) (Lorenz, 1981). Bowlby saw a strong parallel in the way young babies become attached (or bonded) to their mothers (or other principal carers). He argued that a baby becomes distressed and resists separation because of a biologically adaptive mechanism which evolved to protect the young of the human species by ensuring an infant remains in close proximity to their mother.

One of the most controversial features of Bowlby's early theories is that he took the bold step of trying to prescribe children's needs for care. In a famous report to the World Health Organization he argued that some ways of caring for babies are natural and healthy; others are unnatural and harmful. Bowlby's often-quoted conclusion at this time was:

> [W]hat is believed to be essential for mental health is that an infant and young child should experience a warm, intimate, and continuous relationship with his mother (or permanent mother-substitute – one person who steadily 'mothers' him) in which both find satisfaction and enjoyment.

(Bowlby, 1953, p. 13)

Bowlby's work had a major impact on reforming practices in child care, especially in residential and hospital care. At the same time these early theories were criticised on two counts, which centre on the claim that children's emotional needs are an expression of their human nature.

The first set of criticisms drew attention to the dangers of over-generalizing from behaviours of other species. Observations of animal imprinting were translated into theories about mother–infant bonding. The problem is that human infants don't 'bond' with their care-givers in a mechanical or instinctive way equivalent to imprinting. A baby's first relationships are also built on communication, and the beginnings of shared understanding.

The second set of criticisms centred on claims made for 'natural' care. Critics argued that these so-called natural patterns of care were a reflection of Western cultural values, projected onto children as being about their needs. They were seen as a social construction, reinforcing dominant attitudes to family life in post-war Britain, by emphasizing women's responsibilities for meeting the needs of their infants through offering full-time mothering (Tizard, 1991). For example, Bowlby's original work argued that children's needs for love and security are focused on one person (the mother or mother substitute). This principle (known as *monotropism*) was widely criticized for telling as much about mid-twentieth century English attitudes to family, nursery care and gender divisions as about the fundamental needs

In many societies, older children are expected to care for younger children (northern Thailand, 1987).

of children. It contradicted a wide range of evidence from cultural contexts where shared care is the norm, for example, the widespread practice of older siblings (usually older sisters) sharing care of young children (Weisner and Gallimore, 1977).

To summarize, firstly, children have needs for care and nurture, but their attachments aren't necessarily focused on one person and they may be distributed amongst several consistent care-givers. Secondly, developmental theories may be informed by careful empirical research, but the interpretation of that research is shaped by available discourses about children's needs for care and nurture (see Box 3).

Box 3 Cultural dimensions of early emotional development

Robert LeVine and colleagues were interested in the way universal developmental processes may be expressed in different ways in different societies, according to the contexts of care, the demands on parents and other care-givers and the values for children's adjustment. They compared child-rearing practices, in the 1970s, in an urban community in Boston USA with those amongst a rural Gusii community in Kenya.

Amongst the Gusii community, there was a high birth rate, but also a high mortality rate, so careful nurture was a high priority. Mothers kept their babies in close physical contact, breastfeeding on demand and sleeping alongside them. But this nurturing style did not incorporate high levels of stimulation or play between mother and infant. Instead, mothers concentrated on keeping their babies quiet and comfortable, without encouraging lively interactions, so there was little emphasis on playing and talking to babies. These mothers were responsible both for managing their large family and for cultivating the fields. They relied on the help of older children, especially older daughters who would carry the baby on her back, play with it and bring it to the mother for feeding.

LeVine et al. argue that this picture of Gusii childhoods contrasts sharply with the affluent, technically and medically sophisticated US for the very reason that the conditions, priorities and goals for childhood are so different.

For infants growing up in Boston, survival was virtually assured. There were strong expectations on mothers and other carers to establish a close emotional and playful relationship with their infant; a relationship in which there was reciprocity and mutual responsiveness, where the subdued infant was stimulated, and the curious infant encouraged to explore. Children were provided with plenty of psychological space, treated as individuals and encouraged to express their feelings and wishes. Clashes of will were not only expected, but to some extent encouraged, within a framework that emphasized autonomy, assertiveness and independence (LeVine et al., 1994).

Finally, note that extensive research has been carried out since Bowlby originally formulated his theories, especially into the formation of emotional attachments, and the effects of separation or other disturbed relationships (Schaffer, 1996).

SUMMARY OF SECTION 2

- Darwin's observations illustrate the establishment of child study as a research tradition, as well as the links to evolutionary biology.
- One of the goals of early research was to identify norms of development as a standard for measuring children's developmental progress.
- The new scientific approach to childhood was established against a background of social changes in which the new knowledge and techniques could be applied to practical social issues.
- Theories about emotional development and the effects of deprivation illustrate the links between scientific research and theory and cultural discourses about children's needs for specific kinds of care. Cross-cultural studies provide a broader perspective on these issues.

3 STAGES OF DEVELOPMENT

For the rest of the chapter I will be concentrating on children's *intellectual* development, including their understanding of their social world. Probably the most influential developmental theory was constructed by Jean Piaget (1896–1980).

Throughout a lifetime of research, Piaget observed children and conducted experiments, in order to find out how they think and understand the world.

Piaget first became interested in children's thinking abilities when he was working with Binet in Paris, constructing the earliest intelligence tests. He wanted to explain why young children of a certain age tended to make the same kinds of error on simple reasoning tasks, and what led them to make correct judgements a year or so later. He began to study these questions at the Institut Jean-Jacques Rousseau in Paris, but spent most of his long career at the University of Geneva. The connection with Rousseau is no coincidence. Piaget's theory of universal stages in children's development is the most powerful elaboration of Rousseau's basic idea that children's distinctive ways of thinking and behaving reflect their progression through natural phases of development.

Before reading further, revise Piaget's theories from Chapter 1, Section 2, especially how he drew conclusions about stages of development from his observations and experiments with children. Pay particular attention to the experiments described in Chapter 1, Box 1, 'The conservation of liquids task' (p. 13) and Chapter 1, Box 2, 'The three mountains task' (p. 15).

3.1 Piaget's influence

Piaget's image of children as active learners engaging with the world through play and exploration, and progressing through a series of stages towards mature adult understanding has been enormously influential, especially because it connected with powerful discourses in Western societies about what childhood is about and how children should be treated (Walkerdine, 1984). Chapter 1 already illustrated how Piaget's stage theory could be used as a basis for judging children's capacities for understanding and taking responsibility for their actions. In this section, we will look at the impact of stage theory in education. For example:

> The child, the boy, the man, indeed, should know no other endeavour but to be at every stage of development wholly what this stage calls for. Then will each successive stage spring like a new shoot from a healthy bud; and, at each successive stage, he will with the same endeavour again accomplish the requirements of this stage: for only the adequate development of man at each preceding stage can effect and bring about adequate development at each succeeding later stage.
>
> (Froebel, cited by Bruce *et al.* 1995 (first published in 1887), p. 16)

This was written by the German originator of the kindergarten movement, Friedrich Froebel, in 1887. So, the image of the child as an active learner progressing through stages didn't originate with Piaget. What Piaget's theory did was to offer scientific endorsement for progressive, child-centred education. The following extract is taken from an influential official report on British primary education published during the 1960s (known as the Plowden Report), which drew explicitly on child development research, including Piaget's theory:

> At the heart of the educational process lies the child. No advances in policy, no acquisitions of new equipment have their desired effect unless they are in harmony with the nature of the child, unless they are fundamentally acceptable to him. We know a little about what happens to the child who is deprived of the stimuli of pictures, books and spoken words; we know much less about what happens

to a child who is exposed to stimuli which are perceptually, intellectually or emotionally inappropriate to his age, his state of development, or the sort of individual he is.

(Central Advisory Council, 1967, para. 9)

Note the way the authors draw on ideas about children's nature and stages of development in terms of children's readiness for learning. Note, too, that the emphasis is on the individual child's development and learning, with no explicit mention of the role of teaching. Also, note that both quotes follow the convention of the time of using the masculine form 'he' for the child.

Piaget's stage theory is by no means the 'last word' on how children learn to think and how they should be educated. I will conclude this section by showing how enterprising variations on Piaget's classic experiments led some developmental researchers to challenge aspects of stage theory. In Section 4 I will introduce a rather different theoretical framework for studying the child in development, within which social and cultural processes, including teaching, have a more significant role.

3.2 Critical experiments

Allow about 20 minutes

ACTIVITY 3   **Two experiments**

Now study Box 4, in which two experiments are described. They are similar to the Piagetian experiments in Chapter 1. They were first carried out with children in the UK during the 1970s, and were amongst the first to raise questions about Piaget's theory.

Experiment 1 is a variation on the classic conservation of liquids experiment – which was one of the indicators of whether children had reached the operational stage of thinking. This new version of the experiment altered the way the task was presented and the results were rather different. Children were more likely to make the 'correct' judgement from a younger age, suggesting they were capable of operational thinking much earlier than predicted by Piaget.

Experiment 2 is a variation on the three mountains task. Once again, the problem presented to the child is similar to Piaget's experiment, but it is presented in a different way. And, once again, researchers found much younger children showed capacities for perspective-taking than in Piaget's experiments.

For each experiment, think about what might account for the differences in children's ability to make the correct judgements, when compared with the equivalent experiment in Chapter 1. Think especially about the way the problem was presented to children in each case. Also consider the implications of these results for theories about stages in children's intellectual development.

Box 4 Making sense of experimental tasks

Experiment 1: The chipped beaker

Two children were shown two beakers (A and B) filled to the same level (as in Piaget's experiment). In this version pasta shells were used rather than water. The children were asked whether the beakers had the same amount as a preliminary to a game they were going to play with the shells, where it was important for each child to start with the same amount (i.e. so that the game was fair).

When the children judged the quantities to be the same, the experimenter handed them each a beaker in turn, but suddenly 'noticed' one of the beakers was chipped to a sharp edge, then 'found' another container (C) into which they poured the contents of the chipped beaker. (See Figure 2.)

The experimenter then asked the standard question: is there more in the new beaker than in the other beaker, or less, or the same amount?

(Light, 1986)

Figure 2 The chipped beaker task.

Experiment 2: Hiding from policemen

Two intersecting 'walls' were constructed on a board, to form a cross, as in Figure 3. Dolls representing a 'policeman' and a 'little boy' were used as props. With the policeman at the position shown in Figure 3, the little boy was placed in section A and the child asked: 'Can the policeman see the little boy?' The question was then repeated with the little boy placed in position B, C and D. Next, the policeman was placed in a new position, and the child was asked to place the little boy where the policeman couldn't see him. Finally, the task was made more complex, with two policemen positioned at different points, and the child asked to hide the little boy from both policemen. This final task required the child to coordinate two different points of view.

(Hughes, cited in Donaldson, 1978)

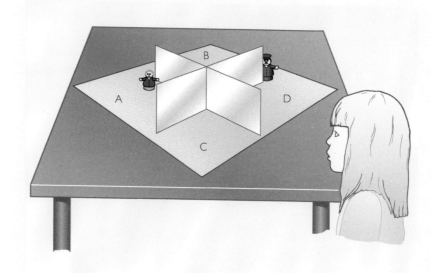

Figure 3 The hiding from policemen task.

COMMENT

Experiment 1 presents the task in the context of a game between two children rather than simply as some kind of test of children's understanding. This is a familiar experience, and even very young children understand the importance of fairness. Pouring the pasta shells into the other beaker also makes more sense to children in this version of the experiment, because it is presented as about avoiding getting hurt. Similarly, in Experiment 2 children reveal much better perspective-taking abilities when the task is presented as a version of hide-and-seek, than when it is about the height and position of mountains.

The difference between these results and those of Piaget drew attention to the ways children make sense of the tasks set by adults. Children seem to understand the task in a different way when it is presented as about chipped beakers or about little boys and policemen, because it makes greater 'human sense' to them in relation to everyday experiences, familiar story themes and games (Donaldson, 1978). So, in the context of making a game fair, replacing a chipped beaker in Experiment 1 doesn't alter children's views on whether quantities are the same. In Experiment 2, while most children don't have direct experience of being chased by policemen, this kind of situation is one they recognize and draw into their play.

These examples illustrate the way results of well designed experiments can lead researchers to abandon (or at least modify) a well established theory. They offered a challenge to any attempt to link ages to stages in a rigid way, since children's reasoning abilities apparently varied according to the way the task was presented and the way it was understood. More broadly, these studies illustrated the dangers of representing child development as a generalized progression through stages, as if 'the developing child' is an isolatable unit that can be studied in a vacuum.

SUMMARY OF SECTION 3

- Piaget's influential account of stages in intellectual development links to progressive traditions of theory and practice in education.
- A comparison between Piaget's classic investigations into children's thinking and more recent experiments highlights how 'human sense' alters children's apparent competence.
- These experimental studies illustrate scientific methods of hypothesis-testing, and show how empirical research can challenge dominant theories.

4 DEVELOPMENT IN CONTEXT

Think about the following question: If we want to study child development, what should we study? This may seem an odd question at first. The answer seems obvious – we should study a child, or children in general. So, in order to understand physical development, measurements can be taken of children's growth at various ages. For motor development, milestones can be recorded from sitting to crawling to walking. For mental development, we study children's abilities to solve problems at various ages, as Piaget did to arrive at his account of the stages of development. The problem is that measuring developmental milestones stripped of context constructs an image of development as happening *within* a child. We turn now to a very different view, in which development is seen as something that happens *between* a child and others in specific social and cultural settings.

This view is especially linked to Lev Vygotsky, a Russian psychologist and contemporary of Jean Piaget (they were both born in 1896). Vygotsky challenged the idea that development is a universal, natural process. He described child studies of this kind as a search for the 'eternal child'. He proposed that child psychologists should instead study the 'historical child', arguing that any particular child's development – their social relationships, sense of self, ways of thinking and so on – is embedded in the social and cultural contexts of their life at a particular point in history.

One implication of Vygotsky's view is that features of child development (including the modern Western childhoods that are often taken as a standard for all) are understood as a product of specific economic, social and cultural contexts. For example, in the introduction to the chapter, I drew attention to the neglect of work as a major influence in the lives of most of the world's children. What I called 'textbook childhood' is constructed as a time of dependency, play and learning, carried out mainly at home and school. By contrast, a cultural approach emphasizes the ways children's development is constructed within particular settings and communities, and is more cautious about assuming that commonly found patterns of development are necessarily universal. On this view, there is nothing fundamentally 'natural' about children's care and learning, either at home or within a school setting. The environments children inhabit and the ways they are treated are shaped by generations of human activity and creativity, and are mediated by complex belief systems, including about the 'proper' way for children to develop and learn. The cross-cultural contrasts in Box 3 (p. 106) illustrate the point, as does the way advice on child-rearing practices has changed over the past century, even within Western societies (Hardyment, 1984).

4.1 Naturally social

Some researchers take the argument a step further, claiming that one of the few universal features of human development is children's inclination to engage in social relationships, cultural activity, communication and meaning making, in all its diversity. According to this view, the most significant features of any child's environment are the humans with whom they establish close relationships and learn to communicate, and from whom they seek guidance and receive instruction and training. The baby becomes connected psychologically, not least through the processes of attachment discussed in Section 2.3. And babies become more – not less – psychologically interconnected as they grow and learn in the context of social relationships. They learn with others and they learn through others – parents, brothers and sisters, friends, grandparents, teachers and so on. Through these close relationships children's experiences are structured and given meaning. By learning to communicate, especially through language, children gain access to shared knowledge and cultural understanding. In this way, mental development is closely tied to social and emotional development. It is not primarily an individualized process (as charts showing stages of development tend to emphasize). It is a social and a cultural process. Vygotsky placed great emphasis on the idea that psychological development is not something that happens *within* the child. Development of human skills, knowledge and beliefs during childhood takes place through relationships *between* the child and others able to guide, communicate and scaffold their learning.

Mutual recognition? Babies are strongly oriented to features of the human face.

Children develop skills and understanding in the context of human relationships and activities.

Studies of early infancy suggest that human babies may be 'pre-adapted' to engage in these early communicative relationships. Very soon after a baby is born, it is common for parents to feel that their newborn already recognizes them, and that they are able to communicate with each other, many months before the first words are uttered. Research with very small babies provides some clues as to why parents may feel this way. A newborn baby's vision is still immature in lots of ways. But in one respect babies are quite discriminating – they prefer looking at other human faces. For example, experimental studies have demonstrated that newborns try to track a picture of a human face when it is moved, but they are much less interested in other equally complex patterns (Johnson and Morton, 1991). Very soon, they begin to discriminate between faces, showing preferences for their mother or other main caregiver. The fact that babies show a special interest in the human face from birth isn't just the starting point for establishing relationships. Reading faces becomes one of the basic tools through which babies learn about other aspects of their social world, especially as their attention gradually begins to incorporate the world of objects as well as people:

> What happens when you show a baby something new, something a little strange, maybe wonderful, maybe dangerous – say a walking toy robot? The baby looks over at Mom quizzically and checks her out. What does she think? Is there a reassuring smile or an expression of shocked horror? One-year-olds will modify their own reactions accordingly. If there's a smile, they'll crawl forward to investigate; if there's horror, they'll stop dead in their tracks.

> (Gopnik *et al.*, 1999, p. 33)

While this US baby was learning how to react to toy robots, other babies in other settings might use similar techniques to learn about what is fun and what dangerous in their environment. At the same time as babies are monitoring facial expressions they also listen for cues in the sounds they hear, about how to react to people and events in their lives. For example, the tone of voice adopted by a parent is sufficient signal as to whether the four-legged furry creature coming towards them is friendly or frightening. Just as for vision, from birth babies seem especially oriented to listen to the sound of the human voice. Even when they are only a few days old, they already show preferences for their mother's voice compared with a female stranger's voice (DeCasper and Fifer, 1980).

These are a just few examples of ways that babies are actively oriented to making sense of their social environment and learn from watching others. From studies like these, Trevarthen goes a step further, arguing that human babies are born with a capacity for 'inter-subjectivity' which is the foundation for many distinctively human qualities: social sensitivity, empathy, imaginative play, communication, conversation, teaching and learning (Trevarthen, 1998). Or, as Gopnik *et al.* put it:

> For human beings, nurture *is* our nature. The capacity for culture is part of our biology, and the drive to learn is our most important and central instinct ... our unique evolutionary trick, our central adaptation, our greatest weapon in the struggle for survival, is precisely our dazzling ability to learn when we are babies and teach when we are grown-ups.

> (Gopnik *et al.*, 1999, p. 8)

4.2 Understanding children

As further evidence for young children's skills in relating to others, I turn finally to a study by Judy Dunn. This study belongs to the continuing tradition of detailed child observation illustrated by Reading A, written more than a century earlier. Towards the end of Reading A, Darwin comments on the early development of 'moral sense'. As evidence, he refers to several incidents between two-year-old Doddy, his sister and his father: Doddy pretends to be angry; Doddy praises his own generosity, echoing the words a parent might use; Doddy is sensitive to what he believes is ridicule; and Doddy tries to deceive his father over the sugar. Indicators of very young children's capacities for social and moral understanding were also the starting point for Dunn's study. She also uses careful narrative records as evidence for children's capacities at various ages, and explores some of the processes that drive their developing understanding.

This is Sally.

Sally has a basket.

This is Anne.

Anne has a box.

Sally has a marble. She puts the marble into her basket.

Sally goes out for a walk.

Anne takes the marble out of the basket and puts it into the box.

Now Sally comes back.   She wants to play with her marble.

Where will Sally look for her marble?

The story of Sally and Anne is used to find whether children can understand another child's point of view.

Source: Frith, 1989, p. 160.

Observation is a strong tradition of developmental research, but so is experimentation, using specially designed tasks like those used by Piaget and his successors (such as in Box 4, pp. 110–11). Dunn became aware of a discrepancy between her observational work and the findings of experimental studies on the same topics. Recall Piaget's investigation into children's ability to understand a situation from another person's point of view (Chapter 1). His work has been extended in recent investigations, using the so-called 'false-belief' paradigm. Dolls and toys are used as props in telling stories like the following (see illustration on previous page):

> Sally and Anne are playing together. Sally puts a marble in her basket and then leaves the room. While Sally is outside, Anne takes the marble out of the basket and hides it in a box. Sally comes back into the room and looks for her marble. Where will she look for it?

Wimmer and Perner (1983) found three year olds consistently expected that Sally would look for the marble in the box – where the children themselves knew it had been put. From the age of four children began to be able to make a judgement based on Sally's perspective – her (false) belief that she would find the marble in the basket. These experiments seemed to confirm the children's stage-like progression from naivety about everyday social situations towards reasoned understanding and sound judgement.

READING

Now study Reading B by Dunn, 'Young children's understanding of other people', which summarizes her work on the social understanding of very young children. She begins by reviewing the evidence of babies' sensitivity to other people. She summarizes four aspects of two and three year olds' day-to-day encounters, and then draws some conclusions about the influences on their development.

As you read, make notes on Dunn's evidence for the following:

Very young children have a practical understanding of other people's feelings and intentions, indicated by knowing what teases their sibling, by selectively appealing to mother for help according to who had initiated the dispute; and by distinguishing an intentional from an accidental act.

During their third year, children become skilled contributors to shared play with their siblings, adapting their play to their partner's intentions, and adopting a repertoire of 'pretend' roles.

They display growing curiosity about other people's feelings and social rules, as expressed through their use of questions.

They are already learning to make jokes, including differentiating between siblings and parents in terms of which kinds of joke they will react to.

Children seemed to become most sophisticated in using reason in support of their self-interest and rights.

Children's understanding about other people's feelings and intentions appears to be enhanced where their families engage in discussion about these themes.

In short, by observing children in familiar settings – in everyday interactions with siblings and parents – Dunn sees much stronger evidence of their practical understanding of other people's point of view, than is suggested by tests that require children to make a judgement about a hypothetical, story situation. Her research emphasizes children's active engagement in making sense of their social world. They are active participants in the cultural practices that structure and shape their childhood:

> By 36 months of age, the children 'managed' their family lives very effectively: they anticipated and manipulated the reactions of others, 'read' their emotions, used others to reach their own ends, and influenced the feeling states of others intentionally and practically by teasing, comforting, and joking. They questioned and disputed the application of social rules to themselves and others and they successfully redirected blame onto others.

(Dunn, 1998, p. 114)

Knowing what teases another is an early sign of social understanding.

Dunn's study is based on close observation of children's engagement with everyday cultural life in specific domestic settings within Britain and the US. As Dunn herself acknowledges, children's experience of early social interaction – play, talk, jokes, disputes and teasing – may be quite different within other settings or cultural contexts. The assumption of much developmental research is that children are seen as individuals, dependent during infancy, but gradually growing towards autonomy. In this respect researchers may share the same cultural assumptions about children's development as the families they research. Anthropologists have long pointed out that this is a dangerous assumption to make:

The Western conception of the person as a bounded, unique, more or less integrated motivational and cognitive universe, a dynamic center of awareness, emotion, judgment, and action organized into a distinctive whole and set contrastively both against other such wholes and against its social and natural background, is, however incorrigible it may seem to us, a rather peculiar idea within the context of the world's cultures.

(Geertz, 1975, p. 29)

For example, the data from fieldwork in Dunn's study have been collected in settings where it is accepted that very young children have strong feelings. Their vocal assertion of their wishes is tolerated, or even encouraged, in a cultural context which recognizes these outbursts as an important feature of becoming a separated identity. In many English-speaking countries, children who are beginning to assert their sense of self are described as the 'terrible twos'. But cross-cultural studies suggest it may be wrong to assume these experiences of child development are natural, normal and universal:

> ... the classic account of the toddler's drive for autonomy and separateness ... appears incorrect as a thematic description of toddler development in many non-Western cultural communities ... For example, in Zinacantan, Mexico ... the transition from infancy to early childhood is not typified by resistant toddlers demanding and asserting control over toileting and other self-help skills (the familiar 'no, I can do it') but instead by watchful, imitative children who acquire toilet training and other elements of self-care with a minimum of fuss.

(Edwards, 1995, p. 47)

Finally, the image of the developing child conveyed by Dunn's account is rather different from the image conveyed by conventional theories about stages in normal development. First, there is the evident precocity of children's understanding of many aspects of their social world, especially within the intimate environment of their homes. These children seem to have quite a strong practical 'moral sense' even by the age of three, when they would still be very immature in terms of more formal tests on these themes (such as on Kohlberg's scales of moral reasoning). Secondly, the children in Dunn's study appear very 'worldly' by the age of three. They are close observers of the day to day events around them, and keen to understand what is going on. They are already learning how to tease and upset their siblings, engage in 'word play on forbidden topics' and negotiate their self-interest. These social skills also coincide with children's developing sense of empathy. Young children can be highly sensitive to expressions of pleasure and pain in others and they are capable of quite touching expressions of sympathy towards a parent who feels unwell or upset.

This line of research raises intriguing questions about how young children are thought about and understood. Are they best seen as dependent innocents in need of protection, or as assertive individuals, interested and engaged in their social world? The power of cultural beliefs about children's innocence will be discussed in greater detail in Chapter 6.

SUMMARY OF SECTION 4

- Lev Vygotsky represents a tradition of developmental research that draws attention to the ways that childhood is a social and a cultural process.
- Research into early infancy suggests human babies are pre-adapted to social interaction and cultural learning.
- In Dunn's research, very young children appear highly socially competent in everyday situations at home, raising questions about cultural beliefs about young children's innocence.

5 CONCLUSION

I've come a long way from the story of the Wild Boy of Aveyron, which captured the imagination of the French public in the winter of 1799. During the intervening two centuries, the idea that childhood is a period of development that can be studied systematically has becoming increasingly significant both as an end in itself (in research and teaching about child development) and in the design of systems of child care and education. This final section draws together some of the main themes of earlier sections, by asking how the study of child development constructs its subject – the child.

In the early sections of the chapter, I explained that early scientific studies of childhood concentrated on identifying normal patterns of children's physical, emotional and cognitive development, as well as variations from the norm. I drew attention to the risks that attach to these normative accounts of developmental processes, especially in so far as they construct an image of a universal child, even though it is mainly based on Western cultural contexts and expectations for childhood. At the core of much developmental theorizing is the idea that childhood is an extended period, during which all children progress through a series of stages from immaturity to maturity, which tends to overlook respects in which routes to maturity, as well as maturity itself, are culturally defined. Positioning children on a developmental trajectory related to their age is seen as a distinctive feature of modern societies. From a social constructionist perspective, developmentalism is a discourse within which children are constructed as 'not yet adults', as in a 'process of becoming', rather than persons in their own right (Burman, 1994; James *et al.*, 1998). They are a set of potentials, a project in the making (Verhellen, 1997). So developmental theories can be seen as a powerful discourse (or discourses) on childhood.

But developmental research also claims status as a field of scientific enquiry. I have tried to show what this means in practice, by illustrating a range of research traditions, including examples where a new experiment or set of careful observations can serve to challenge a powerful theory or paradigm. In the final section especially, I contrasted Piagetian approaches that convey an image of the individual child progressively constructing mature capacities for reasoning and thinking, with Vygotskian theory which emphasizes child development as a social, interactive, and cultural process. For me, the lesson of social constructionism is not to abandon scientific research and theory building but to be aware of the various ways theories, research methods and findings construct the child in development (as also argued in Chapter 1).

This leads to the final point – about the status of the child in research and theory. I have tried to convey a sense of the challenges of studying child development within a scientific framework, especially how the child is understood as a growing human organism, as a social actor, and as a subject for research.

Who's studying whom?

The cartoon illustrates one of the most basic dilemmas. Compare it with the cartoon at the beginning of the chapter (p. 88). These cartoons sum up some features of two very different ways of studying children. The first represents a strictly scientific approach, the parent/scientist studies the child's learning, much as a chemist might record what happens to chemicals in a test-tube. It may remind you of the objective methods of observation and experimentation, symbolized by Gesell's observation dome (Box 2, p. 99). In the second, the scientist is also making a systematic study of the child. What he may not have observed is that the child is equally intent on making his own study of the scientist and will probably react to the situation according to his understanding of what is going on. The second cartoon is a reminder that the child is not a passive object of research. Researching children's development is not like carrying out a chemistry experiment, because a human relationship is involved, researcher and child are both accessing cultural knowledge to make sense of what is going on. They are also relying on cultural communicative practices, notably language, to share their understanding. In other words, while the researcher is trying to make sense of the child, the child may be trying to make sense of the researcher. Each in their own way is a participant in the process of human meaning making (Woodhead and Faulkner, 1999).

Asking about the status of children as participants in research is part of a much broader question about their status in society – how far they are viewed as immature and dependent or as citizens with rights. These questions are the subject of the next chapter.

REFERENCES

BARNES, P. (1995) 'Growth and change in adolescence' in Barnes, P. (ed.) *Personal, Social and Emotional Development of Children*, Oxford, Blackwell/The Open University.

BEEKMAN, D. (1977) *The Mechanical Baby: a popular history of the theory and practice of child raising*, New York, New American Library.

BLANCHET, T. (1996) *Lost Innocence, Stolen Childhoods*, Dhaka, University of Dhaka Press.

BOWLBY, J. (1953) *Child Care and the Growth of Love*, Harmondsworth, Penguin.

BOYDEN, J. (1997) 'Childhood and the policy-makers: a comparative perspective on the globalization of childhood' in JAMES, A. and PROUT, A. (eds) *Constructing and Reconstructing Childhood*, London, Falmer Press.

BRUCE, T., FINDLAY, A., READ, J. and SCARBOROUGH, M. (1995) *Recurring Themes in Education*, London, Paul Chapman.

BURMAN, E. (1994) *Deconstructing Developmental Psychology*, London, Routledge.

CENTRAL ADVISORY COUNCIL FOR EDUCATION (1967) *Children and their Primary Schools*, London, HMSO (The Plowden Report).

CHISHOLM, J. S. (1996) 'Learning "respect for everything": Navajo images of development' in HWANG, C. P., LAMB, M. E. and SIGEL, I. E. (eds) *Images of Childhood*, Hillsdale (New Jersey), Erlbaum.

DAS GUPTA, P. (1994) 'Images of childhood and theories of development' in OATES, J. (ed.) *The Foundations of Child Development*, Oxford, Blackwell/The Open University.

DECASPER, A. J. and FIFER, W. P. (1980) 'Of human bonding: newborns prefer their mother's voices', *Science*, **208**, pp. 1174–6.

DONALDSON, M. (1978) *Children's Minds*, London, Fontana.

DUNN, J. (1988) *The Beginnings of Social Understanding*, Oxford, Blackwell.

EDWARDS, C. P. (1995) 'Parenting toddlers' in BORNSTEIN, M. H. (ed.) *Handbook of Parenting*, Hillsdale (New Jersey), Erlbaum.

FRITH, U. (1989) *Autism: explaining the enigma*, Oxford, Blackwell.

GEERTZ, C. (1975) '"From the native's point of view": on the nature of anthropological understanding', in Goldberger, N. R. and Veroff, J. B. (eds) (1995) *The Culture and Psychology Reader*, New York, New York University Press.

GESELL, A. (1925) *The Mental Growth of the Pre-school Child: a psychological outline of normal development from birth to the sixth year, including a system of development diagnosis*, New York, Macmillan.

GOPNIK, A., MELTZOFF, A. and KUHL, P. (1999) *How Babies Think*, London, Weidenfeld and Nicolson.

HARDYMENT, C. (1984) *Dream Babies: child care from Locke to Spock*, Oxford, Oxford University Press.

HENDRICK, H. (1997) *Children, Childhood and English Society 1880–1990,* Cambridge, Cambridge University Press.

ITARD, J. (1962; first published in 1806) *The Wild Boy of Aveyron (L'enfant sauvage)*, translated by Humphrey, G. and Humphrey, M., New York, Meredith Publishing.

JAMES, A., JENKS, C. and PROUT, A. (1998) *Theorizing Childhood,* Cambridge, Polity Press.

JOHNSON, M. H. and MORTON, J. (1991) *Biology and Cognitive Development: the case of face recognition*, Oxford, Blackwell.

KAGAN, J. (1976) 'Emergent themes in human development', *American Scientist,* **64**, pp. 186–96.

LEWIS, M. and BROOKS-GUNN, J. (1979) *Social Cognition and the Acquisition of Self,* New York, Plenum.

LEVINE, R. A., LEVINE, S., LIEDERMANN, P. H., BRAZELTON, T. B., DIXON, S., RICHMAN, A. and KEFFER, C. H. (1994) *Child Care and Culture: lessons from Africa*, Cambridge, Cambridge University Press.

LIGHT, P. (1986) 'Context, conservation and conversation' in Richards, M. and Light, P. (eds) *Children of Social Worlds,* Cambridge, Polity Press/The Open University.

LORENZ, K. Z. (1981) *The Foundations of Ethology*, New York, Springer-Verlag.

MORROW, V. (2003) 'Moving out of childhood' in MAYBIN, J. and WOODHEAD, M. (eds) (2003) *Childhoods in Context*, Chichester, Wiley/The Open University (Book 2 of course U212 Childhood).

NEWSON, J. and NEWSON, E. (1974) 'Cultural aspects of child-rearing in the English-speaking world' in RICHARDS, M. P. M. (ed.) *The Integration of a Child into a Social World*, Cambridge, Cambridge University Press.

SCHAFFER, H. R. (1996) *Social Development*, Oxford, Blackwell.

SHAFFER, D. R. (1993, 3rd edn) *Developmental Psychology*, Pacific Grove (Calif.), Brooks/Cole.

SMITH, P. K., COWIE, H. and BLADES, M. (1998, 3rd edn) *Understanding Children's Development*, Oxford, Blackwell.

SROUFE, A. L., COOPER, R. G., DEHART, G. B. and MARSHALL, M. E. (1996) *Child Development: its nature and course*, New York, McGraw-Hill.

TIZARD, B. (1991) 'Working mothers and the care of young children', in PHOENIX, A. and WOOLLETT, A. (eds) *Social Construction of Motherhood*, London, Sage.

TREVARTHEN, C. (1998) 'The child's need to learn a culture' in WOODHEAD, M., FAULKNER, D. and LITTLETON, K. (eds) *Cultural Worlds of Early Childhood*, London, Routledge/The Open University.

VERHELLEN, E. (1997) *Convention on the Rights of the Child,* Leuven, Garant Publishers.

WALKERDINE, V. (1984) 'Developmental psychology and the child-centred pedagogy: the insertion of Piaget's theory into primary school practice' in HENRIQUES, J. *et al.* (eds) *Changing the Subject*, London, Methuen.

WEISNER. T. and GALLIMORE, R. (1977) 'My brother's keeper: child and sibling caretaking', *Current Anthropology,* **18**(02), pp. 169–90.

WIMMER, H. and PERNER, J. (1983) 'Beliefs about beliefs: representation and constraining function of wrong beliefs in young children's understanding of deception'. *Cognition,* **13**, pp.103–128.

WOODHEAD, M. (1999) 'Reconstructing developmental psychology: some first steps', *Children and Society,* **13**(1), pp. 3–19.

WOODHEAD, M. and FAULKNER, D. (1999) 'Subjects, objects or participants: dilemmas of psychological research with children', in CHRISTENSEN, P. and JAMES, A. (eds) *Conducting Research with Children*, London, Falmer Press.

A biographical sketch of an infant

Charles Darwin

[...] During the first seven days various reflex actions, namely sneezing, hickuping, yawning, stretching, and of course sucking and screaming, were well performed by my infant. On the seventh day, I touched the naked sole of his foot with a bit of paper, and he jerked it away, curling at the same time his toes, like a much older child when tickled. The perfection of these reflex movements shows that the extreme imperfection of the voluntary ones is not due to the state of the muscles or of the coordinating centres, but to that of the seat of the will. At this time, though so early, it seemed clear to me that a warm soft hand applied to his face excited a wish to suck. This must be considered as a reflex or an instinctive action, for it is impossible to believe that experience and association with the touch of his mother's breast could so soon have come into play ...

With respect to vision, – his eyes were fixed on a candle as early as the 9th day, and up to the 45th day nothing else seemed thus to fix them; but on the 49th day his attention was attracted by a bright-coloured tassel, as was shown by his eyes becoming fixed and the movements of his arms ceasing. It was surprising how slowly he acquired the power of following with his eyes an object if swinging at all rapidly; for he could not do this well when seven and a half months old. At the age of 32 days he perceived his mother's bosom when three or four inches from it, as was shown by the protrusion of his lips and his eyes becoming fixed; but I much doubt whether this had any connection with vision; he certainly had not touched the bosom. Whether he was guided through smell or the sensation of warmth or through association with the position in which he was held, I do not at all know.

The movements of his limbs and body were for a long time vague and purposeless, and usually performed in a jerking manner; but there was one exception to this rule, namely that from a very early period, certainly long before he was 40 days old, he could move his hands to his own mouth... When between 80 and 90 days old, he drew all sorts of objects into his mouth, and in two or three weeks' time could do this with some skill; but he often first touched his nose with the object and then dragged it down into his mouth. After grasping my finger and drawing it to his mouth, his own hand prevented him from sucking it; but on the 114th day, after acting in this manner, he slipped his own hand down so that he could get the end of my finger into his mouth. This action was repeated several times, and evidently was not a chance but a rational one.

[...]

Affection. This probably arose very early in life, if we may judge by his smiling at those who had charge of him when under two months old; though I had no distinct evidence of his distinguishing and recognising anyone, until he was nearly four months old. When nearly five months old, he plainly showed his wish to go to his nurse. But he did not spontaneously exhibit affection by overt acts until a little above a year old, namely, by kissing several times his nurse who had been absent for a short time. With respect to the allied feeling of sympathy, this was clearly shown at 6 months and 11 days by his melancholy face, with the corners of his mouth well depressed, when his nurse pretended to cry. Jealousy was plainly exhibited when I fondled a large doll, and when I weighed his infant sister, he being then 15 months old. Seeing how strong a feeling jealousy is in dogs, it would probably be exhibited by infants at an earlier age than that just specified, if they were tried in a fitting manner.

Association of Ideas, Reason, &c. The first action which exhibited, as far as I observed, a kind of practical reasoning, has already been noticed, namely, the slipping his hand down my finger so as to get the end of it into his mouth; and this happened on the 114th day. When four and a half months old, he repeatedly smiled at my image and his own in a mirror, and no doubt mistook them for real objects; but he showed sense in being evidently surprised at my voice coming from behind him. Like all infants he much enjoyed thus looking at himself, and in less than two months perfectly understood that it was an image; for if I made quite silently any odd grimace, he would suddenly turn round to look at me. He was, however, puzzled at the age of seven months, when being out of doors he saw me on the inside of a large plate-glass window, and seemed in doubt whether or not it was an image. Another of my infants, a little girl, when exactly a year old, was not nearly so acute, and seemed quite perplexed at the image of a person in a mirror approaching her from behind. The higher apes which I tried with a small looking-glass behaved differently; they placed their hands behind the glass, and in doing so showed their sense, but far from taking pleasure in looking at themselves they got angry and would look no more.

[...]

Moral Sense. The first sign of moral sense was noticed at the age of nearly 13 months: I said 'Doddy (his nickname) won't give poor papa a kiss, – naughty Doddy.' These words, without doubt, made him feel slightly uncomfortable; and at last when I had returned to my chair, he protruded his lips as a sign that he was ready to kiss me; and he then shook his hand in an angry manner until I came and received his kiss. Nearly the same little scene recurred in a few days, and the reconciliation seemed to give him so much satisfaction, that several times afterwards he pretended to be angry and slapped me, and then insisted on giving me a kiss. So that here we have a touch of the dramatic art, which is so strongly pronounced in most young children. About this time it became easy to work on his feelings and make him do whatever was wanted. When 2 years and 3 months old, he gave his last bit of gingerbread to his little sister, and then cried out with high self-approbation 'Oh kind Doddy, kind Doddy.' Two months later, he became extremely sensitive to ridicule, and was so suspicious that he often thought people who were laughing and talking together were laughing at him. A little later (2 years and 7_ months old) I met him coming out of the dining room with his eyes unnaturally bright, and an odd unnatural or affected manner, so that I went into the room to see who was there, and found that he had been taking pounded sugar, which he had been told not to do. As he had never been in any way punished, his odd manner certainly was not due to fear, and I suppose it was pleasurable excitement struggling with conscience. A fortnight afterwards, I met him coming out of the same room, and he was eyeing his pinafore which he had carefully rolled up: and again his manner was so odd that I determined to see what was within his pinafore, notwithstanding that he said there was nothing and repeatedly commanded me to 'go away,' and I found it stained with pickle-juice; so that here was carefully planned deceit. As this child was educated solely by working on his good feelings, he soon became as truthful, open, and tender, as anyone could desire ...

Source

DARWIN, C. R. (1877) 'A biographical sketch of an infant' in KESSEN, W. (ed.) (1965) *The Child,* New York, Wiley, pp.118–126.

Young children's understanding of other people

Judy Dunn

In infancy, babies are apparently both interested in and responsive to the emotions and behavior of other people. They are born predisposed to attend to stimuli with the characteristics of the human face and voice, and they develop quickly 'remarkable abilities to perceive the actions and expressions of other people' (Spelke and Cortelyou, 1981). They learn rapidly about stimuli that change in a manner that is contingent upon their own behavior – as does the behavior of other people interacting with them. By 2 months of age, they respond differently to a person who intends to speak to them than to one who speaks to someone else (Trevarthen, 1977). By the second half of their first year, they have begun to share a common communicative framework with other family members, and, as we have learned from the elegant experimental studies of *social referencing* (Klinnert, Campos, Sorce, Emde, and Svejda, 1983), in situations of uncertainty, they monitor the emotional expressions of their mothers and change their behavior appropriately in response to those expressions. As the work of those studying early language has shown particularly clearly, their comprehension of social procedures is surprisingly subtle. Bruner, for example, has persuasively argued that children have mastered the culturally appropriate use of requests, invitations, and reference well before they are correctly using the conventional linguistic forms (Bruner, 1983).

[...] The findings that I discuss (described fully in Dunn, 1988) are drawn from three longitudinal studies of secondborn children in their second and third years: six children followed at 2-month intervals through the second year, six followed similarly through their third year and 43 families studied when the secondborn children were aged 18, 24, and 36 months. The families were middle- and working-class families living in and around Cambridge in England, and all the observations, which were unstructured, were made while the children were at home, playing, fighting, and talking with their mothers and siblings. Examples are also cited from an ongoing study of children in Pennsylvania ...

[...]

Disputes

Within each domain that we studied – disputes, jokes, empathetic and prosocial behavior, cooperation, pretend play, and conversations about other people – we found evidence for children's growing grasp of the feelings of others, of their intended actions, and of how social rules applied to other people and to themselves. In disputes, for example, the children showed a growing sophistication in teasing – actions that demonstrated a practical grasp of what would upset or annoy a particular person. Early in the second year, acts that we categorised as teasing were pretty simple; for example, children in disputes with their older siblings often seized or removed their siblings' transitional object or most special toys, or attempted to destroy something that had special significance for the siblings. In the course of the second year, such teasing acts became more frequent and more elaborate. One 24-month-old, for instance, whose older sister had three imaginary friends called Lily, Allelujah, and Peepee, would, in the course of disputes with this sister, announce that *she* was Allelujah. It was an act that was reliably followed by anger or distress on her sister's part, and it was also an act of notable sophistication for a 24-month-old, because it involved both some grasp of what would upset her sister and a transformation of her own identity.

Our analysis of disputes between the siblings showed, too, that early in the second year the children's attempts to enlist the aid of their mothers on their own behalf differed sharply according to whether the siblings had acted in an aggressive or hostile fashion first or whether they themselves had done so. The probability that the children would appeal to their mothers was high (66%) if the sibling had been the first to act in an aggressive or teasing manner. In contrast, they rarely appealed to their mother for help in incidents when they *themselves* had acted in such way: in only 4% of such incidents did they do so. Such a distinction in the children's behavior, and indeed the evasive actions that second-year children take to avoid future punishment (see Dunn, 1988), indicate some anticipation of the mothers' actions, although, of course, they imply no elaborate understanding of the mothers' *minds*. This grasp of how other people can be expected to behave in relation to social rules becomes strikingly evident during the third year, when children's language abilities increase ...

Particularly illuminating were the excuses that the children used in their attempts to avoid disapprobation. The nature of the excuses that the children used in disputes showed an increasingly elaborate grasp of how social rules applied to different peoples in different contexts and of how these ruled could be questioned. For our present purposes, it is excuses of intent that are of special interest. In our culture, we see as crucial the distinction between acts that are intended to harm others or transgress rules of conduct and acts that have similar consequences but are accidental (Darley and Zanna, 1982). The question of when children begin to make this distinction is, however, a matter of some dispute. Piaget (1965) considered that there was 'some reason to doubt whether a child of 6–7 could really distinguish an involuntary error from an intentional lie ... the distinction is, at the best, in the process of formation' (p. 145). In contrast to this view, Shultz (1980) reported observations that children as young as 3 may make such a distinction. The children in our studies made the excuse that they 'didn't mean to' rather infrequently during the observations. However, among the incidents when they did refer to intentions were some that involved children as young as 26 months:

Example 1: Child aged 26 months (Study 3)
Child climbs on Mother to investigate light switch:
M: You're hurting me!
C: Sorry. Sorry. I don't mean to.

This example could be interpreted as a 'rote-learned' strategy for getting out of trouble, rather than evidence that the child really understood the significance of his intentions for his mother... However, the wide variety of situations and the appropriateness with which these phrases are used should be borne in mind ... The following example comes from an observation of a 33-month-old girl in the Pennsylvania study, who came crying to her mother after her brother had deliberately bitten her on the forehead:

Example 2: Child aged 33 months (Pennsylvania study)
C: Look what Philip did!
            He bited me!
            (crying)
M: He bit you on the head?
C: Yes.
M to Sib: Philip is that true?
S: No.
C to M: Yes!
            On purpose!
M to C: He did it on purpose?
C: Yes.
M to Sib: Come on over, Philip.
Sib to M: I didn't do it on purpose Mom.
C to M: Yes he did.
[...]

Co-operative pretend play

The analysis of children's behavior in co-operative play, in response to others' distress, as humorists, and in conversation about others, provides further evidence on the nature of their understanding of other people in their world. During the third year, children's participation in joint pretend play, for example, changed dramatically. Between 18 and 24 months, they joined their older siblings' pretend play as compliant participants who obeyed (usually) the managerial – and often dictatorial – instructions of their siblings (Dunn and Dale, 1984). In the course of the third year, their co-operation became a far more active affair, in which they were innovative actors who not only anticipated the goals and intentions of their partner in play, but who, in their own original contributions, demonstrated some understanding of the intentions and feelings of the pretend 'other' whose role they were enacting. In the example that follows, the 30-month-old girl was playing a game of mothers and babies with her older sister. The game began with a command from the older sister to 'pretend you're a baby or my mummy.' The sequence was not unusual in its length or complexity. It lasted for 140 conversational turns and Annie, the younger sister, made a number of contributions to the play narrative, relevant to her role as baby. She also acted both compliantly and noncompliantly:

Example 5: Child aged 30 months (Study 3)

Child's innovations in the joint pretend play, for her role as Baby:
    Makes babbling noises.
    Crawls.
    Says she can't put slippers on: 'I'm baby.'
    Designates 'baby bed.'
    Asks for porridge.
    Plays guitar in a way she designates as 'a babby way ... Me babby.'
    Addresses sibling as 'Mummy.'
    Acts naughty with the guitar.
    Pretends to get lost.
    Snores.
    In answer to sibling enquiring why she is crying ('What's wrong babbu?') replies 'Me can't get to sleep.'
    Instructs sibling on what she should say, as Mummy.

Child's disputes and noncompliance with sibling over course of pretend play:
    When told to babble and not to cry, cries.
    Criticizes sibling's action in terms of role: 'No you not a baby.'
    Denies that they are both tired in the game.
    Refuses to go on 'Mummy's' knee.

Child's compliance with sibling's actions or suggestion in the game:
    Sibling goes to sleep: Child pretends to sleep.
    Sibling gives 'drink': Child pretends to drink.
    Sibling gives 'food': Child pretends to eat it.

Such innovations in joint pretend became increasingly evident from the middle of the third year. The ability to imagine being another person with intentions and feelings that are different from one's own is surely important evidence for children's growing understanding of others – evidence that parallels the signs of children's ability to deceive ...

Conversations about others

From the transcripts of the observations of the six children observed at 2-month intervals during their third year, we examined all the children's questions about other people, categorising such inquiries according to whether they were about the whereabouts, actions, or inner states of the people concerned or about the application of social rules to those others. ... [I]nquiries about inner states and social rules were absent during the first months of the third year but showed a sharp increase in the second half of that year.

A similar analysis of the 43 children in the large study as 36-month-olds provided an encouraging replication of these findings, with very similar proportions of questions about the inner states and feelings of others. What is particularly notable about such conversations, for our present concern, is that a relatively high proportion of the conversations included discussion of the cause or consequence of the feelings or inner state of the person discussed (Dunn, Brown, and Beardsall, 1990). The rise of questions about others at this time and our analysis of the pragmatic context of such questions indicate that, as their ability to reflect on other minds develops there is a growth of 'disinterested' curiosity about others. [...]

Jokes

A further instance of the children's sensitivity to the interests and feelings of the different people in their social world was provided by an analysis of the children's humor. Even before they are using many words, children find the behavior of others in their world a source of amusement, as they do jokes that can be pointed out and shared with others. Sharing a joke implies, at some level, an expectation that another person will also find this distortion of the expected absurd or comic. What our examination of the children's jokes showed was that children made different jokes to their siblings than to their mothers or the observer. With parents, play with naming jokes, true-false assertions, transgressions of the social rules, and with the emotional dynamics of their relationships stood out ...

With their siblings, the children enjoyed and developed ritual insults, scatological jokes, and word play on forbidden topics. The results strongly suggest that, by 36 months, children already have a considerable and differentiated understanding of what familiar others will find funny or offensive.

The developmental course of children's understanding of others in the second and third year

In summary, the results of these observations within the family suggest the following course of development: children's understanding of others' feelings grows early in the second year from an 'affective tuning' to the distress or amusement of others (see Stern, 1985) to a grasp of how certain actions lead to disapproval or anger in others, how certain actions can comfort other family members (see Yarrow, Zahn-Waxler, and Chapman, 1983), and what action can be a shared source of amusement with others. They respond empathetically to others' distress early in the second year, and they show in both their nonverbal and verbal behavior much interest in the feeling states of others. With increasing explicitness, they show curiosity about and understanding of the causes of pain, anger, distress, pleasure, dislike, fear, comfort in others. They play with and joke about these feelings in others and tell stories about them.

They also, during the second year, show increasing sensitivity to the goals and intentions of others – understanding that is evident in their disputes, pretend, narratives, and questions. Understanding of mental states, as opposed to emotional states and intended actions, appears to develop somewhat later, during the second half of the third year.

[...]

The possible importance of the emotional context

In considering the ways in which family interactions might play a special role in fostering the development of social understanding, it is surely important to examine the possible role of affective experience. One provocative set of findings here came from our analysis of the disputes between children and their mothers and siblings (Dunn and Munn, 1987). We were interested in the relations between the emotions that the children expressed during the disputes, the topic of these disputes, and the likelihood that they would *reason*, rather than behave in a less mature way (such as resorting to hit or howl). The results showed that as 18-month-olds they were most likely to be angry or distressed in disputes over the topic of rights and interests (usually their own!) ...

Eighteen months later, when the children were 36 months old, it was in these disputes over rights and interests that they showed their most 'mature' behavior, by marshalling justifications and excuses for their actions. The children, that is, showed their most mature behavior over the issues that their earlier emotional behavior had suggested they cared most about. One inference from these findings might be that children use their intelligence on what matters most to them emotionally. Another, which is not incompatible with the first, is that the experience of mild distress and anger during these family conflicts may actually contribute to the children's learning – that the arousal they experience may heighten their vigilance and attentive powers.

[...]

The possible significance of family discourse

... The evidence from studies in both the United States and Britain shows that young children in our cultures grow up in a world in which there is much conversation within families about the feelings and behavior of others and about their motives, intentions and the permissibility of their actions ... Children are participants in conversations about such matters from a very early age: they monitor, comment on, and join in such discussions between others, and they question, joke about, and argue as to the causes and consequences of the feelings and behavior of others. It appears very likely that children's differentiated understanding of other minds is influenced by such discourse. Here, the analysis of individual differences supports such a contention. Differences between families in the frequency and extent of discussion of others' feelings, motives, and behavior are striking; in our studies in Cambridge, correlations were found between such differences in the first three years of children's lives and in a variety of 'outcome' measures, such as the child's own participation in conversation about inner states (Dunn, Bretherton, and Munn, 1987), their friendly behavior towards their younger siblings (Dunn and Kendrick, 1982), and, most strikingly, their performance three to four years later on affective perspective-taking tasks (Dunn, Brown, and Beardsall, 1990) ...

References

BRUNER, J. (1983). *Child's talk*. New York: Norton.

DARLEY, J.M. and ZANNA, M.P. (1982). Making moral judgements. *American Scientist, 70*, 515–521.

DUNN, J. (1988). *The beginnings of social understanding*. Cambridge, MA: Harvard University Press.

DUNN, J. and DALE, N. (1984). I a Daddy: Two-year-olds' collaboration in joint pretend with mothers and siblings. In I. BRETHERTON (Ed.), *Symbolic play: The development of social understanding* (pp.131–158). New York: Academic Press.

DUNN, J. and KENDRICK, C. (1982). *Siblings: Love, envy and understanding*. Cambridge, MA: Harvard University Press.

DUNN, J. and MUNN, P. (1987). The development of justification in disputes with mother and with sibling. *Developmental Psychology, 23*, 791–798.

DUNN, J., BRETHERTON, I., and MUNN, P. (1987). Conversations about feeling states between mothers and their young children. *Developmental Psychology, 23*, 132–139.

DUNN, J., BROWN, J., and BEARDSALL, L. (1990). Family talk about feeling states, and children's later understanding of others' emotions. *Developmental Psychology, 26*.

KLINNERT, M.D., CAMPOS, J.J., SORCE, J.F., EMDE, R.N., and SVEJDA, M. (1983). Emotions as behaviour regulators: Social referencing in infancy. In R. PLUTCHIK and H. KELLERMAN (Eds), *Emotion: Theory, research and experience* (Vol. 2, pp. 57–86). New York: Academic Press.

PIAGET, J. (1965). *The moral judgement of the child*. New York: Free Press.

SHULTZ, T.R. (1980). The development of the concept of intention. In A. COLLINS (Ed.), *Minnesota symposium on child psychology* (Vol. 13, pp. 131–164). Hillsdale, NJ: Lawrence Erlbaum Associates.

SPELKE, E.S. and CORTELYOU, A. (1981). Perceptual aspects of social knowing: Looking and listening in infancy. In M.E. LAMB and L.R. SHERROD (Eds), *Infant social cognition* (pp. 61–84). Hillsdale, NJ: Lawrence Erlbaum Associates.

STERN, D. (1985). *The interpersonal world of the infant*. New York: Basic Books.

TREVARTHEN, C. (1977). Descriptive analyses of infant communicative behaviour. In H.R. SCHAFFER (Ed.), *Studies in mother-infant interaction* (pp. 227–270). London: Academic Press.

YARROW, M.R., ZAHN-WAXLER, C., and CHAPMAN, M. (1983). Prosocial behaviour. In P.H. MUSSEN (Ed.), *Handbook of child psychology: Volume 4. Socialization personality and social development* (pp. 469–545). New York: Wiley.

Source

Dunn, J. (1991) 'Young children's understanding of other people' in WOODHEAD, M., FAULKNER, D. and LITTLETON, K. (eds) (1998) *Cultural Worlds of Early Childhood*, London, Routledge/The Open University, pp. 101–116.

Chapter 4
Children and rights

Rachel Burr and Heather Montgomery

CONTENTS

When you have studied this chapter, you should be able to:

1   Understand the concept of human rights and examine how they apply to both children and adults;

2   Recognize some of the ways in which rights can be complex and contradictory;

3   Understand the main provisions of children's rights documents such as the United Nations Convention on the Rights of the Child and the African Charter on the Rights and Welfare of the Child, and discuss the effects this legislation is having on children's lives.

4   Discuss cultural relativism versus universal implementation of human and children's rights.

I INTRODUCTION

So far this book has introduced two ways of considering childhood – from a social constructionist approach (Chapter 2), and a developmental approach (Chapter 3). This chapter will use a third perspective – an applied approach – to examine children's rights. It will analyse the impact of children's rights on children, looking at what they mean to children, the extent to which children are able to exercise them and whether they have made any real differences to children's lives. In particular, this chapter will concentrate on one of the most important documents protecting children's rights, the United Nation Convention on the Rights of the Child (UNCRC) and look at the effects of this, and other international legislation, on children's lives.

This chapter will start by examining human rights in order to put the UNCRC into context. It will then discuss the philosophical basis for children's rights and describe some of the problems of acknowledging that children have rights. In particular, it will look at children's rights to participation in society. This can mean a number of things but one of the key ideas is the importance placed on listening to children and encouraging their participation in decisions that affect them. The expectation that adults must listen to, and take into account, children's viewpoints has significant implications, particularly if this challenges past experiences, power relationships and assumptions that adults know best. This chapter will then turn to specific pieces of children's rights legislation before examining the impact of children's rights at a local level.

2 WHAT ARE HUMAN RIGHTS?

2.1 The development of human rights

The idea that every person has the same rights is about 200 years old, beginning with the French and American Revolutions. The original draft for the American Declaration of Independence began with the words 'We hold these truths to be sacred and inalienable: that all men are created equal and independent, that from equal creation they derive rights inherent and inalienable, among which are the preservation of life, liberty, and the pursuit of happiness.' But the writers of these words did not apply the 'inherent and inalienable' rights to women, slaves or children. Indeed, slaves were seen as not human and having no rights.

Box 1 (overleaf) is an extract from a novel written by a white woman, Martha Browne, about a slave who was born in Kentucky in 1808. On the death of her master she was sold and was separated from her mother. It is clear that she has notions of the inherent dignity of human beings and equality among them, and there are comments that look forward to a time of universal 'rights'. She makes the point that under the system of slavery in the American South, USA, animals have more rights than people.

Martha Browne's experiences may seem a historical curiosity but the example of slavery shows how, at certain periods in history, people have been seen as less than human and as having no inherent worth.

It was not until 1948, in the aftermath of the Second World War, that international human rights were first codified. The 1948 UN Declaration of Human Rights asserted for the first time that everyone had rights due to them, not because of the property they owned, the colour of their skin or their sex but simply because they were human. Being human gave them certain inalienable rights, such as the right to life or the right to freedom of conscience. After the horrors of the Holocaust, a codified system of legal rights was seen as necessary to prevent any such atrocities ever happening again. Over the years this Declaration has been extended into a complex web of international legislation but the most important thing to note is that all international human rights laws are interconnected, whether they are global, regional or national, or whether they focus on specific issues (such as torture) or groups (such as migrant workers or women). They supplement and complement each other and draw their inspiration from the 1948 UN Declaration of Human Rights. Rights are indivisible. This means that governments cannot pick and choose which rights they uphold, giving people free education for instance, while banning freedom of religion. States must uphold all rights.

States must also be held accountable. Governments do torture people, prevent them from practising their religion or imprison them without a fair trial. If governments sign the UN Declaration, however, they should be accountable to the international community for these infringements. In signing human rights treaties, governments have agreed not only to

Box 1 Selling a child

A tall, hard-looking man came up to me, very roughly seized my arm, bade me open my mouth; examined my teeth; felt of my limbs; made me run a few yards; ordered me to jump; and, being well satisfied with my activity, said to Master Edward, 'I will take her.' Little comprehending the full meaning of that brief sentence, I rejoined the group of children from which I had been summoned. After awhile, my mother came up to me, holding a wallet in her hand. The tear-drops stood on her cheeks, and her whole frame was distorted with pain. She walked toward me a few steps, then stopped, and suddenly shaking her head, exclaimed, 'No, no, I can't do it, I can't do it.' I was amazed at her grief, but an indefinable fear kept me from rushing to her.

'Here, Kitty,' she said to an old Negro woman, who stood near, 'you break it to her. I can't do it. No, it will drive me mad.' … At length Aunt Kitty approached me, and, laying her hand on my shoulder, kindly said:

'Alas, poor chile, you mus' place your trus' in the good God above, you mus' look to Him for help; you are gwine to leave your mother now. You are to have a new home, a new master, and I hope new friends. May the Lord be with you.' So saying, she broke suddenly away from me; but I saw that her wrinkled face was wet with tears …

What could she mean by new friends and a new home? Surely I was to take my mother with me! No mortal power would dare to sever *us*. Why, I remember that when master sold the gray mare, the colt went also. Who could, who would, who dared, separate the parent from her offspring? Alas! I had yet to learn that the white man dared do all that his avarice might suggest; and there was no human tribunal where the outcast African could pray for 'right!'

(Browne, 1857, pp. 13 and 14)

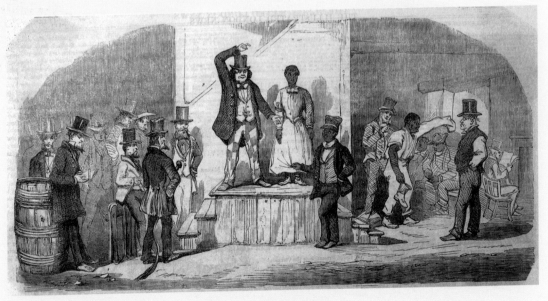

Slave girl sold at auction.

recognize rights but to *enforce* them. For example, Article 26 of the UN Declaration of Human Rights states that:

> Everyone has the right to education. Education shall be free, at least in the elementary and fundamental stages.

If a person has a right to education, then the government has a duty and a responsibility to provide that education. If people do not have free elementary education then their rights are being infringed and someone must be held accountable for that.

2.2 Human rights — universal or relative?

The UN Declaration states that it applies to all humanity, whatever their 'race, colour, sex, language, religion, political or other opinion, national or social origin, property, birth or other status' (Article 2). However, whatever the ideal, the Declaration conflicts with belief systems in some parts of the world, where, for example, women are not given full rights or seen as equal to men. This problem becomes even more acute when discussing children, but before we go on to discuss children's rights specifically, we need to look at why the idea of universal human rights is problematic. The ideals of the UN Declaration appear noble and well intentioned, so why are they contested?

Cultural relativism rejects notions of right or wrong in relation to other cultures, arguing that they must be judged by their own logic and standards and not those of others. It rejects the notion of one universal standard.

One of the most difficult issues is that of cultural diversity. There are instances where local cultural practices conflict with notions of universal rights. Countries such as Saudi Arabia which do not allow women equal rights to men, and claim religious authority for doing so, pose obvious problems. Which is the more important: respecting devout religious belief or setting universal standards? Are such societies simply to be condemned for infringing human rights or should outsiders attempt to understand their beliefs? There are no easy answers to these questions – one extreme position would be that of a cultural relativist, someone who argues that all aspects of all cultures are equally valid and that to interfere is wrong, even with the best of intentions. Using this reasoning, practices such as female circumcision, physically dangerous male initiation rituals and child marriage cannot be condemned as long as they are part of a culture. Others would argue that if the UN Declaration is to have any validity at all, it must be implemented equally for all people without exception, even if this appears to impose Western cultural values on others' societies. Most people might argue for flexibility, allowing certain cultural practices which do not cause harm and forbidding those that do. However, this is a very difficult line to draw. So even when the intention is to safeguard fundamental rights, there is disagreement about how to do this and often irreconcilable tension between the demands of local practice and international law.

One particular problem in introducing the UN Declaration of Human Rights has been that the relationship of individuals to each other and to the state is so different across cultures that it becomes very hard to set universal standards. The 1948 Declaration of Human Rights is based on the idea that each human is an autonomous individual. However, this understanding of the person is based on Western, liberal humanist philosophy and does not easily translate into other societies. In many other societies the idea of a person existing as an individual, autonomous person, simply does not exist. Commenting on Japan, anthropologist Roger Goodman writes: 'when the concept of 'rights' was introduced into Japan ... a whole new vocabulary had to be developed to explain it, as did the idea of the individual who could be endowed with such rights. Even today, individualism has strongly negative connections in Japan and is frequently associated with Western concepts of selfishness' (Goodman, 1996, p. 131).

Allow about 10 minutes

ACTIVITY 1   Chinese families and human rights

Read the text below about Chinese family life and make a note of the ways in which the philosophy of Confucius has helped shape relationships among people in China. What implications might this have for human rights in China?

The Chinese philosopher Confucius (551–479 BCE) has greatly influenced how Chinese societies and families are organized. Confucius believed that the greatest level of responsibility should reside within the family unit, rather than among its individual members. Thus individuals should subvert their own wishes to those of the family as a whole. For example, during the feudal period it was acceptable for a younger and less important son within a family unit to serve a prison sentence where a more powerful brother within the same family had committed a crime. Because the collective sense of self was so important, the older brother was punished enough by experiencing his younger brother undergoing hardship on his behalf.

The family unit was more significant than any one individual in it. The Confucian family worked within a firm hierarchy with particular value being attached to men of the household. The oldest male of each household held the most power, followed by any other male, including male children, residing under the same roof. Women were of little importance in this system, so much so that girls were often not named (Mao Zedong's mother,

for example, was called simply 'Daughter Number Three'. Mao was leader of China from 1954 to 1976).

It was not until the Communist era that women were given equal rights to men in such matters as education and work. While women's standing in society improved under Communism, the legacy of Confucianism still influences their position and rights. Generally women still have lower status than men. Family structures and hierarchies remain traditional and very strong. The individual autonomous self is not nearly as pronounced as it is in the North. Instead a collective sense of identity, in which individuals act for the greater good of the family, is still very much the norm.

COMMENT

You might have noted that the family unit in China takes precedence over the individuals who make up that collective. This has enormous bearing on how people operate within their society and also on how they understand rights. From the brief description of family life above, it is clear that individual human rights are subordinate to those of the needs of the family. Individuals do not have specific rights which take precedence over the family or the right of the oldest man in the family to enforce his position. Rights, in this context, are not enjoyed by all people equally but are dependent on a rigid hierarchy of age and gender.

Japan and China are by no means the only societies that emphasize a collective rather than an individually based sense of the person. When we move on to look at children's rights later in the chapter, we will see that throughout Asia and Africa the family group is often of more importance than any particular individual. There are many examples of the collective needs of the family taking precedence over the needs and desires of the individual that makes up a part of that whole. One such example would involve a person's career being decided by the family even where that person is not happy about that choice, which is often the case in some Asian societies.

There is a tension therefore at the heart of all human rights legislation and that is between universal acceptance of such rights and how different cultures understand them. This tension will be even more pronounced in the discussion of children's rights because the idea that children are independent and autonomous is alien to many belief systems.

SUMMARY OF SECTION 2

- Universal human rights have been discussed for over two centuries.
- They were written down and codified in 1948. The UN Declaration was designed to prevent global war ever happening again.
- The UN Declaration claimed that human rights are indivisible (they cannot be separated from each other) and inalienable (they cannot be taken away).
- Human rights are based on the idea that each person is an autonomous individual.
- Human rights have thus proved hard to implement in some societies which retain very different notions about the nature of the individual and the relationships between people.

3 CHILDREN'S RIGHTS

3.1 Do rights apply to children?

While the idea of human rights is well established, the idea of children having rights is newer and more problematic. Some people might feel that children do not need specific rights because they are covered by the 1948 UN Declaration which ensures equal rights for everyone regardless of age. Others might think that rights do not apply to children because they are too immature to understand them. Others, however, argue that children have particular interests which need to be protected and which are different from adults. In their view, children need special provision in international and national treaties to protect their interests because:

- Children are still growing. As a rule, children are less mature and in many ways more vulnerable than adults, especially if they are deprived of adequate food, care and shelter. They are also more dependent on adults for these things.

- Children may not know as much about the world. They are less experienced and in many ways less competent to make judgements about what is best for them.

- Children may not be able to use language as well. They may not be so skilled in communicating their feelings or explaining their wishes.

- Children have less power. They are more at risk of being abused and exploited by more powerful people.

READING

In Reading A (p. 170), de Vylder looks at why specific rights for children are necessary. He argues that children's rights often get overlooked in macro-economic policy and that attention needs to be paid to the effects on children of national and international economic policies. Look out for particular examples which support his argument that children do not figure in economic policies. In order to understand this article more fully, you should note that NGOs stands for non-governmental organizations (such as aid agencies). Structural adjustment programmes are economic programmes often demanded by the World Bank or the International Monetary Fund before they will loan money to a country. Often they demand the repaying of foreign debt and the move to a capitalist, market economy, away from nationalized industry and investment in social welfare. Article 28 refers to a particular article of the UNCRC which will be discussed in greater detail later in the chapter. Now please read Reading A, 'The big picture'.

COMMENT

In this article, de Vylder shows how children often suffer through the unintentional effects of large-scale economic policies. Children need a specific set of rights because they are weaker, more vulnerable and are subject to economic forces that they cannot control. It is too easy to leave children out of planning processes or to ignore the effects that policies will have on them. Because of this lack of power, children are often the first to suffer. Children's rights are not separate from adults' concerns or from human rights but are very firmly linked to wider concerns of the family and the state. When parents are made unemployed because of government policy, it is the children who suffer. When governments introduce fees for healthcare or education, both adults and children suffer but children do so disproportionately. For this reason, specific safeguards for children are necessary.

3.2 Protection and participation rights

Allow about 10 minutes

ACTIVITY 2   **What rights do children have?**

Read the following list of rights that are guaranteed to children. Can you see differences between them? Are some rights concerned with practical aspects of children's lives and some with more abstract aspects? Can you identify different types of rights?

Children have a right to:

> Food
> Shelter
> Education
> Privacy
> Legal representation and a fair trial
> Protection from abuse
> Protection in times of armed conflict
> A say in decisions about their life
> Freedom of conscience
> Hold and express their opinion freely

COMMENT

Some of these rights are concerned with practical, tangible aspects of children's lives such as providing food and shelter. Others are more concerned with issues about freedom. Others deal with preventing abuse of children's rights and protecting children if their rights are threatened.

Many people who write about children's rights therefore, group rights together, under four headings. These are often referred to as the 'four Ps' of children's rights; they are:

- **Provision rights.** These rights enable children's growth and development. They include rights to food, housing and education.
- **Prevention rights**. These rights are concerned with putting systems in place that prevent abuse of children or infringements of their rights. Such rights include legal representation or privacy.
- **Protection rights**. These rights are concerned with protecting children against exploitation and abuse and intervening once their rights have been infringed. For example, refugee children and child soldiers are given special protective rights in consequence of their vulnerability. Children who suffer abuse in the home can be protected by state intervention.
- **Participation rights**. These enable children to take part in decisions made on their behalf. They also include the right to hold an opinion and to freedom of conscience.

Obviously some of these rights overlap and the four Ps are not meant to be mutually exclusive. Protection and prevention rights in particular are often very closely linked. It is also important to emphasize that some of these rights are more controversial than others. For example, most people would agree that children have a right to food, health services and education and that measures should be taken to prevent and protect them from abuse. However, participation rights are more problematic. They relate to the idea that children must be consulted about any decisions that shape their future. Participation rights mean that children must be seen as full human beings, not simply as dependants of their parents or the property of families, but as full members of society who have a right to be consulted about any decisions concerning them. In practice, there may be a clash between adults and children over children's right to participate in such decisions. The best known example comes in Article 28 (mentioned in Reading A by de Vylder) which gives children a right to *compulsory* education. Children are not allowed to refuse this right and even if they have strong opinions about not going to school, they have no choice. This potential clash is further illustrated in Activity 3.

Allow about 15 minutes

ACTIVITY 3   Hiep – a street boy in Vietnam

The case below is taken from a conversation Rachel Burr had with a fourteen-year-old boy called Hiep who worked, cleaning shoes, on the streets of Hanoi, Vietnam. Hiep's story raises some interesting questions about the tension between protection and participatory rights. Read what Hiep has to say about his position in society and then write a paragraph detailing the extent to which you think he is able to exercise his right to participate in decisions about his future.

In 1997, when Hiep was speaking about his experiences, the Vietnamese government had set up a repatriation programme that took children who had migrated to the city for work off the streets and returned them to their province of birth and their family members. The government wanted to dissuade children from moving to the city because there was genuine concern that living away from home did not serve their best interests. Also international pressure on Vietnam was mounting because of international concern about child labour.

An international aid agency, PLAN International, supported the repatriation project by training local people as outreach workers on the streets. They believed that the children's best interests would be better served by returning them to their family. Under this policy it was felt that Hiep, like many other children, was better off living with his parents in the countryside.

Hiep explains the reasons why he feels he is better off working on the streets.

> I am fourteen years old and have worked for the last couple of years on the streets after I moved here from the countryside to earn money that would pay for my schooling and would provide an additional income to my parents in the countryside. Now the government and some aid agencies are introducing a program of repatriation to the countryside for children like me who they want to return home to live with our parents. I don't want to do this because my parents cannot afford to support me along with all my younger brothers and sisters and I'd rather carry on working to earn a living and help them out.
>
> Since moving to Hanoi two years ago I have earned enough money to support myself, sent small amounts of money home and pay to go to school in the afternoons. I am studying hard and would like to go to university in four years' time. I could not afford classes in the countryside because I did not earn money [in Vietnam education is only free up to eleven years of age]. They say it is wrong for children to work on the streets but this gives me many opportunities.
>
> (Burr, 2000)

COMMENT

Even though he is only fourteen, Hiep has worked on the streets since he was twelve and during that period has been able to pay for a standard of education that he says he could not receive in the countryside. At the same time he has earned enough money to support himself and send money home to his parents.

However, because of his age, both the government-run child protection organizations and the international aid agency want to return him to live in the countryside with his parents, which they consider to be in his best interests. Outreach workers assume that Hiep is better living at home where adults will be able to take care of him. However, from Hiep's point of view this policy prohibits his ability to participate properly in society. As he had already proved himself able to live independently he resented the policy of returning him to his village of birth. In this instance Hiep's rights to participate are severely compromised and such an example forces us to ask questions such as whether it is right to force a decision on a child against their will. At what point should we take into account and respect a child's point of view, particularly when it goes against our own ideas about what is best for a child? Should we ensure a child's right to safety over any right of that child to take risks? Two key concepts are at the centre of these questions: 'best interests' and 'competence'. These will be more fully discussed in sections 3.3 and 3.4.

In the aftermath of this meeting Hiep was repatriated to his parents in the countryside but three months later he had returned to Hanoi and was more determined than ever to stay. As a result of his treatment during repatriation Hiep also vowed that he would have nothing to do with the government-hired outreach workers. In light of this it might be argued that by taking a decision on Hiep's behalf adults had made it less likely that he would seek out support from adults who sought to protect him. Was the repatriation therefore misplaced or was Hiep unable to see the wider issues of protection involved?

Hiep's case shows the potential clash that can occur between protection, provision and prevention rights and participation rights. In this instance, the government and aid agency are offering Hiep a *protectionist* form of support. This protectionist approach legitimizes decision-making that is adult-centred.

In contrast, Hiep asked for participatory rights, the right to be consulted, to live on the streets if he chooses to and the right to make independent decisions which he feels he is capable of making.

We will be exploring this debate between protectionist and participatory approaches in later sections. Note that various models of children's rights exist and different authors use terms which mean very similar things. For the purposes of clarity we have listed them in Table 1. The two separate columns represent quite different ways of treating and understanding children: on the one hand, according to values laid out in the left-hand column, society is expected to impose protective limitations upon children while the right-hand column presents us with the idea that children are capable of making many decisions for themselves. In this chapter we begin to ask questions which focus on this debate, such as how much children are both included and excluded from decision making in society, and to what extent children should be listened to and have their viewpoints validated and supported.

> Protectionist forms of support are where governments and parents make decisions on behalf of the child. They assume responsibility for the child and the child has minimal say in decisions.
>
> Participatory support is where adults empower children to make their own decisions. The child assumes responsibility for these decisions.

Table 1 Protectionist and participatory approaches.

Philosophies that view children as needing adult protection and help, where adults make decisions on behalf of the child	Philosophies that view children as needing empowering, where children make decisions on their own behalf
Protectionist	Participatory
Welfarist	Rights-based
Care-taker	Liberationist

3.3 The best interests of the child

> The 'best interests of the child' mean that adults who act on behalf of children should always act in ways that place the child's welfare and best interests above all other considerations.

In the UNCRC, the guiding principle when adults act on behalf of children is that they should always act in 'the best interests of the child'. The way that rights are interpreted depends on the age and maturity of children, but one of the most important principles behind them is that adults should promote the 'best interests' (or maximum welfare) of a child or a group of children. Broadly speaking the UNCRC demands that children are looked after to the highest possible standards, not simply the minimum acceptable ones. Children should benefit from the best possible practice at all times. It means that the child's best interests are set above the interests of adults. Although in practice this is not always apparent, it is the basis and the most important concept of both international and national legislation. The concept of best interests is further elaborated in Reading B.

Achieving a consensus on what is a child's best interest is, however, highly problematic (as Activity 3 demonstrated). 'Best interests' is open to a range of interpretations and there is sometimes an irreconcilable clash between children's interests and children's wishes. As the case of Hiep shows, children's and adults' views of the best interests of a child may not coincide. Although children's rights to hold an opinion and to be consulted about their future are enshrined in law, often adults may decide that a child's best interests are better served by ignoring their wishes. Examples of this include cases where children who have refused surgery have been overruled because the courts believe it is in their best interests for doctors to operate on them. Other more extreme cases exist in countries like the Netherlands whose legislature places great emphasis on participatory rights for children. They have allowed terminally ill children over the age of twelve to request euthanasia if they believe it is in their best interests to do, even when it is against the wishes of their parents (BBC News Online, 1999). Many people, including many in the Netherlands, are profoundly uncomfortable with this and it raises many difficult questions about the conflict between children's best interests and children's wishes. There are also further clashes when different groups of adults disagree on what is in a child's best interests. One of the obvious examples here is the case of Jehovah's Witnesses, who are opposed, on religious grounds, to blood transfusions. Yet very often, when Jehovah Witness children need a blood transfusion, doctors in Britain and in Europe will appeal to the courts to overrule parents. The courts usually rule that it is in children's best interests to have a transfusion.

3.4 Children's rights and children's competences

Much of the controversy between protectionist and participatory perspectives on children's rights centres on the issue of children's competence. This issue has been mentioned in several of the previous chapters. Chapter 1 used 'When does childhood end?' as a starting point for looking at moral competence and responsibility, using the British age of criminal responsibility as an example. Chapter 2 examined different discourses around childhood and in her reading in that chapter, Jane Ribbens discussed the ways that many parents saw their children 'as small people' with rights and needs based on their competences. Much of Chapter 3 was devoted to studying children's developing competences, and many of the examples concerned evidence for children's intellectual, social and moral competence. Children's rights therefore must be discussed in terms of the relationship between rights and competence.

In his book, *Children: rights and childhood*, David Archard (1993) draws a distinction between 'child liberationists' and 'caretakers' in relation to children's rights (those who wish to empower children and those who wish to protect them – see Table 1). The former group, lead by educationalists

John Holt (1975) and Richard Farson (1974) argue that children are imprisoned in childhood, that they *are* not incompetent but are *made* incompetent by adult attitudes and that they must be liberated from this state. Holt proposes 'that the rights, privileges, duties, responsibilities of adult citizens be made *available* to any young person, of whatever age, who wants to make use of them' (Holt, 1975, p. 15). Holt argues that giving children rights will bring them freedom and that it is only through being given all the rights of adults, including the right to vote, to work and 'the right to do, in general, what any adult may legally do' (Holt, 1975, p. 16), that children's rights will be truly fulfilled. Neither Holt nor Farson are explicit about the extent of these rights and such a position gives rise to some obvious absurdities – a baby cannot drive a car or vote so what is the point of giving children rights that they cannot use? Farson recognizes the 'obvious inability' of a baby to do these things but does not say when a child obviously *is* able to vote or drive.

The caretaker thesis argues that children should not be given full rights because they do not have full autonomy. They are not able to understand their rights and they need protection from the consequences of their actions. While this viewpoint may be seen as paternalistic, some would argue that there is nothing wrong with this because children 'have not yet developed the cognitive capacity to make intelligent decisions in the light of relevant information about themselves and the world, and because they are prone to emotional inconstancy such that their decisions are likely to be wild and variable' (Archard, 1993, p. 53).

The question of competence is central to this debate. Is there any point claiming rights for children that they cannot understand or cannot use? At what stage *can* children genuinely participate in society and decisions about their lives, such as those regarding when are they physically mature enough to choose to have sex or to have the strength and judgement to drive a car? In the UK, the rather arbitrary distinction of age is drawn – the age of seventeen to drive a car for instance – but this is based on assumptions about certain levels of maturity that can be expected of most people of that age. However, given the fact that the rate of car accidents among men aged 17 to 25 is three times as high as that of people (and men in particular) in their 30s and 40s, maybe giving this right to 17-year-old boys is misguided.

In Box 2 (overleaf) David Archard discusses the issue of arbitrariness and rights and points to some anomalies in using age as a criterion for rights.

As Box 2 shows, the issue of age and competence is a difficult one. As Chapters 1 and 3 have discussed, there is no chronological age when all children achieve the same level of competence. Indeed competence itself is a slippery idea, dependent on cultural context. In the Netherlands, for instance, the age when children are deemed competent to make an informed choice about sex (and indeed about hospital treatment and euthanasia) is twelve. In Britain, they are not considered competent to make these choices until they are sixteen (and in the case of euthanasia not at all, even when adult). Although international children's legislation claims that a child is anyone under eighteen, there are obvious differences between children in this category. It is clear from Chapter 3 that a fifteen year old has physically and mentally more in common with an adult than he or she does with a five-

Box 2 Age and rights

If nothing else, children are younger than adults. The child liberationist [such as Holt or Farson] is correct to argue that a distribution of rights on the basis of age *alone* would be unfair. It would be morally arbitrary and unjust to deny children rights merely because they were younger than adults. It would be as arbitrary and wrong as denying rights to humans who were shorter than average, had fewer hairs or a lower pitch of voice than others. Clearly some of the rhetoric of children's rights appeals to the general arbitrariness of age in this sense.

However, the denial of rights to children is not based solely on age. It's done on the basis of an alleged correlation between age and some relevant competence. The young are denied rights because, being young, they are presumed to lack some capacities necessary for the possession of rights. The argument from arbitrariness charges that it is unfair to correlate incompetence with some particular age.

Let me spell this out. Either one has a right or one does not. If age is to be the criterion then some particular age must be fixed as the point at which the right is first held. If it is, for instance, 18 then this means 17-year-olds on the eve of their eighteenth birthday lack the right but acquire it the next day. This prompts the charge of arbitrariness. How can a matter of hours, minutes, seconds even, make all the difference between being someone who can legitimately and someone who cannot legitimately hold a right? What possible capacity or competence of sufficient importance to warrant holding a right can be acquired within minutes? I shall term this criticism 'the arbitrariness of any particular age'.

It should be kept distinct from another criticism with which it is sometimes conflated. This is what might be termed the 'unreliability of correlation by age' and runs as follows. Some 17-year-olds, indeed some 16 and 15-year-olds have those competencies judged necessary for the holding of the right in question, whereas some 18-year-olds, indeed 19 and 20-year-olds lack them. The use of 18 as a single point of transition is thus unfair.

Finally there is a view, which could be called the 'preferability of a competence test', and which is usually run in tandem with either or both of these two criticisms. It may be summarized as follows. It is one's competence or incompetence which is relevant to the possession or non-possession of the right rather than one's age as such. Thus it would obviously be fairer to accord rights if this competence is displayed by an individual than to do so simply when some designated age has been reached.

(Archard, 1993, pp. 58–9)

month-old baby, even though they are both considered children. British law also recognizes this, allowing fourteen year olds to be tried in court but not four year olds. These anomalies raise important questions about how child participation should be understood. Many adults might seriously consider giving a sixteen year old the right to vote but would not countenance it for a six year old. This is because they recognize that children's physical, emotional and intellectual competences do change over time and levels of competency are different among different children.

The final section of this chapter will explore a further issue, that of the emotional effects of giving children rights, especially participation rights. Is it putting an unfair burden on children to ask them to make critical decisions that have far-reaching effects on their lives? Although children may be competent to make these decisions, is competence the only issue?

SUMMARY OF SECTION 3

- Children's rights are an integral part of human rights legislation. Children have rights because they are human. However children are different from adults and need special protection because they are more vulnerable.

- The 'best interests of the child' is a guiding principle of legislation on children's rights.

- Children's rights legislation aims to give children rights in four categories. These relate to:

  provision (for growth and development);

  prevention (of harm);

  protection (against exploitation);

  participation in decisions made on their behalf.

- The first three are relatively uncontroversial but the fourth, participation, can be problematic and participation and protection rights can come into conflict.

- Participation rights are difficult because they raise important issues about children's competence. It is very hard to know when children are physically, mentally and emotionally competent to participate fully. Most governments use age as the criterion for competence although this is problematic.

4 CHILDREN-FOCUSED HUMAN RIGHTS ACTS

4.1 The UN Convention on the Rights of the Child (UNCRC)

Having examined the philosophical basis and problems of human and children's rights, we will now turn to specific international conventions concerning children's rights. The UNCRC is a central part of human rights legislation as well as a culmination of six decades of work for children's rights and special protection for children. As far back as 1924, the special status of children was noted and marked out for protection in the Declaration of the Rights of the Child, a declaration that was modified in 1959 and which was the fore-runner of the 1989 Convention on the Rights of the Child (Van Bueren, 1995). Alongside this ran various human rights treaties which expressly acknowledged the vulnerability of children and their right to special protection. The 1948 Universal Declaration of Human Rights, the 1966 International Covenant on Economic, Social and Cultural Rights and the International Covenant on Civil and Political Rights, also 1966, all made special mention and provision for the protection of children. None of these documents indicated how these provisions could be achieved yet their inclusion into a larger framework of human rights emphasizes that children's rights are an integral part of the human rights movement (Alston, 1994; Van Bueren, 1995; Ennew, 1998).

In 1989 the General Assembly of the United Nations adopted the Convention on the Rights of the Child (UNCRC), which states that all children have the same rights as adults and, in addition, rights which recognize their particular vulnerability. It aims to protect and promote children's rights and welfare through a set of principles made up of 54 legally binding articles. It covers children's health, education, nationality, the role of the child in the family and society. It has been one of the most ratified conventions in the history of the United Nations and has been signed and ratified by every country in the world except the United States and Somalia. The Convention has also led to the development of a wide range of new, supplementary international human rights agreements concerning children. These include special provision for especially vulnerable children such as child workers, child prostitutes, child soldiers and child refugees. The UNCRC emphasized that children may need special protection because of their age or emotional development but that children's rights spring from the inalienable fact of their humanity. The two most important points about the UNCRC is that it emphasizes that children's rights are not separate from human rights and that children's rights apply to every child regardless of which state they live in.

Those who drafted the Convention viewed children's rights in terms of the four Ps, outlined earlier in the chapter: protection, provision, prevention and participation. Therefore children are guaranteed rights to do with provision (for example, Article 1 claims that all children have a right to survival and development, Article 24 recognizes children's rights to health care and Article 28 says that children have a right to compulsory, free primary education). Children are also given prevention rights such as legal representation if they are accused of crimes so their rights are not infringed at a later date (Articles 37 and 40) or against commercial sexual exploitation (Article 34). By banning child pornography and criminalizing the soliciting of children under the age of 18 for sex, the UNCRC aims to prevent sexual abuse of children by preventing them coming into contact with abusers. While it is concerned with protecting them once they have been abused, it also recognizes the need to prevent the abuse in the first place. The UNCRC guarantees children protection rights if they are involved in armed conflicts (Article 38) or become refugees (Article 22) or if their rights are being infringed in their family setting and they need to be removed (Article 20). Finally the UNCRC ensures children's participatory rights through the right to hold an opinion (Article 12).

However, as we said earlier, not all these Ps have been adopted equally enthusiastically. As Geraldine Van Bueren, one of the legal experts who drafted the Convention, commented, 'Participation rights are the most radical and the ones which governments have done the least to implement' (Van Bueren in The Open University, 2003). This is echoed by Gerison Lansdown, an author who has written widely on the subject of the UNCRC, particularly in relation to Britain. She argues that the UNCRC is a radical document which challenges adult power and may be threatening to some:

> [The UNCRC supports] the rights of children to be heard, to express their views and freedom of religion and so on. And in that respect there is a challenge to every society in the world in relation to children because children traditionally have not had rights to articulate their views, to be heard properly in political decisions, in social decisions, in family decisions, in education and so on.

> (Lansdown in The Open University, 2003)

Lansdown recognizes that the UNCRC is a radical and challenging document that both individuals and governments might find threatening. Indeed, the USA is one of the two countries in the world to refuse to sign the UNCRC (the other is Somalia, which has not signed it because it currently lacks a functioning government). Some people in the USA believe that the particular, federal form of the US constitution makes it very difficult to sign up to the Convention because it would mean the government depriving the states of their independence. Other have stronger ideological objections to it, believing that children's rights are best dealt with on a familial level according to the laws of each state and that such a convention would erode parental freedom. The US government sees parents' rights and family privacy as giving better protection and provision for children than international rights legislation (Amnesty International, 2001).

4.2 Advocates of the Convention

READING

In Reading B (p.173), Gerison Lansdown recaps on some of the issues previously mentioned in the chapter. She specifically refers to the British context of children's rights. Note the importance she places on the concept of the best interests of the child. She looks at welfarist or protectionist rights for children (see Table 1), and why these are not adequate to safeguard children's rights fully. Think about how far you agree with her on this. She then relates this to the UNCRC, looking at why specific rights that it mentions for children are necessary. Again, do you agree with her? Is it more important that children should be protected or that they participate?

COMMENT

In this reading Lansdown discusses the two approaches that can be taken when dealing with children in society – a rights approach and a welfare approach. Having rejected the welfare approach, because adults cannot always be trusted to look after children's rights and because sometimes adults' and children's interests clash, she concentrates on the rights approach, through an examination of the UNCRC. In her view, the UNCRC is necessary to enforce children's rights in Britain and she approves particularly of the emphasis that it places on participation. For her, participatory rights are the most important rights in the Convention, and especially relevant to children in the UK. She stresses the point that the best interests of the child can only be effective if adults listen properly to children and children can fully participate. She also claims that children who are respected will find the confidence to challenge any abuse of their rights.

The existence of the UNCRC has also inspired nation-states to create their own laws that support children's rights and some have also opted to include laws that are relevant to the local environment. The British 1989 Children Act set a precedent under British law because for the first time the opinion of the child was placed alongside that of his or her parents (see Box 3).

On an international level, charities such as Save the Children have emerged as strong advocates for the UNCRC. The UNCRC has had a fundamental impact on the way they work at the grass roots level. In the past Save the Children might have addressed the issue of health care by building a health centre in a village. Today they would not view this as adequate and might also find out whether villagers had informal sources of health care that might be incorporated into a project and also what local people, including children, felt they needed:

> The impact that the UN Convention has on Save the Children's work at grass roots level has really been to move away from single project approaches from vertical programming where you might just work on health in a particular community, to looking at it in a much broader way and a much more holistic way.

> (Caroline Harper, Head of Research, Save the Children Fund UK, in The Open University, 2003)

Box 3 The Children Act

The 1989 Children Act established that children should have the right to be heard about matters affecting their welfare. For the first time in the history of the British legal system this meant that the courts must have regard for the wishes and feelings of the child concerned (considered in the light of his or her age and understanding). This meant that children would be invited by the courts and the welfare system to voice opinion in such matters as where they would prefer to live after a parental divorce, or whether they wished to remain at home or go into care when there were concerns about child protection issues. The Children Act also upholds the right of children to apply for court orders in their own right.

Responses to the Act were very mixed. Some child advocacy groups (particularly those that supported the UNCRC) were very enthusiastic about the level of autonomy the Act sought to offer children (see for example Brayne and Martin, 1990). They viewed the Children Act's support for children's participation in decision making very positively. Other groups however, while broadly supportive of the provision and protection aspects of the Act, disliked the participatory rights it gave to children. They were concerned about what they saw as being the potential for the Act to undermine parental responsibility and adult power over children. Some commentators called it a 'brat's charter' when it was first made law (Lansdown, 1994) and warned of children divorcing their parents because they didn't have enough pocket money or demanding the right to do whatever they wanted.

Organizations like Save the Children have also realized the value of children's participation. Not only does it empower children themselves but it can be beneficial for the whole community.

> We know of a group of community workers who know every inch of the village in which they work, who are accepted by everyone, who want to help their community, who will work hard (for short periods of time) and cheerfully (all the time). Last month the health worker asked them to collect information about which children had been vaccinated in the village. Next Tuesday some of them will help remind the villagers that the baby clinic is coming and they will be at hand to play with the older children when mothers take their babies to see the nurse. Next month they plan to help the school teacher in a village clean up campaign. These health workers are the boys and girls of the village.
>
> (Hawes and Scotchmer in Save the Children, 1995, p. 36)

4.3 Critics of the Convention

The UNCRC is the most widely ratified convention in the history of the United Nations. However, there are some, who, while welcoming the interest it shows in children and acknowledging that it has put children's rights on the international agenda, are unhappy with some aspects of it.

The two main causes of concern are the difficulty of applying general principles to local situations and the cross-cultural differences concerning the concept of the child.

General principles and local situations

One of the big differences between national laws that focus on children and the international human rights laws such as the UNCRC is that national laws tend to be more detailed and less generalized. Burman points out:

> The discourse of rights necessarily invokes general claims. That is, these function as appeals to general entitlements, the generality of which is used to strengthen demands for their application in a specific situation. But how well do general statements about children map on to the conditions and positions of children in particular contexts?

> (Burman, 1996, p. 46)

A number of critics have pointed to the problem that the Convention is written in the abstract and offers over-generalized intentions. For example, under international child rights legislation all children are to be given facilities for the treatment of illness (Article 24, UNCRC). How this quite abstract right is interpreted at the national level, is dependent on many influences, including whether health care is free or fee-paying and whether people have equal access to health care. At the very local level this right will also be affected by the attitude of a child's parents or main caregiver and in addition by their caregivers' ability to access health care. Issues such as a child's social class, gender, ethnicity, religion and cultural practices will also inform the extent to which their attainment of particular rights are made possible. Giving children a right to health care is fine as a generalized principle but is dependent on the very specific context.

Allow about 5 minutes

ACTIVITY 4   Maya, a mother in Bangladesh

Read the case study below about Maya and note how local cultural practices have influenced her ambition to continue her education and complete secondary education. Write a short paragraph on what rights you think she should have in terms of her marriage and her education. Why do you think she might not be able to claim these rights?

Maya

Maya is fifteen years old and lives in Bangladesh. The year before she had eloped from her parents' home to marry her boyfriend (aged sixteen) of whom her father did not approve. After marriage she had been determined to avoid pregnancy and to continue to go to school because she wanted to study to be a doctor. However, a year after getting married she gave birth to a daughter. Although Maya very much wanted to continue to go to school her husband forbade her to do so. Under the UNCRC (Article 28), of which the Bangladeshi government is a signatory, Maya should have a legal right to go to school. Section (e) of the article reads: 'States parties take measures to encourage regular attendance at schools and the reduction of drop-out rates'.

COMMENT

Maya's ability to claim such a right, however, is impeded by local custom that makes it difficult for her to go against her husband's wishes (even though he too is technically still a child) and also by lack of formal apparatus to uphold and support her wish to return to school. In this case local custom overrides any expectation of returning to school for a young girl once she is married and has become a mother. We do not know if Maya's parents still want her to go to school, but they would have difficulty upholding such a wish because as a result of marriage Maya is beholden to her husband's wishes.

As Maya's experiences demonstrate, a child's ability to attain rights is determined by numerous factors, only some of which are determined at the international level. It would probably be quite difficult for Maya to access legal support to fulfil her desire to return to school. Therefore at the national and family level her rights are interpreted and shaped in a particular way that does not reflect the intentions set down in the UNCRC. In Maya's immediate community there are no mechanisms in place that allow her to use the UNCRC to her advantage to challenge her husband's decision that she should not finish her schooling. Social expectations also made it very difficult. This example highlights how difficult it can be to offer children particular rights. It also shows that what is meant by children's rights varies from place to place and is very dependent not only on support for child rights at international and government levels but also on a child's immediate community and family setting (or at the local level).

If you compare Maya's situation to that of fifteen-year-old girls in other countries, there may have been different outcomes. Marriage at the age of fifteen would be considered illegal in some societies. In other cases a girl in a similar situation to Maya may have had access to contraception and would not have become pregnant. In other communities, girls of Maya's age would also be able to date more freely without adult figures of authority being aware, or being unduly concerned. They might also be compelled to attend school, raising further problems about a child's right to autonomy and decision making.

The UNCRC is only as effective as particular states allow it to be and the extent to which they can enforce its provisions. Most countries have ratified it but there are not enough checks in place for enforcement to be guaranteed. But the UNCRC is still relatively new. Supporters of the Convention argue that the UNCRC provides human rights activists with a mechanism for challenging the systems that discriminate against children. With the UNCRC in place it is now possible to, at the very least, document human rights violations specifically aimed at children.

Cultural differences and the UNCRC

Another fundamental criticism of the UNCRC is that it upholds and supports a Western understanding of childhood (an issue that was touched on briefly in Section 4 of Chapter 3). Earlier we discussed the Chinese and Japanese support of the hierarchically structured family unit over the individual, and pointed out that in China the individual is

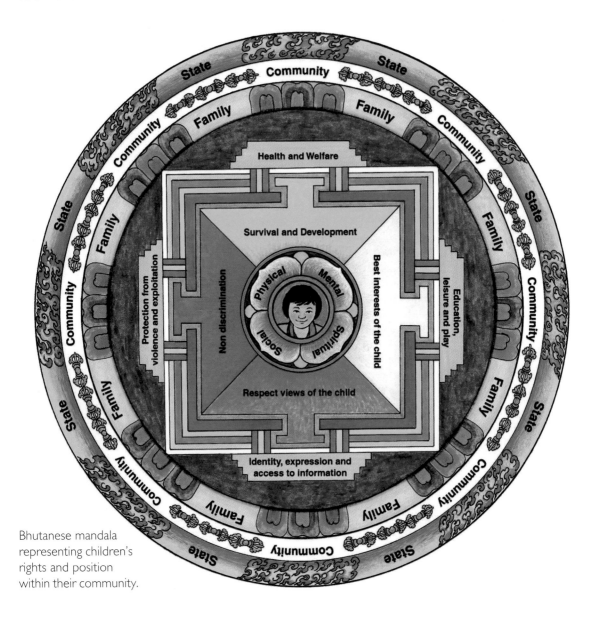

Bhutanese mandala representing children's rights and position within their community.

subordinate to the family. Yet in the UNCRC the child is consistently given rights as an individual based on a Western understanding of the child as an autonomous individual. However, in many other societies this idea of a child simply does not exists. Speaking for the aid agency Alliances for Africa, Iheoma Obibi commented on African children:

> Within many African societies the child is seen as part of a wider network, but not as an individual. In fact you'll find that many children are part of a family, community, and the Convention is very individualistic, and that is a problem because many cultures don't operate like that.

(Iheoma Obibi in The Open University, 2003)

Clearly, as Chapter 2 also showed, there are vast differences in people's conceptions of childhood and consequently great differences of opinion at the local and international level around what constitutes appropriate support for children. It is this issue that is at the centre of much debate over whether or not the UNCRC is fulfilling its human rights objectives.

As discussed earlier, the most important intention of the UNCRC is that it claims to be universal. The premise behind all human rights legislation is that concepts such as human rights or children's rights are not negotiable at local level. All children everywhere have rights and all children are equally entitled to these rights. However, as the previous section showed, this presents difficulties in practice. The most obvious instance is the first article of the UNCRC which states that a child is defined as anyone below the age of eighteen. In British society, people can marry, join the army and go to work from the age of sixteen while technically still children. In developing countries, the difficulties of setting a standard age of eighteen are even more obvious. In many societies, children's births are not registered and they have no idea when exactly they reach eighteen. In other cultures, boys and girls marry much younger, often at puberty, they work as soon as necessary and even have their own children, at ages that the UNCRC would still refer to as childhood. There have been campaigns against child marriage (Anti-Slavery International, 1995) and attempts to encourage later marriages among young women but these do not always have the desired outcome. If custom and culture promote early marriage, then it is debatable whether international legislation could or should have any effect on this. There may well be grounds for legitimate concern about the possibility of abuse when children marry early or have children very young but even so, a child marrying at fifteen in full accordance with traditional norms and local custom in India is very different from a child marrying at fifteen in the UK (Montgomery, 2001).

The role of the regional charters on children's rights, such as the African Charter on the Rights and Welfare of the Child, emphasizes the tensions between the benevolent ideals of international law and the complexities of grass roots implementation. If children have to work, tend to marry early and anyway have no way of knowing when they reach the age of 18 because their births were not registered, then implementing the UNCRC becomes problematic. Many countries have changed their laws in response to the UNCRC but questions have to be asked about which rights become more important – the right to be protected until the age of eighteen or the right to be part of a culture in which early marriage, for example, is practised and welcomed.

4.4 African Charter on the Rights and Welfare of the Child

Given that the UNCRC is almost universally ratified, the existence of national and regional children's rights treaties may seem redundant. Yet other treaties have come into being which, while drawing their inspiration from the 1948 UN Declaration of Human Rights, recognize specific local contexts.

One of the most significant of these is the African Charter on the Rights and Welfare of the Child, which came into force in 1990. It was set up by the Organization of African Unity, a group made up of African governments which provides a regional forum for African issues. The various member states in this organization felt that the UNCRC needed to be made more relevant to the concerns of the region. The African charter therefore, deals with issues that are of particular importance to African people, such as apartheid, refugees and children in armed conflict and acknowledges the special difficulties that African countries face: 'severely depressed economic situations, shortage of basic social amenities, widespread occurrence of armed conflict, and resultant displacement of populations' (OAU 1990).

The charter also recognizes the particular qualities of an African childhood and refers specifically to 'the historical background and the values of African civilization' at its heart. Importantly, it stresses both the rights and the *responsibilities* of the child and gives equal weight to the concurrent

responsibilities of the community towards the child. Its first section is not called 'Children's Rights' but 'Rights and Duties'. The African Charter places significantly more emphasis than the UNCRC on responsibility and sets out clearly the responsibility that parents have to their children (Article 20) and the duties and responsibilities that children have towards their parents (Article 31). In contrast, in the UNCRC, the words 'responsibilities' and 'duties' never feature in relation to children, only to the adults caring for them.

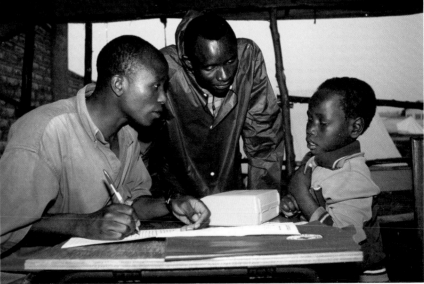

Allow about 20 minutes

ACTIVITY 5 **The UNCRC and the African Charter**

Compare the following. The first is Article 27 taken from the UNCRC. The second is Article 31 from the African Charter on the Rights and Welfare of the Child. What is the first thing you notice when you compare them? Look particularly at the relationship between the state, the parent and the child. What is different?

Article 27, UNCRC – Parental Responsibilities

1 States Parties recognize the right of every child to a standard of living adequate for the child's physical, mental, spiritual, moral and social development.

2 The parent(s) or others responsible for the child have the primary responsibility to secure, within their abilities and financial capacities, the conditions of living necessary for the child's development ...

Article 31, African Charter on the Rights and Welfare of the Child – Responsibility of the Child

Every child shall have responsibilities towards his family and society, the State and other legally recognized communities and the international community. The child, subject to his age and ability, and such limitations as may be contained in the present Charter, shall have the duty;

(a) to work for the cohesion of the family, to respect his parents, superiors and elders at all times and to assist them in case of need;

(b) to serve his national community by placing his physical and intellectual abilities at its service;

(c) to preserve and strengthen social and national solidarity;

(d) to preserve and strengthen African cultural values in his relations with other members of the society, in the spirit of tolerance, dialogue and consultation and to contribute to the moral well-being of society;

(e) to preserve and strengthen the independence and the integrity of his country;

(f) to contribute to the best of his abilities, at all times and at all levels, to the promotion and achievement of African Unity.

COMMENT

The biggest difference between these articles, and indeed between the two conventions, is the issue of the child's duties and responsibilities. The word 'duty' is never mentioned in the UNCRC except in relation to the State, the word 'responsibility' is not mentioned except in relation to parents. Nowhere in the UNCRC is a child seen to have duties and responsibilities as well as rights. There is no equivalent in the UNCRC to Article 31 of the African Charter. Instead the UNCRC concentrates on what parents should do for children. Elsewhere in the UNCRC, Articles 5 and 18 deal explicitly with parental responsibilities; parents must care for children emotionally and materially to their best of the ability. The UNCRC sets out to codify the ways in which the state and parents should work together to ensure children's rights and enable them to participate in decision making processes. The African Charter has a very different focus. The individual, autonomous child who is the rights bearer in the UNCRC does not exist to the same extent in the African Charter. Children are expected to care for their families, their communities and indeed Africa in general. The African Charter views families as much more interdependent – parents must rely on children as much as children on parents and therefore rights come with responsibilities. This charter recognizes, unlike the UNCRC, that both adults and children have duties as well as rights.

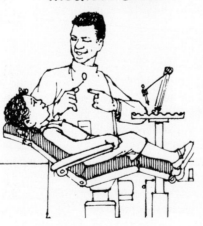

These illustrations are pages from a booklet produced by Molo Songololo, a children's rights organization in South Africa. The booklet matches rights to responsibilities.

Children have the right to be loved and protected from harm...

...and the responsibility to show others love and caring.

Children have the right to be proud of their heritage and beliefs...

...and the responsibility to respect the origins and beliefs of others.

SUMMARY OF SECTION 4

- The UNCRC came into force in 1989. It took as its basis the notion that a child is an individual, autonomous person with inalienable rights which parents and the state must protect.

- The UNCRC emphasizes that children's rights are not separate from human rights – they are integral to them.

- The UNCRC gives all children in the world particular rights that are theirs regardless of which state they live in.

- However, there have been problems with the UNCRC. Some countries have found that it does not adequately address the particular circumstances of African people and have claimed that it is based on a political philosophy that they do not share. Consequently additional treaties such as the African Charter on the Rights and Welfare of the Child have been drawn up.

- The African charter has a different focus to the UNCRC. It concentrates less on the individual child and more on the child as part of a community. It emphasizes the duties of children as well as their rights.

5 HAS THE UNCRC IMPROVED CHILDREN'S LIVES?

The recognition of children's rights at an international and national level has forced governments and non-governmental organizations to look seriously at the ways that they treat children. There have subsequently been many initiatives at the international and national level to improve children's lives through rights legislation. As this chapter's readings show, recognizing and supporting children's rights entails looking seriously at all aspects of economic and legal policy to examine the effects that they have on children. But questions remain. Has the UNCRC made any difference to children's lives? Have the ideals it champions actually translated into actions which improve children's lives?

There have been been problems and criticisms of the UNCRC and, as this chapter has shown, difficulties in fully realizing children's rights at a local level. However, looking seriously at the impact of policy decisions on children's lives has led to differences in policies towards children and in some instances to improvements in children's lives. For example, aid agencies are now required to look at the implications of their projects on children. It is no longer enough to look only at the benefit of the community or to employ a 'trickle-down approach' to children's rights – that is, if you give money and help to a child's parents, benefits will automatically trickle down to the child. An example of this approach is a particular water project in Gambia:

During a participatory research exercise with a group of women in Jarumeh Koto (in Gambia), the benefits and disadvantages of a donor government installation of a hand-pump in the village were discussed. The benefits stated were: that the water drawn was now clean and good for drinking which meant better health; that it was safer than the open well which was dangerous as children could fall inside; and it was cheaper in terms of the costs of buying buckets and ropes. However, when the bore hole was dug it sucked the water out of three of the wells in the village, which can no longer be used. This means that they now have four wells in the village – two of which have hand pumps. At the hand-pump, only two people can draw water at once, while at the old well they could have between 10–15 people drawing water at once. This means now that it takes longer to collect water, especially considering they have also lost three of their wells. The area around the pump is always full of people waiting to use it.

Because of this, many women send their children more often to fetch water. Since it is easier and less dangerous to use the pump they have started sending younger children, as young as seven. Previously children under about fifteen would not have used the wells. After the wait at the pump children may be late for school, and because of the weight of the water, children are physically affected, causing chest pain.

This is one example of how the installation of a pump has affected children – mainly girls – in a development project that might have been seen to be beneficial to the whole community.

(Johnson *et al.*, 1995, p. 68)

An aid donor would perhaps not make the same mistake now as they are mandated to look after the best interests of the child. They have to take into account the effect of such a project on children and if it could be seen to be harmful, then the damage to children must outweigh any benefits to the rest of the community.

In many situations, children are now listened to, encouraged to participate and have their best interests taken into account. While there is still a long way to go (and serious problems with the international and national legislation), undoubtedly there is a will to take children's rights seriously and use this legislation to start to improve children's lives.

Allow about 15 minutes

ACTIVITY 6 **Children's rights and quality of life**

Read the two short scenarios below concerning UK children. What effects has giving children rights had on these children? What are the positive and negative effects here?

1 Simon is twelve and has a debilitating heart condition. He has spent most of his life in and out of hospital and is mature and knowledgeable about medical procedure. There is now the possibility of a heart transplant but it is risky and will involve a great deal of pain. He is not sure that he wants it. The doctors and his parents want him to go ahead and have the operation but believe

that it should be his decision. In what ways might availing himself of this right make his life better and in what ways worse?

2   Angela is fourteen. Her parents are undergoing a very acrimonious divorce and are fighting over custody of her in the courts. The Children Act gives legal weight to her opinion and the courts have asked her to decide which parent she wants to live with. How might this right improve her life? What difficulties might having this right cause her?

COMMENT

In both cases, these children have rights about which they might feel ambivalent. Simon is still very young and is having to face a profoundly important decision in his life. If he agreed with his family and doctors there would be no conflict. However, if he finds that he and his family want something different, this will cause problems. He may feel that he does not have enough knowledge to make this decision but it is left up to him to make it. He may wish that he did not have the responsibility and that he would rather someone else was in control. However, twenty years ago he would not have been consulted, he would have been told that the operation was going ahead and he would have had no say in that decision.

In Angela's case, her right to participate in decisions about her future is legally recognized. This may bring positive benefits and she might want to be able to choose freely which parent she lives with. However, it may be more complicated than this and it may put her under unwanted pressure. She might feel torn between her parents and unwilling and unable to choose between them. She may rather that the decision was made for her so the responsibility was not hers.

Both children in the above scenarios have been judged, either by the courts or their parents, as competent to make these decisions but there are further issues which need to be taken into account. There can be no right or wrong answer to the question of whether respecting children's rights makes their lives better. For some children, the chance to participate and express their views is undoubtedly positive. For others it may bring unwanted responsibility. However, the fact that governments are taking children seriously and realizing that they have their own views and that they should be given a chance to express them is a positive development, which, it is to be hoped, can be built upon.

It must be remembered that giving children rights is not an end in itself. They must be implemented, any violations investigated and rectified and the far less tangible issue of children's *quality of life* must be examined. For instance, there may be a distinction between the types of freedoms children enjoy depending on where and when children grow up. Some children may enjoy particular types of freedoms that go unacknowledged because of the present dominant child rights discourse. For example, children in the UK fifty years ago did not have international legislation protecting their interests but it could be argued that they had more freedom to play in the areas they wished to, to walk to school, to roam their neighbourhood streets without curfew or parental control. They enjoyed more time to do what they wanted. In contrast today's British children are less likely to play outside, are more often driven to school, have to account for their movements, are encouraged to take part in more extra-curricular activities and continually tested in school. However, they have different freedoms, such as the freedom to voice an opinion. Today's children are far more likely to be seen as having an autonomous voice and to be respected by their elders. Many children today are consulted by their parents on issues such as choice of schools, choice of holiday destination or new houses. Respecting children's rights is important, and understanding them in the widest possible context even more so.

SUMMARY OF SECTION 5

- An acknowledgement of children's rights means looking at the impact of policies on children. Aid agencies have realized that some policies have had adverse effects on children, even when they have been beneficial to others in the community.

- In some cases giving children rights might involve giving them too much responsibility which they do not want. It is very important to strike a balance.

- However, analysing the implementation of children's rights might not be the only way of measuring improvements in children's lives. It is worth looking at children's quality of life as well as the extent that their rights are being upheld.

6 CONCLUSION

The children's rights movement is relatively recent. Although childhood has long been marked out for special protection in national and international law, the idea of children as individual rights bearers, as being equal to adults, has a short history. It is still fiercely debated and many people remain unhappy with this challenge to adult power over children. This is why, while the majority of governments and indeed adults would support the notion that children need protection, provision and prevention from harm, they find it much harder to agree that children should also participate if they are to enjoy full rights. As long as children cannot fully participate, they are unlikely to be treated as equal to adults, and yet full participation is problematic because children are limited by their physical, mental and emotional competences. Rights, and particularly those to do with participation, remain complex and sometimes contradictory notions in relation to children.

Children's rights become even more problematic in an international context. Although the UNCRC was supposed to be universally applicable, many have argued that the language and philosophy behind it, especially the emphasis on the individual child separate from the family, are alien to their culture and do not reflect the realities of children's lives within these cultures. Therefore regional charters have been signed which aim to counterbalance these Western ideas.

Despite criticisms of the UNCRC, it has put children's rights on the agenda. Few countries in the world now deny that children need rights; agreeing on exactly what those rights should include and how they might be implemented is much harder.

REFERENCES

ALSTON, P. (1994) 'The best interests principle: towards a reconciliation of culture and human rights' in ALSTON, P. (ed.) *The Best Interests of the Child – Reconciling Culture and Human Rights*, Oxford, Clarendon Press.

AMNESTY INTERNATIONAL (2001) 'Convention on the Rights of the Child: frequently asked questions', *Children's Human Rights*, on-line, http//www.amnesty-usa.org/children/crn_faq.html Accessed 19 February 2002.

ANTI-SLAVERY INTERNATIONAL (1995) 'Contemporary forms of slavery requiring action by governments: examples of a large-scale and persisting problem in the 1990s', paper prepared in June 1995 by Anti-Slavery International for the United Nations Working Group on Contemporary Forms of Slavery.

ARCHARD, D. (1993) *Children: rights and childhood*, London, Routledge.

BBC NEWS ONLINE (1999) 'Holland edges towards legal euthanasia', 11 August 1999, on-line, http://news.bbc.co.uk/hi/english/world/europe/newsid_417000/417110.stm Accessed 18 December 2001.

BRAYNE, H. and MARTIN, G. (1990; 1st edn) *Law for Social Workers*, London, Blackstone.

BROWNE, M. (1857) *Autobiography of a Female Slave*, New York, Redfield, reproduced on-line by the Academic Affairs Library, University of North California at Chapel Hill http://docsouth.unc.edu/browne/menu.html Accessed 19 February 2002.

BURMAN, E. (1995) 'Local, global or globalized? Child development and international child rights legislation', *Childhood*, **3**(1), pp. 45–66.

BURR, R. (2001) *Understanding Children's Rights*, unpublished PhD thesis, London, Brunel University.

ENNEW, J. (1998) 'The African context of children's rights', paper presented at the ANPPCAN, CODESRIA, Childwatch International and Redd Barna Conference, 'The African context of children's rights', Harare, Zimbabwe.

FARSON, R. (1974) *Birthrights*, London, Macmillan.

GOODMAN, R. (1996) 'On introducing the UN Convention on the Rights of the Child into Japan' in GOODMAN, R. and NEARY, I. (eds) *Case Studies on Human Rights in Japan*, Kent, Curzon Press, Japan Library.

HOLT, J. (1975) *Escape From Childhood: the needs and rights of children*, London, Penguin.

JOHNSON. V., HILL, J. and IVAN-SMITH, E. (1995) *Listening to Smaller Voices: children in an environment of change*, London, Actionaid UK.

LANSDOWN, G. (1994) 'Children's rights' in MAYALL, B. (ed.) *Children's Childhoods: observed and experienced*, London, Falmer Press.

MONTGOMERY, H. (2001) 'Imposing rights? A case study of child prostitution in Thailand' in COWAN, J., DEMBOUR, M-B. and WILSON, R. (eds) *Culture and Rights*, Cambridge, Cambridge University Press.

THE OPEN UNIVERSITY (2003) U212 *Childhood*, Audio-cassette 2, Side 1, Band 3, 'The UN Convention on the Rights of the Child', Milton Keynes, The Open University.

ORGANIZATION OF AFRICAN UNITY (OAU) (1990) 'Report of the Inter-Governmental Expert Group Meeting on the Draft African Charter on the Rights and Welfare of the Child', 17–20 April, 1990, Addis Ababa.

SAVE THE CHILDREN (1995) *Towards a Children's Agenda*, London, Save the Children.

VAN BUEREN, G. (1995) *The International Law on the Rights of the Child*, Dordrecht, Martinus Nijhoff.

The big picture

By Stefan de Vylder

Macroeconomics have a direct impact on children's lives, but the links are only starting to be recognized

Macroeconomic policies are rarely discussed in connection with children. This means that most people working for the rights of the child regard macroeconomics with indifference or suspicion; and most of the work of economists is blind to children's needs.

Globally, young people under the age of 18 represent one third of the world's population, and in many developing countries children constitute the majority. Still, economic decisions very rarely take into account the interests of the child, or the impact on them. Indeed children do not merit even a mention in most major economic textbooks. At best, there is a paragraph or two about 'human capital' and the importance of investing in education.

The children's own voices are never heard, despite the fact that many economic decisions directly or indirectly affect them.

There is no such thing as 'child-neutral' economic policies. There is a need to make children more visible in economic policy-making. There is also great scope for better cooperation and understanding between economists and children, and between economists and advocacy groups working on children's behalf.

Economic analysis can be used to demonstrate that good economic policies and the best interest of the child often go hand-in-hand, and that while the financial costs of creating a more child-friendly society are often small, the social and economic benefits of linking these interests are enormous. To invest in children is a win-win strategy: the individual child and society benefit as a whole.

To illustrate the ways in which economic policies affect the situation of children, imagine a set of concentric circles moving outwards (see Figure 1). At the hub are policies and legislation that explicitly target children including public provision of primary health and education, and regulations against the exploitation of child labour.

In a second circle are policies and institutions that have a strong but less direct impact. Here are traditional social security and welfare policies, most redistributive tax and public expenditure policies, and in general, policies that directly affect the family.

In a third circle are macroeconomic policies in a conventional sense where the impact may be more indirect, but still strong. This includes fiscal policies (policies related to taxes and government expenditure); monetary policies (which influence the interest, inflation and exchange rates), as well as trade policies, the managing of external capital flows and the foreign debt.

Figure 1
The child at the centre.

In a final circle is the overall policy environment or framework, including the choice of development strategy and the globalization process.

While the policies in the inner circle are usually discussed in connection with the rights of the child, policies belonging to the outer circles also affect children either directly or indirectly through their effect on the family's economic and social situation. There are examples where the links between macroeconomic policies and children demonstrate the direct impact the one has on the other. The relationship between trade liberalization and child labour in export industries is an obvious example.

The choice between inflation and unemployment represents the classic dilemma of macroeconomic policies. Far from being child neutral, inflation affects countries, social classes and age groups in quite different ways. In high and medium-income countries with relatively well-developed financial markets, young families with children tend to finance the purchase of new homes with the help of credit from the formal credit market. Among low-income households, especially in poor countries, money for a new house is often raised on the informal credit market, which includes relatives, friends or local moneylenders. Generally, debts are incurred by families when children are small and repaid when the children have grown up.

For this reason, moderate inflationary policies tend to have a less negative impact on young families with children, who are often indebted. The erosion of their debts through inflation may even be in their interest. On the other hand, austere monetary policies, which reduce the rate of inflation while raising the real rate of interest, tend to be particularly harmful for young parents with children.

Monetary policies leading to high real rates of interest can thus be labelled child-hostile, since they have a direct bearing on the affordability of acceptable dwellings. Moreover, if there is a choice between some inflation and unemployment, many young families would probably prefer more employment, even if this were to mean a slightly higher inflation.

This would make sense since there is a wealth of evidence that suggests that unemployment (especially long-term) is very harmful to children economically, socially, and psychologically.

In poor countries the effects of unemployment can be dramatic because economic margins are small or non-existent. The child's very right to survival may be threatened by the parents' unemployment. In addition to suffering severe economic loss, family disintegration often tends to follow. Clearly, these associated costs of unemployment, which include family disintegration and possibly increased child labour, rising drop-out rates and even juvenile delinquency due to parents' unemployment, are not fully captured in conventional economic analyses.

An anti-poverty, child-friendly strategy must therefore pay much attention to job creation without embarking on imprudent policies that lead to a high rate of inflation. Parents need employment in order to support their children; and children and adolescents need to feel that education is a worthwhile investment and that they will be welcome in the labour market.

Fiscal policies, or policies related to taxes and government expenditure, are at the core of macroeconomic policy choices. A state budget reflects the overall priorities of the government. It is essentially a political not a technical instrument as it translates policies and political platforms into expenditures and taxes. The analysis of state budgets is of paramount importance in order to assess the links between macroeconomic policies and children. The choices behind state budgets have an impact on children's lives both directly and indirectly.

Children are affected indirectly by budget expenditures and revenues, which determine the development of fiscal deficits or surpluses, the sources of finance, and the amount of foreign borrowing. These fiscal policies influence inflation, unemployment, income distribution, foreign debt obligations, taxes, and subsidies that affect the families' social and economic situation and consequently children.

State budgets can have a direct impact in areas of concern for children such as: nutrition, child and maternal health, water and sanitation, early childhood development and basic education, social welfare, leisure and cultural activities, and child protection measures.

From a child's perspective, massive foreign indebtedness is exceedingly harmful. Foreign credit may appear a comfortable short-term option and, if the borrowed money is invested wisely, may have some positive long-term effects. But taking up foreign loans today also implies a mortgaging of the future and often boils down to theft from tomorrow's children and adolescents who will have to repay the debts.

External economic policies such as trade policies, the managing of external capital flows and of foreign debt, and, more broadly, the so-called process of globalization fall into the definition of macroeconomics and do impact children. Structural adjustment programmes and foreign debt are good examples of how macroeconomic policies can neglect children's rights.

Many structural adjustment programmes have been designed in open contradiction to provisions in the Convention on the Rights of the Child. Article 28 of the Convention, for example, states in unequivocal terms that governments have the obligation to "make primary education compulsory and available free to all". The introduction of school fees, which has often accompanied structural adjustment, is simply incompatible with the CRC ...

The point to stress here is that macroeconomic policies are far from age- or gender-neutral. A perspective which recognizes the rights of children and women has to be present while macroeconomic policies are being designed, not after they are finalized. The best interest of the child should permeate macroeconomic policies, embracing fiscal policies, monetary policies, and exchange rate policies, as early and as comprehensively as possible. It is not enough to advocate that a larger share of public expenditure goes to social sector development. Trade and exchange rate policies may have more of an impact on child development than, for example, the relative size of the state budget allocated to health and education.

It is imperative to avoid the situation where hard core economic policies are decided in isolation from human development objectives while NGOs, United Nations organizations and bilateral donors are called upon to look after humanitarian aspects and give relief assistance to victims of devastating macroeconomic policies.

Source

VYLDER, S. DE (2000) 'The big picture', *CRIN Newsletter*, no. 13, pp. 11–13.

READING B

Children's welfare and children's rights

By Gerison Lansdown

Children's interests are often disregarded in public policy

Children's interests are frequently disregarded in the public policy sphere in favour of those of more powerful interest groups. It is not necessarily the case that children's welfare is deliberately disregarded but that children, and the impact of public policy on their lives, are not visible in decision-making forums and, accordingly, never reach the top of the political agenda. Just consider, for example, the impact of public policy [in the UK] on children during the 1980s and 90s. In 1979 one in 10 children were living in poverty. By 1991 the proportion had increased to one in three (DoH, 1993). That alone is a sufficient indictment of our neglect of children. Even more significantly, however, it is children who bore the disproportionate burden of the increase in poverty during that period: no other group in society experienced a growth in poverty on a comparable scale. The consequences of that poverty on children's life chances are profound, impacting on educational attainment, physical and mental health, emotional well-being and employment opportunities. At a collective level, then, our society failed to promote and protect the welfare of children over two decades.

There is little analysis of public expenditure to assess whether the proportion spent on children and their well-being reflects either their level of need or their representation within the community. What little we do know indicates that the lack of data is likely to cover very significant inadequacies in spending on children, indicating their weak position in the lobbies that influence public agendas and expenditure. We know, for example, that health authorities spend 5 per cent of their mental health budgets on children and adolescent mental health services, even though this age group represents 25 per cent of the population (Audit Commission, 1999). It is of course likely that services for older people will necessitate a disproportionate claim on these budgets, but no systematic assessment has been made of whether the current balance in any way reflects comparative levels of assessed needs. Also, as long as children lack powerful advocates in the field of health, such discrepancies will not be effectively challenged.

Similarly, in the field of housing, countless estates have been built in which the needs of children have been completely disregarded – no play spaces or facilities, dangerous balconies, and lifts with controls out of the reach of children (Freeman *et al.*, 1999). We have also grown increasingly intolerant of children in the public arena. Far from developing towns and cities that are designed with children in mind, that are child-friendly, as befits a society with the welfare of children at its heart, we now tend to view children as undesirable in streets and shops, particularly when they are in groups. The introduction of powers to impose child curfews, the refusal of many shops to allow children in and the decision by the Millennium Dome to refuse entry to the under-16s if they are not accompanied by an adult are all testimony to a perception of children as threatening, hostile and outside the legitimate bounds of society. Public spaces are seen to be 'owned' by adults, young people's presence in those spaces representing an unwanted intrusion. Yet these are the adults on whom children rely to promote their best interests. These are the adults who are responsible for protecting children's welfare.

Children's competence and contribution

The welfare model of childcare has perpetuated the view that children lack the capacity to contribute to their own well-being or do not have a valid and valuable contribution to make. Yet a failure to involve children in decisions that affect their own lives has been the cause of many of the mistakes and poor judgements exercised by adults when acting on children's behalf. There is now a growing body of evidence that children, both in respect of individual decisions that affect their lives and as a body in the broader public policy arena, have a considerable contribution to make to decision-making (Alderson, 1993; John, 1996; Marshall, 1997). Children, even when very young, can act, for example, as peer counsellors, mediators or mentors for other children. Local and health authorities have successfully involved children in the development of new hospitals, anti-poverty strategies and advice services. In other words far from being 'in waiting' until they acquire adult competencies, children can, when empowered to do so, act as a source of expertise, skill and information for adults and contribute toward meeting their own needs.

Moving beyond a welfare perspective

Once it is acknowledged not only that adults are capable of the abuse of children, but also that children's welfare can be undermined by conflicting interests, neglect, indifference and even hostility on the part of adults, it becomes clear that it is not sufficient to rely exclusively on adults to define children's needs and be responsible for meeting them. Indeed, the welfare model has failed children. The traditional perception of children as having needs – for love, care, protection – is now challenged by a recognition that children are subjects of rights, a concept that has gradually developed during the course of the twentieth century, culminating in the adoption by the UN General Assembly in 1990 of the UNCRC. The Convention now has almost universal acceptance, having been ratified by 191 countries throughout the world. Only the USA and Somalia have not yet made the commitment under international law to comply with the principles and standard it embodies. The Convention is a comprehensive human rights treaty encompassing social, economic and cultural as well as civil and political rights.

The recognition of children as the subjects of rights rather than merely the recipients of adult protective care introduces a new dimension to adult relationships with children. It does not negate the fact that children have needs but argues that children therefore have rights to have those needs met. The rights contained in the Convention fall into three broad categories, each of which imposes different obligations on adults: freedoms to protection from the state, protection by the state to ensure respect for individual rights, and rights to the fulfilment of social and economic needs. The discourse in respect of human rights traditionally centred on the need for boundaries to the abusive exercise of power by the state to protect the civil and political rights and freedoms of individual citizens. While those protections remain important – there is still a need for powers to constrain the intrusion of the state into individual liberties – there has been a growing recognition that rights are not only abused by the state but also perpetrated by individuals against other members of a society. There is thus a need for the state to play an active role in protecting the rights of citizens from violations of their rights by others. This is particularly true of children. Because they lack autonomy, and their lives are substantially circumscribed by the adults who have responsibility for them, there is a clear onus on the state to intervene actively to protect those rights. In addition, children have socio-economic rights and impose obligations on the state to make available the necessary resources to ensure that children's well-being is promoted.

For example, if a child has a right to protection from discrimination, the government has the responsibility to introduce the necessary legislation, backed up by enforcement mechanisms, training and public education. If a child has a right to free full-time education, it is the responsibility of the state at a local and national level, as well as the child's parents, to ensure that education is made available and that the child is able to benefit from it
...

One of the underlying principles of the Convention is that the best interests of the child must be a primary consideration in all actions concerning the child (UNCRC, 1989, Article 3). This principle does not, however, merely take us back to a welfare approach: a commitment to respecting the human rights of children requires an acceptance that promoting children's welfare or best interests requires more than the good will or professional judgment of adults. The Convention injects two fundamental challenges to traditional practices in respect of children.

First, the means by which the best interests of children are assessed must be the extent to which all their human rights are respected in any particular policy, action or legislation. In other words the rights embodied in the Convention must provide a framework with which to analyse the extent to which proposals promote the best interests of children (Hodgkin and Newell, 1998). This approach also extends both to matters affecting the rights of an individual child and to children as a body. In providing child protection services, for example, do interventions that seek to protect the child from abuse also respect the child's right to privacy, to respect for the child's views and evolving capacities, to continuity in family life, to contact with the immediate and extended family? In a proposed local housing development, have the rights of children to adequate play facilities, safe road crossings and leisure services been properly considered? Similarly, one can apply a comparable analysis to decisions taken within families. Many parents currently drive their children to school and justify so doing in terms of the potential dangers of both traffic and abduction or assault to which the children might otherwise be exposed. A rights-based approach would necessitate a broader analysis of rights of children. What impact does driving children to school have on their right to the best possible health, to freedom of association, to play, to a growing respect for their emerging competence?

In all these examples it can be argued that unless a comprehensive rights-based approach is taken, there is a risk that a decision or intervention is made that responds to one aspect of the child's life and in so doing fails to acknowledge other rights or needs. Indeed, it may inadvertently impact adversely on the child.

Second, if children are subjects of rights, they themselves must have the opportunity to exercise those rights and be afforded the means of seeking redress when their rights are violated. In other words they must have opportunities to be heard. Article 12 of the Convention embodies the principle that children have the right to express their views on matters of concern to them and to have those views taken seriously in accordance with their age and maturity. It is a procedural right that has increasingly been recognized as necessary if children are to move beyond their traditional status as recipients of adult care and protection and become social actors entitled to influence decisions that affect their lives (Lansdown, 1996; Willow, 1997). Children are entitled to be actively involved in those decisions which affect them as individuals – in the family, in schools, in public care, in the courts, and as a body in the development, delivery, monitoring and evaluation of public policy at both local and national levels.

Listening to children and taking them seriously is important because children have a body of experience and views that are relevant to the development of public policy, improving the quality of decision-making and rendering it more accountable. Beyond this, it is an essential element in their protection. Children who experience respect for their views and are encouraged to take responsibility for those decisions they are competent to make will acquire the confidence to challenge any abuse of their rights. The active participation of children must also be backed up by clear and accessible complaints and appeals procedures and the availability of independent advocacy if they are to be able to challenge failures to respect their rights.

It is in the field of education that the failure to recognize the importance of listening to children as an essential component of promoting their best interests is perhaps most evident. The current government has placed a considerable emphasis on education whose focus has been almost exclusively the issue of academic attainment. Certainly, the UNCRC includes the right of children to an education on the basis of equality of opportunity, and the determination of the current government to ensure that high aspirations and opportunities exist for all children is consistent with the fulfilment of that right.

However, unlike children in most other European countries, children in the UK are denied the right to express their views and have them taken seriously within the education system (Davies and Kirkpatrick, 2000). There is no right to establish a school council, and children are expressly excluded from sitting on governing bodies. Children are not consulted over the National Curriculum, teaching methods, school policies or proposed legislation. Children, as opposed to their parents, have no right of appeal against a permanent school exclusion. There are no complaints procedures that can be followed in the event of injustice, discrimination or abuse. There are no regional or national networks of school students to act on behalf of pupils. In other words the government agenda in respect of children perpetuates the view that education is something that adults do to or for children, the child being constructed as the recipient. It fails to recognize the obligation to respect children's human rights within the education system – the right to be listened to, to be respected, to learn through day-to-day experience about the meaning of democracy and human rights. Children's best interests can only be promoted if these rights, alongside the right of access to education, are realized.

Conclusion

There is a continuing resistance to the concept of rights in this country, particularly when applied to children. It is a resistance shared by many parents, politicians, policy-makers and the media. It derives, at least in part, from a fear that children represent a threat to stability and order if they are not kept under control. Furthermore, it reflects the strong cultural tradition that children are 'owned' by their parents and that the state should play as minimal a role as possible in their care. Attempts by the state to act to protect children are thus viewed with suspicion and hostility.

But promoting the rights of children is not about giving a licence to children to take complete control of their lives irrespective of their level of competence. It is not about allowing children to ride roughshod over the rights of others, any more than adult rights permit such abuses. It is, rather, about moving away from the discredited assumption that adults alone can determine what happens in children's lives without regard for children's own views, experiences and aspirations. It means accepting that children, even very small children, are entitled to be listened to and taken seriously. It means acknowledging that, as children grow older, they can take greater responsibility for exercising their own rights. It involves recognizing that the state has explicit obligations towards children, for which it should be held accountable. A commitment to respecting children's rights does not mean abandoning their welfare: it means promoting their welfare by an adherence to the human rights standards defined by international law.

References

Alderson, P. (1993) *Children's Consent to Surgery*, Buckingham, Open University Press.

Audit Commission (1999) *Children in Mind*, London, Audit Commission.

Davies, L. and Kirkpatrick, G. (2000) *The Euridem Project, Children's Rights Alliance for England, for evidence of democracy in education in Sweden, Denmark, Germany and Holland*, London, Children's Rights Project.

DoH (Department of Health) (1993) *Households below Average Income 1979–1990/1*, London, HMSO.

Freeman, C., Henderson, P. and Kettle, J. (1999) *Planning with Children for Better Communities*, Bristol, Policy Press.

Hodgkin, R. and Newell, P. (1998) *Implementation Handbook on the Convention on the Rights of the Child,* New York, UNICEF.

John, M. (1996) *Children in Charge: the child's right to a fair hearing*, London, Jessica Kingsley.

Lansdown, G. (1996) *Taking Part*, London, Institute for Public Policy Research.

Marshall, K. (1997) *Children's Rights on the Balance: the Participation–Protection Divide*, London, Stationery Office.

Willow, C. (1997) *Hear! Hear! Promoting Children and Young People's Democratic Participation in Local Government*, London, Local Government Information Unit in Association with the Children's Rights Office.

Source

LANSDOWN, G. (2001) 'Children's welfare and children's rights' in Foley, P., Roche, J. and Tucker, S. (eds) (2001) *Children in Society: contemporary theory, policy and practice*, Basingstoke, Palgrave/The Open University, pp. 91–7.

Chapter 5

Gendered childhoods

Wendy Stainton Rogers

CONTENTS

When you have studied this chapter, you should be able to:

1 Describe the main biological differences between human males and females and outline some of the processes and mechanisms that produce these differences.

2 Outline the research into how rewards and punishments, imitation and role modelling and developing social understanding account for how boys learn to be boys and girls learn to be girls.

3 Explain what is meant by the social constructionist claims that gender creates sex and that gender is something that people 'do' rather than something that they 'are'.

4 Outline the main contributions that social constructionist research has made to our understanding of gender in childhood.

5 Outline some of the ways in which a child's gender affects their educational experiences and their opportunities, and the effects this can have on their own children.

6 Review some of the implications for policy and practice of seeking to promote equal educational opportunities for boys and girls.

1 INTRODUCTION

So far in this book you have looked at childhood from a range of perspectives, exploring cultural and historical variations in the treatment of children and the different ways childhood can be understood. In this chapter I take the argument a stage further by asking about the significance of gender. How far does it make sense to talk about children and childhood without distinguishing 'masculine' childhoods from 'feminine' childhoods? Can we fully make sense of childhood without acknowledging that there are separate 'girls' worlds' and 'boys' worlds'?

1.1 Sex and gender

What are little girls made of?
Sugar and spice and all things nice.
What are little boys made of?
Slugs and snails and puppy dogs' tails.

Let's start by establishing terminology. Traditionally people thought and spoke about femaleness and maleness in terms of *sex* – as in expressions like 'sex differences'. However, during the last thirty years, theorists and researchers have increasingly distinguished between sex and gender. Nowadays, the term 'sex' is usually reserved for those features that arise from biological differences. The term 'gender' has been adopted in order to acknowledge the extent to which femininity and masculinity are also moulded by historical, social, cultural, economic, political and psychological influences.

Allow about 15 minutes

ACTIVITY I   **Sex and gender**

Imagine you are introduced to five-year-old twins, a boy and a girl. Write a list of five ways in which you think they might be different because one is a girl and one is a boy. You don't need any specialist knowledge for this – just draw upon what you expect them to be like, based upon your own experience.

When you have done this, look at the differences on your list and put them into one of three categories:

1   **Sex** differences – those that you think the children are born with, and have a biological basis. We sometimes describe these as originating in a child's 'nature'.

2   **Gender** differences – those that you think the children have acquired through their childhood experiences, upbringing and so on. We sometimes describe these as arising from a child's 'nurture'.

3   Those you think are a mixture of nature and nurture.

COMMENT

For this activity, I imagined twins growing up in the English village where I live. My list included the obvious physical difference between boys and girls. I assumed Kylie would have a vagina and Jarvis would have a penis, and I put these firmly into the biological sex differences category. I also included the fact that they would probably be dressed differently. Kylie would be more likely to wear girls' colours (like pink) and clothes (like dresses) whereas Jarvis would wear 'boys' clothes' – no pink and without any flowers or frills. I thought Kylie would be more likely to have long hair and Jarvis short. I put these into the gender differences category, as I know that conventions like these vary between cultures and over time. Most of the other features I recognized as less certainly one or the other. I thought Jarvis might be more likely to play aggressively, Kylie might be more talkative; that Kylie might well be more cuddly in her behaviour, and Jarvis less likely to cry (although these are big generalizations, and individual children vary considerably on these things). I also thought they would have different interests. Jarvis would be more likely to play with cars and Kylie with dolls, for example. It was obvious to me that some aspects of these differences were learned, but I recognized that they might also arise from biological predispositions.

1.2 Nature and nurture

Theorists have long argued – and continue to argue – about the relative influences of 'nature' and 'nurture'. Some take the position that the differences between boys and girls always have a biological basis, and continue to use the term 'sex differences' to describe them. Moir and Moir argue, for instance, that:

> differences in the brain lead to sex differences in abilities, interests, levels of aggression, motives and emotional characteristics, and these in turn will influence what boys and girls choose to do in school.

(Moir and Moir, 1998, p. 119)

Others counter this position by claiming that biology is relatively unimportant, and that it is nurture that almost entirely accounts for gender differences. The sociologist, Barrie Thorne, for example, stresses that:

> The phrase *sex category* refers to the core, dichotomous categories of individual sex and gender (female/male; girl/boy; woman/man) – dualisms riddled with the complexities of biology/culture and age/gender. While these categories appear to be rock-bottom and founded in biology – hence 'sex' category – they are deeply constructed by cultural beliefs and by social practices of gender display and attribution.

> (Thorne, 1997, p. 196)

Yet others propose an interactionist model. They argue that a child's development is a product of the interplay between 'nature' and 'nurture'. For example, the developmental psychologist Martin Richards writes:

> throughout development there is an essential tension between the biological and the social. The infant and his [*sic*] social world are in constant interaction; just as the biological infant structures and modifies his social environment, so he is socially structured by it and his biology is modified.

> (Richards, 1974, p. 1)

You will see as the chapter develops that these are not just theoretical arguments; they have practical implications and consequences. The main reason for this is that while biology is difficult to alter (though it can be, by medical treatment, for example), upbringing can be changed. Thus the theoretical position taken can have a very strong influence upon, for example, arguments about whether we should pursue equal opportunities (in schooling, for instance) for boys and girls.

1.3 Scientific approach versus social constructionism

However, there is another important theoretical debate going on. Underlying the terminological distinction made between 'sex' and 'gender', there are two contrasting approaches to the relationship between them. You have met these already: the scientific approach and the social constructionist approach.

From the scientific perspective, sex is seen as the biological foundation upon which a child's gender is built. In other words, nature provides the basic building-blocks of sex, upon which 'nurture' overlays gender. Social constructionism takes the opposite view. It views the nature/nurture debate as irrelevant. Rather, it argues that sex as well as gender is a product of human meaning-making. Indeed, the strongest form of this argument proposes that it is gender that produces sex, not sex that produces gender. Without gender, the argument goes, sex would not matter, and it is *mattering* that turns a concept (such as 'sex') into a thing – it's what gives it reality.

This may strike you as a bizarre claim, and certainly it can be a difficult argument to take seriously at first. Possibly it is easiest to follow the argument in another context: that of disability.

The social construction of disability

At first it may appear that disability is a natural, physical reality – it is just a matter of what people's bodies (including their brains) can and cannot do. But think about it. I have a friend (who is right-handed) who lost all the fingers of his right hand in an accident. He was lucky – the surgeons managed to reconstruct his hand so he has a 'finger' made out of some of the bones that were left, held together by skin grafts. It looks a bit like a pincer, and after several operations now works so well that he can grasp firmly with it. It means he can do most things that people in his community need to do – write, use a knife and fork, carry a bag – so he describes himself as hardly disabled at all. Until, that is, he goes to China! Chopsticks are his downfall, since they require much more right-hand dexterity than using a knife, and so he's aware of being much more 'disabled' there.

It's possible to argue, then, that it's not bodily incapacity that produces disability, but disability that produces bodily incapacity. To make this argument work it is necessary to define disability. What does 'disability' mean? One definition is that it means *not being able to do the things that people do*. There are lots of things that people can't do that other animals can. Unlike bats, people can't use a kind of radar to find their way around. People are not able to see certain bands of light like bees and other insects can. People can't hear some of the sounds that dogs can. People can't swim as fast as dolphins, or run as fast as horses. But that does not make all humans 'disabled' – just human.

Now, think about the way human society can construct a disabling world. Steps are an obvious example – they disable everybody who cannot walk up and down them (as anybody who tries to get around with a child in a pushchair can tell you).

Well, this certainly buggers our plan to conquer the Universe.

From this argument, it is the human-built environment that creates some forms of disability. If houses were built with their ceilings set low, for example, it would be able-bodied people who were 'disabled' and wheelchair users who would be free to move around. Disability may be sited in the body – in that it arises from a bodily incapacity. But that *in*capacity is not there in nature – it is an incapacity in relation to *expected* capacities. The human world is organized around the expectation that people can walk, climb stairs, hear certain sounds and see certain kinds of light. But people aren't expected to be able to fly, hear very high-pitched sounds, or to be able to echo-locate as a bat can do.

In London, even in a Chinese restaurant, a person wouldn't be expected to be able to use chopsticks as they would in China. So 'disability' is not simply about what a particular person can and cannot do. It's about whether or not they can do the things that *matter* – the things people are expected to be able to do. Micheline Mason, a campaigner for disabled people's rights, wrote: 'Although we do, of course, have medical conditions which may hamper us, the major disability we face is that caused by the social and environmental barriers placed upon us by the structures of our societies' (Mason, 1992, p. 223).

1.4 Gender producing sex?

Let's return now to the argument that it is gender that produces sex. Imagine a world in which an individual's sexual characteristics go unnoticed. This is hard to do, since gender is so very obvious to us. But try to just imagine, for the purposes of this exercise, what life would be like in a world where people are indifferent to the physical differences between the sexes.

It would be a world in which things like clothes and hairstyle would not act as markers, and so the bodily differences would be a lot less obvious. But there would still be some that it might be possible to discern – such as having a different body shape. People would be *capable* of perceiving the differences, but they would not see them. As far as they were concerned, they would not exist. 'Hang on,' you might say, 'What about childbirth – that's impossible to ignore!' In Marge Piercy's science fiction novel *Woman on the Edge of Time* (Piercy, 1976) she got round that one by inventing birthing machines, so neither men nor women experienced childbirth.

In a genderless world a person's sex would not exist, so it could not have any influence on how they are treated, how they act or what they can and cannot do. Sex would be 'there' in just the same way as gamma rays have always been 'there', but it would not exist for people – just as gamma rays did not exist until people found ways to observe and conceive of them. It is in this sense that social constructionists claim that sex would not 'exist' without gender.

Now think about what the consequences for children would be. The physical differences between boys and girls would also go undetected and so boys and girls would not be distinguished as different from each other. They would not even think of themselves as 'boys' or 'girls' but simply as children. They would have no need to learn what 'gender' means, or, indeed, acquire a gender. In such a world childhood would be very different from the world in which we live, where gender not only matters, but matters enormously. Again, this kind of gender-free world has been conjured up in science fiction. Ursula LeGuin's novel *The Left Hand of Darkness* (LeGuin, 1969) is a good place to start if you would like to explore what a genderless society might be like. She achieves this by creating a race where sex differences only arise in adulthood, and then only for short periods in a state she calls 'kemmer'.

This idea of gender producing sex is the stance taken by social constructionist theory, and is explored in Section 4. Social constructionism, as you have learned already, regards the 'realities' we take for granted (such as disability or gender) as socially constructed – the product of human meaning-making. This directs our attention to the social, historical, cultural and economic forces that create and mould adult gender – and hence create the gendered world into which children are born and in which they grow up. Social constructionism thus allows us to examine the gendered aspects of childhood in a different way from conventional scientific approaches. It ignores the nature/nurture debate, and, instead, focuses upon the way that human meaning-making constructs both sex and gender.

1.5 Chapter outline

In this introduction I have outlined some of the basic controversies that surround the study of gendered childhoods. In the rest of the chapter I will look at these controversies from the perspectives outlined in earlier chapters, the scientific, social constructionist and applied approaches. You will examine scientific approaches to sex and gender in Sections 2 and 3. Section 2 focuses on 'nature'. It outlines the biological mechanisms and processes that produce the sexual differentiation between males and females. Section 3 then focuses on 'nurture'. It looks at gender acquisition – how boys learn to be masculine, and girls learn to be feminine, and how children gain an understanding of what maleness and femaleness mean.

In Section 4 you will examine the approach to gender taken by social constructionism, both in theoretical terms and empirically in its approach to research.

The chapter then goes on to address an applied approach. Section 5 briefly explores the impact of a child's gender on her or his experiences of childhood, their aspirations and expectations, and their life-opportunities. Finally, in Section 6, the chapter reviews different theories and explanations of gender and standpoints on it in terms of their implications for policy and practice. It looks at what each advocates, for example, about child care, child rearing and the services (such as education) that should be offered to children.

SUMMARY OF SECTION 1

- Researchers distinguish 'sex differences' arising from biology from 'gender differences' arising from social, cultural and psychological influences. This is often presented as an issue about 'nature' versus 'nurture' and about the interactions between the two.

- The ways people are disabled by social attitudes, including the design of places and processes, provides an illustration of the social constructionist approach.

- One scientific perspective sees sex as the biological foundation upon which a child's gender is built. Social constructionists reverse the argument. They see awareness of and interest in sex differences as a product of human meaning-making. From this point of view it is gender that produces sex.

2 THE BIOLOGICAL BASIS OF SEX DIFFERENCES

In this section you will look, briefly, at what a scientific approach can tell us about the biological mechanisms and processes that account for sex differences in children. These include differences in the structure and chemistry of the body and the organization of the brain.

2.1 Producing females and males

Scientific research has established many of the mechanisms that produce 'maleness' or 'femaleness' at a biological level. The basis of these are biochemical operations within and between cells, the tiny units of living matter which make up human bodies. Inside the nucleus of each cell in a human body are rod-like things called 'chromosomes'. Chromosomes are made up of 'genes' which encode information, rather like a computer program, and this genetic information provides instructions for all the biological processes that enable humans (and other animals) to develop and to sustain life. Examples include 'blueprints' for constructing organs (such as the eye or a finger), and instructions for continuing processes (such as growth, digestion and blood circulation). Humans have 46 chromosomes, which are organized in the cell nucleus as 23 pairs.

In humans, a new life starts when two special cells, one derived from a man (a sperm cell) and one derived from a woman (an ovum or egg), fuse to form one cell. Their genetic material joins together in a single nucleus inside this cell. Rapidly this cell divides, forming first a hollow ball of cells and then, slowly, it takes shape as a foetus.

In the production of sperm and egg cells, and in their fusion, the chromosomes do something which is different from ordinary cell reproduction. The cells making up the rest of the body reproduce by division, and in this ordinary cell division each chromosome pair is

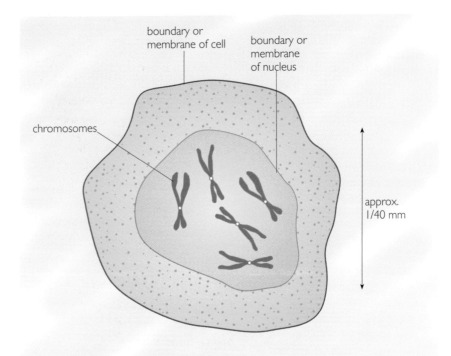

boundary or
membrane of cell

boundary or
membrane
of nucleus

chromosomes

approx.
1/40 mm

Figure 1
Diagram of a human
cell showing the
nucleus containing
chromosomes.

simply copied. In the cell division which produces sperm and egg cells, only one of each pair of chromosomes is generated and each cell, therefore, has only a half-set of chromosomes. When the sperm and egg cells fuse, these sets then combine to produce a full set of paired chromosomes, one of each pair coming from the sperm, and one from the egg. So half of the genetic information in the new cell comes from the female parent, and half from the male.

Of the 23 pairs of chromosomes in a human cell, 22 are similarly shaped pairs. However, the other pair (pair 23) are usually in one of two distinctive configurations: either an XX set or an XY set (their names reflect their shapes, like an X and like a Y). In most instances, people possessing an XX pair are female; people possessing an XY pair are male.

The configurations arise through the coming together of the half-set of chromosomes from each parent. Women produce only X chromosomes in their egg cells; men produce about half X-carrying and half Y-carrying sperm. When an X chromosome from the man meets the X chromosome from the woman, the resulting foetus is female. When a Y chromosome is in the sperm that fuses with the egg cell, the result is a male foetus.

For the first six weeks or so male and female foetuses are the same except at the genetic level. At this point each has the capacity to develop either a male or a female body-form and each has the capacity to develop either the male reproductive system or the female reproductive system – each foetus contains both systems in undeveloped forms.

But from about six weeks, things begin to change (see Figure 2). Where the foetus has an XY (male) pairing of sex chromosomes, it produces two kinds of hormones. One sort (androgens) stimulates the male reproductive-system-to-be, to make it begin to grow. At the same time the other hormone

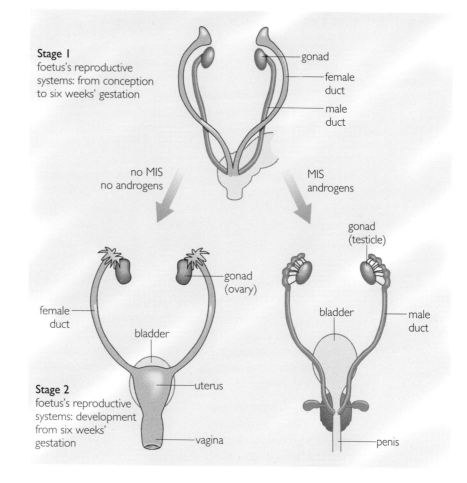

Stage 1 foetus's reproductive systems: from conception to six weeks' gestation

gonad

female duct

male duct

no MIS no androgens

MIS androgens

gonad (testicle)

gonad (ovary)

female duct

bladder

male duct

bladder

Stage 2 foetus's reproductive systems: development from six weeks' gestation

uterus

vagina

penis

Figure 2 The effects of hormones on the foetus's reproductive systems.

(the Müllerian Inhibiting Substance, MIS for short) inhibits the female reproductive-system-to-be, and makes it degenerate. Where the foetus has an XX (female) pairing of sex chromosomes, it produces no androgens or MIS, and it is the female reproductive-system-to-be which develops. Biologically speaking, femaleness is the default state – a foetus develops a female reproductive system unless it is masculinized by the androgens and MIS.

2.2 The action of hormones

Hormones are sometimes called 'chemical messengers'. This gives a good clue as to what they are and do: they are chemicals which travel around the body in the bloodstream, produced by specialized glands. Particular cells in the body are receptive to particular hormones – they possess a biochemical receptor site which, when activated by a hormone, 'turns on' or 'turns off' a particular process.

What happens when hormone production and reception do not work properly? If there are problems with production or reception of masculinizing hormones in an XY foetus, it will not develop its masculine reproductive system properly. So the foetus develops with what looks like female rather than male physical characteristics. This does occasionally

Box 1 5-alpha-reductase deficiency syndrome

There are several genetic causes of failure of masculinization. One of them is especially interesting, as masculinizing doesn't work properly in the foetus, but works at puberty. The baby appears to be female, but has a 'natural' sex change at puberty and does not develop into a woman but a man. This condition results from the foetus's lack of a chemical called 5-alpha-reductase, and the technical, scientific term for this condition is *5-alpha-reductase deficiency syndrome*. Boys with this condition have, at birth, male genitals that are not developed. Their penis is very small and looks more like a clitoris, and their scrotum looks like labia. Often (but, as you will see later, not always) babies with this condition are assumed to be – and are raised as – girls. However, at puberty their hormonal system works to masculinize their bodies. Their voice lowers, penis grows (although it remains small), their testes descend, they grow pubic hair and their muscles increase in mass. Such individuals appear to transform from a girl into a man as they become adult.

happen. When the child is born it *looks* female, and the baby will often be assumed to *be* – and hence raised as – a girl (see Box 1).

The reason why this condition is so interesting is that it provides, in effect, a 'natural experiment'. By looking at what happens to such individuals when they reach puberty and undergo a 'sex change', it is possible to explore the interplay between biology and social and cultural forces in constituting a person's gender. You will look at these in Section 4.

The hormonal system is largely controlled by a gland sited beneath the brain – the pituitary gland. This gland produces a number of hormones, which, in turn, stimulate the release of other hormones. For example, the action of the pituitary stimulates the sex organs (called gonads – the testes and the ovaries) to secrete gonadal hormones. Hormones control a large number of body processes.

Sex hormones

The sex hormones can be divided into two main classes: the androgens (such as testosterone), which you met above, and the oestrogens. It is often assumed that androgens are 'male' hormones and oestrogens are 'female' hormones, as if only men have androgens and only women have oestrogens. But this is not so – *both* sexes produce *both* types. In general, men have a lot more of each androgen and less of each oestrogen operating in their bodies; and women have a lot more of each oestrogen and less of each androgen.

Hormones and puberty

During infancy and childhood, the level of sex hormones circulating in the body is low. But at puberty a number of hormones come into play. The pituitary releases growth hormones, which results in the adolescent growth spurt. This is when bones (especially the long bones in legs and arms) and muscles grow faster, so that the child rapidly gains adult size and proportions. The pituitary also releases two other hormones: follicle-stimulating hormone (FSH) and luteinizing hormone (LH). These stimulate the gonads to increase the production of oestrogens and androgens, which results in the maturation of the gonads and the development of what are called secondary sexual characteristics (the primary ones being the internal and external genitalia) – body hair in both sexes, and the distinctive body shapes of adult females and males.

In adolescent boys the production of androgens is proportionately higher than their production of oestrogens; in adolescent girls the situation is reversed, with relatively more oestrogens and less androgens being produced. Again, it is important not to assume that androgens are simply 'male hormones' and oestrogens 'female hormones'. One of the androgens, for example, is responsible for the growth of pubic and under-arm hair in both boys and girls. Equally, FSH and LH are involved both in the development of egg cells in women and in the production of sperm in men, and LH contributes to the maturation of egg cells in women and the maturation of sperm and the production of testosterone in men.

Currently in the affluent parts of the world, puberty usually happens between the ages of about ten to fourteen. It is not at all uncommon for a girl to have her first period at eleven, and it is unusual if it does not happen before she is sixteen. But 100 years ago very few girls had their first period at eleven and it was not at all uncommon for first menstruation to occur at age sixteen. Scientists have attributed this shift mainly to the much better nutrition that children in affluent contries have today compared with 100 years ago. This conclusion is based on studies that scientists have carried out on baby animals that compare their rate of development in relation to the amount and quality of food given. These studies have shown that development tends to happen faster the better fed the animal.

The earlier sexual maturation of girls in these circumstances demonstrates that their genetic make-up is not the only factor in sexual development. Environmental factors – such as diet – also play a role.

2.3 Sex differences in mental functioning

So far we have concentrated on the biological processes that lead to physical differentiation between the sexes, especially during foetal development and at puberty. Are there also psychological differences between girls and boys, and are these differences linked to biological differences, especially in the organization of the brain?

Intelligence tests have consistently shown that women and girls score higher, on average, on tests of verbal ability, and men and boys on tests of mathematical problem-solving and spatial ability (see Maccoby and Jacklin, 1974, for a review). One of the most controversial explanations offered for these findings is that they are linked to sex differences in the brain. The cerebral cortex of the brain is divided into two halves – two hemispheres. As children develop, each hemisphere specializes in certain tasks, a process called lateralization. Typically (the pattern is somewhat different for left-handed and ambidextrous people), the left hemisphere specializes in language skills, while the right hemisphere specializes in spatial skills. Some evidence indicates that men, on average, tend to be more lateralized than women; the specialization of each hemisphere is more complete. For example, Shaywitz *et al.* (1995) used a magnetic resonance imager (MRI) to map neurological activity in the brain, and got men and women to solve problems involving language use. In all the men in their study, only the left hemisphere was seen to be active when working on these problems. Many of the women, however, seemed to be using both hemispheres. Shaywitz *et al.* concluded that: 'Our data provide clear evidence for a sex difference in the functional organization of the brain for language ... We have demonstrated remarkable differences in the functional organization of a specific component of language, phonological processing, between normal males and females' (Shaywitz *et al.*, 1995, p. x).

There are always problems with attributing a direct biological cause to behaviour. Moreover, recent work has drawn attention to the dangers of exaggerating the extent of psychological differences between girls and boys, which may in any case be gradually reducing in societies in the North. In the case of verbal abilities, Brannon (1998) suggests the difference is very small, and only shows up in some verbal abilities (such as spelling) and not in others (such as verbal reasoning). Equally, research into mathematical ability shows a much more complicated picture than was originally apparent. Boys' and men's advantage is concentrated in mathematical skills that involve spatial reasoning. On some spatial tasks, men and boys seem to have a consistent, but small, advantage over women and girls (Kimura, 1992).

Recent data on the performance in the UK of girls and boys in the public examinations taken at ages 16 and 18 (GCSE and A Levels) confirms that social and cultural forces are probably much more powerful than biology. In 1999, girls' performance in A-level mathematics for the first time outstripped that of boys.

SUMMARY OF SECTION 2

- Biological processes are largely – but not entirely – responsible for the development of 'sex', in the sense of female and male physical differences.
- An individual's sex is determined by one pair of the 23 pairs of chromosomes. Those with an XX pair are usually female, those with XY are usually male. However, a small number of individuals are born with genetic defects which can mean an individual has their gender 'wrongly' assigned.
- Both sexes have male and female hormones, though in different proportions. The action of hormones produces primary sexual characteristics before birth (such as a penis or a vagina), and produces secondary sexual characteristics during puberty (such as menstruation in girls and facial hair in boys).
- Small differences in mental abilities have been found between males and females. Females tend, on average, to achieve better on verbal tests and males, on average, achieve better on problem-solving and some spatial tasks. However, changing relative performance between girls and boys suggests social and cultural factors play a significant role.

3 ACQUIRING GENDER

Section 2 looked at the 'nature' of sex differences. This section turns to scientific theories and research about the significance of 'nurture' and to what developmental psychologists have said about the processes by which children acquire gender. How do male infants become boys and female infants become girls? There are many different theories in this field, but I am going to look at just a few ways of studying how children learn gender.

Allow about 10 minutes

ACTIVITY 2   **Learning gender**

Jot down notes while you think about how children learn to act in gender-appropriate ways. How, for example, might a two-year-old girl or boy learn what is considered appropriate in their society? What other things might they learn as they get older? You might like to think back to the five-year-old twins in Activity 1. Think about the role adults might play in shaping how children behave. Think as well about how far children learn for themselves about what is gender-appropriate behaviour.

COMMENT

You might have thought about the toys parents buy for their children, the TV programmes they encourage them to watch or the ways they comment when a young child does something that they don't see as gender appropriate. A girl might be encouraged to play with a doll, while a boy might be told, 'Don't be a cissy!' You might also have thought of situations where a child is exposed to gender role models, again through television, or through who does the washing-up or the car maintenance at home. Finally, you might have thought about children's developing understanding about gender, especially the role that talk plays in shaping gender identity. Each of these aspects of gender development has been studied extensively. In this section we will concentrate on three lines of research.

3.1 Rewards and punishments

The first line of research derives from a general theory of learning called 'behaviourism'. This theory is built on the basic principle that behaviour that is rewarded tends to be repeated, whereas behaviour that is punished or ignored tends not to be, and, indeed, may be extinguished. If every time a two-year-old girl plays with dolls, she gets a lot of attention, smiles and approval from those around her, she is likely to play in this way more and more. If she gets ignored or even teased whenever she plays with boys' toys or mimics men's tasks (such as hunting), she is likely to lose interest in them. In this way her feminine behaviour will be reinforced, and her unfeminine behaviour will be, if not always punished, certainly discouraged. For example, a study of American homes during the 1970s found that two-year-old girls were encouraged by their parents to dance, dress up and play with dolls, but were discouraged from jumping and climbing. Boys of the same age were encouraged to play with blocks and trucks but not with dolls. Interestingly, when boys sought help, they were encouraged to be more autonomous in their play (Fagot, 1978).

3.2 Observation, imitation and modelling

The second line of research concentrates on children's role in observing and imitating gender-appropriate behaviour. For example, Bandura and Walters (1963) proposed that children acquire their gender by *observational learning* – observing and modelling the behaviour of others. They looked at how children in various cultures develop gender-roles. In traditional cultures where men's jobs and women's jobs are clearly separate, they observed that girls tended to stay with their mothers, watching and imitating their domestic activities. The boys accompanied their fathers, and were often given child-size tools so that they could copy their fathers' work activities.

In cultures in which children's education is mainly gained through working alongside adults and older siblings, the separation of men's and women's roles is often nearly complete (see, for example, Nsamenang and Lamb, 1998). Hence childhood experiences are highly gendered. But even in cultures where boys and girls are reared together much more, things like the toys they play with and the television programmes they watch mean that observational learning will be different for boys and girls.

Allow about 5 to 10 minutes

ACTIVITY 3   **Observational learning and toys**

Think about the toys that are designed for girls and boys. You can, if you like, go and look at children playing, or look at a catalogue of children's toys. How may these aid observational learning?

COMMENT

Girls' toys often enable girls to mimic the behaviour of their mothers – dolls, toy cleaning or cooking implements, for example. Boys' toys often enable them to mimic their fathers' behaviour. Examples include toy cars, things that can be used for construction and building things and toy guns. Of course there are toys that both boys and girls play with, and these days boys, for example, are often encouraged to 'play cooking' as well as girls. But even so, the general difference is very striking.

Bandura and Walters rejected the idea that all that is going on here was simple mimicry. Rather, they argued, observational learning is a profoundly *social* experience: 'While playing with toys that stimulate imitation of adults, children frequently reproduce not only the appropriate adult-role behaviour patterns but also characteristic or idiosyncratic parental patterns of response, including attitudes, mannerisms, gestures, and even voice inflections ... ' (Bandura and Walters, 1963, p. 48). They gave the term 'modelling' to the process where children not only imitate the behaviour of the people around them, but act out their roles – just as, say, an actor in a drama will 'play the villain' or 'the damsel in distress'. Adults thus become *role models* for children.

Allow about 15 minutes

ACTIVITY 4   Children's role models

Paying particular attention to gender, note down your responses to the following questions:

1   What factors are likely to determine the role models that children adopt?

2   Which people are most likely to act as a child's role models?

3   How can this change as children get older?

COMMENT

In early childhood the most important factor seems to be the amount and nature of the contact the person has with the child. Not surprisingly, then, very young children usually adopt their parent(s) as role models – or whoever is acting in the parental role for them. In most cultures children, as they get older, will tend to be more exposed to same-gender role models. Girls are more likely to spend time with women and boys with men. So girls are more likely to model themselves on women and boys on men. But the amount of contact isn't the only factor influencing role models, since young boys often spend more time being cared for by women than men. Another factor is identification. Children tend to imitate role models they see as similar to themselves. Again, this is likely to lead girls to model themselves on women and boys on men. While parents or other family members are initially likely to be major role models, as children get older they may adopt as a role model another significant adult, such as a teacher or a celebrity.

3.3 Social understanding and gender identity

The third line of research links back to Piaget's and Kohlberg's theories about children's developing understanding (Chapters 1 and 3). It recognizes that children are actively involved in trying to make sense of gender as a key dimension of their social world and asks how this aspect of social understanding develops. For example, at what age do children become aware of their own and other people's gender identity? Research suggests the majority of children can answer the question, 'Are you a boy or girl?' by the age of two, and by three years old most have no difficulty judging others too. By this age children also have clear ideas about what is gender-appropriate behaviour (cited by Miell, 1995).

Recall the study of young children's social understanding by Judy Dunn, Reading B in Chapter 3, especially her emphasis on the role of language as the tool through which children learn about and negotiate their social relationships. In an earlier study, Dunn and Kendrick (1982) observed young children's reactions to the arrival of a new baby. In the following example, two-year-old Sally talks with her father about her teddy and about her little brother Trevor:

CHILD: Teddy's a man

FATHER: What are you?

CHILD: You're a boy.

FATHER: Yeah. What are you?

CHILD: A menace.

FATHER: Yeah, a menace. Apart from that are you a boy or a girl?

CHILD: Boy (laughs)

FATHER: Are you? What's Trevor?

CHILD: A girl (laughs)

FATHER: You're silly.

(Dunn and Kendrick, 1982, pp. 110–111)

This child's responses show that she has a clear sense of gender at an early age. Moreover, her identity is sufficiently well-established to allow her to play with the concept, exploring gender reversals and recognizing what will amuse or provoke an adult. These very early conversations about gender are just a beginning. They draw attention to ways in which gender is constructed amongst children as well as adults. This is the theme of the next section.

SUMMARY OF SECTION 3

- Psychological studies of the way children learn to act and think in gender-appropriate ways stress the influence of the environment in which they grow up.
- One way children learn gender-appropriate behaviour is through rewards and punishments, which often take the form of approval for some kinds of play but disapproval of others.
- Other research claims that children learn gender-appropriate behaviour by observation. They model themselves on others. Boys tend to model themselves on men and girls on women.
- Studies of children's developing social understanding draw attention to children's growing capacity to make sense of gender as an aspect of their social and cultural world.

4 THE SOCIAL CONSTRUCTION OF GENDER

In this section you will examine the social constructionist approach to gender: that gender is not a product of biology, nor merely of socialization, but is *produced* by human meaning-making. It is people's conceptualization of gender and the significance they accord to it that makes the sexual differentiation between male and female powerful. In other words, a child's sex – their maleness or femaleness – is obvious and meaningful to us only because gender *matters*.

This was shown very clearly in a famous set of experiments where boy babies were dressed in pink and girls in blue, in a reversal of the usual use of clothes' colour to mark gender in British and American societies. When adults were introduced to these babies and were not told their sex, they seem to have assumed that the babies in pink were girls and babies in blue were boys. They then proceeded to treat them very differently. 'Girls' were called pretty, cuddled more and soothed when they banged their toys whereas 'boys' were called big and strong, played with more roughly and encouraged to use their bodies more (cited by Lloyd and Duveen, 1990). Gender in this instance is not simply about pink or blue. What the study showed is how powerful these colours were for adults as symbolic markers of gender, which profoundly altered the ways they treated boy and girl babies, and appeared to override any other indicators in the children's behaviour or responsiveness.

Gender, in all cultures and societies, powerfully determines how the members of those societies and communities perceive and treat children, how children see themselves and relate to others, what children can and cannot do, their access to opportunities and to resources, their life-opportunities and so on.

4.1 Doing gender

Social constructionism therefore argues that gender is something we 'do' rather than something we 'are'. Lorber describes it thus:

> Talking about gender for most people is the equivalent of fish talking about water. Gender is so much the routine ground of everyday activities that questioning its taken-for-granted assumptions and presuppositions is like thinking about whether the sun will come up. Gender is so pervasive that in our society we assume it is bred into our genes. Most people find it hard to believe that gender is constantly created and re-created out of human interaction, out of social life, and is the texture and order of that social life. Yet gender, like culture, is a human production that depends on everyone constantly 'doing gender' ...

(Lorber, 1994, p. 13)

Allow about 40 minutes for the recording and reviewing part of this activity, and about 20 minutes for reading and reflection

ACTIVITY 5 Doing gender

Begin by reading the short extract below, taken from ' "Night to his day": the social construction of gender' by Judith Lorber.

> [E]veryone 'does gender' without thinking about it. Today on the subway, I saw a well-dressed man with a year-old child in a stroller. Yesterday, on a bus, I saw a man with a tiny baby in a carrier on his chest. Seeing men taking care of small children in public is increasingly common – at least in New York City. But both men were quite obviously stared at – and smiled at, approvingly. Everyone was doing gender – the men who were changing the role of fathers and the other passengers, who were applauding them silently. But there was more gendering going on that probably fewer people noticed. The baby was wearing a white crocheted cap and white clothes. You couldn't tell if it was a boy or a girl. The child in the stroller was wearing a dark blue T-shirt and dark print pants. As they started to leave the train, the father put a Yankee baseball cap on the child's head. Ah, a boy, I thought. Then I noticed the gleam of tiny earrings in the child's ears, and as they got off, I saw the little flowered sneakers and lace-trimmed socks. Not a boy after all. Gender done.
>
> (Lorber, 1994, p. 13)

For the next week, as you go about your daily life, look for examples of children and/or teenagers 'doing gender'. You can make your observations from the media (watching television, for example) or from real life (such as a visit to the shops) or both. Make notes describing your observations as soon as you can afterwards, and set aside a few minutes each day to review and record your observations.

When you have a number of observations to go on, set aside about twenty minutes to reflect upon your reactions. There are no 'right answers' – indeed, there are not really 'answers' to this activity. The aim is for you to spend some time being more alert to, and aware of, the ways in which children 'do' gender; how it's woven into their daily lives. Think about what you expected – did your observations surprise you? In what ways? To what extent did the experience of observing how gender is 'done' convince you that it is socially constructed?

COMMENT

As I said, there aren't any 'answers' to this activity. I hope, though, that doing it gave you opportunities to experience at first-hand what is meant by the idea of 'doing gender'. This activity may not have convinced you that gender is socially constructed. But it should at least have persuaded you that children and teenagers work very hard at gender, and are by no means simply passive sponges that soak up gender roles. Nor do they all act the same. Some work at being – and being seen as – conventionally gendered: to be 'real' girls and boys. Others resist, and work at not being stereotyped.

Becky Francis (1998), in a study she conducted on children's constructions of gender, argued that conventional learning theories cannot account for the way children acquire gender. She said that if all that were going on was that children gradually learn to adopt appropriate gender roles, then nothing would change. The same roles would be passed on from one generation to another. But, she pointed out, things do change, using as an illustration the shifts that have been observed in England in the relative educational performance of boys and girls between the 1970s and the present-day.

4.2 Discursive positioning

Francis's work is explicitly informed by social constructionism. She adopts, in particular, the theory of *discursive positioning*; that is, the idea that people's identities are not fixed but are fluid, positioned *in* and positioned *by* different discourses. You have met this idea already in Chapters 1 and 2, where discourses on childhood were described, including the Romantic discourse of childhood that positions children as inherently good; and the Puritan discourse that positions children as inherently bad.

In Chapters 1 and 2, the social constructionist definition of discourse was introduced. Discourse is a whole set of interconnected ideas that work together in a self-contained way, ideas that are held together by a particular ideology or view of the world.

Using the theory of discursive positioning, Valerie Walkerdine (1988) looked at why, at the time and place where she conducted her research (Britain in the 1970s) girls tended to do poorly at maths in school. She argued that the then dominant educational discourse positioned girls as doing maths 'the wrong way'. Heavily influenced by Piagetian theory, this discourse defined experimentation and play as the 'right way' of learning mathematical concepts. Since girls tended to work in a more systematic and disciplined manner, they were positioned by their teachers – and, often, by themselves – as less capable than boys of learning maths.

Francis observes that since the 1980s in the UK, educational policy has 'reflected a return to a discourse of "the basics" (the three Rs, well presented coursework and exam success). Boys' constructions of masculinity may not sit so easily with this discourse' (Francis, 1998, p. 166).

Thus part of the explanation for the shift from girls doing badly at maths relative to boys in the 1970s to girls performing better than boys in the 1990s she attributes to the positioning of girls in different discourses. The Piagetian-informed dominant discourse in the 1970s positioned them as less capable than boys. The 'back to basics' dominant discourse of the 1980s and 90s positions them as more capable. Flowing from these discourses are teachers' expectations of the relative competence of girls and boys – and hence the way to treat them. But the discourses also influence boys' and girls' own expectations, and, indeed, those of their parents and others.

As further evidence Francis cited a famous study carried out in the 1970s by Paul Willis, on the construction of male identities by English working-class boys (Willis, 1977). Willis showed that these boys did not simply take on the masculine roles offered to them in a passive or universal manner. They actively constructed their masculinity, often resisting, for example, the guidance and expectations offered by their families and schools. Francis points out that girls, too, 'take up gender roles in multiple and contradictory ways, simultaneously accommodating and resisting them' (Francis, 1998, p. 5).

Resistance is when a less powerful person seeks to undermine or otherwise counter power being exercised over them.

Resistance is a term used to describe how those in powerless positions can act – they need not be passive. They can resist the power exercised to control them – by, for example, finding subtle ways to undermine it. Children are extremely adept at resistance; for instance, in superficially doing what they are told to do, but in ways that defeat its object. An example of resistance would be that of a young woman called Moni who was interviewed in Bangladesh as part of the research for this book. She is a young Bangladeshi woman who has been married against her will and is fighting to have the marriage ended. She said:

I think boys have more freedom than girls. Boys are asked to get married ... [but] most girls don't want to get married ... I think parents should get consent from the girls before they are married ... I wish my mother had asked me for my consent. When she arranged my marriage I felt bad, I didn't like it. And also I didn't like the boy ... I am standing against my marriage because I don't want to get married. I'm fighting against it and I've told people that I don't want to be in this marriage ... In our country boys of my age are never forced into marriage but girls of my age are forced into marriage.

Power

Discursive positioning theory focuses upon the power that is embedded within discourses – power that operates by constructing people in different ways. The traditional discourse positions Moni as obliged to conform to her 'natural' role and the wishes of her parents, and hence as powerless to change her situation. A children's rights discourse positions her as entitled to challenge her marriage. Locating herself in the power-engendering children's rights discourse offers Moni a means of resistance. By seeing herself and demanding to be seen by others as a person with rights, Moni can justify challenging the marriage arranged for her.

In discursive positioning theory, power is seen as far from simple. It's not a question of some people being powerful and others powerless – it's a lot more subtle and complicated than that. Foucault, the originator of the theory of discursive positioning, described it as being like a network or web, with individuals in it both exercising power and being affected by it. It permeates human relationships at all levels, from the personal to the institutional.

4.3   Ambiguous gender

To explore this idea of power as a network, think back to the genetic disorder 5-alpha-reductase deficiency syndrome (page 190). If you recall, the effect is that a child is born looking more female than male, but, at puberty, develops male characteristics. Within a relatively short time the apparent girl has transformed – in a biological sense – into a young man. What happens when this occurs helps us to see how gender is caught up in the dense networks of power that operate in all human societies and cultures. This genetic disorder tends to be more frequent in specific geographical localities and, by consequence, in specific cultures. Two places where it occurs relatively frequently are the Dominican Republic and Papua New Guinea. Even though it is a rare condition, it happens often enough for researchers to have been able to study what happens to individuals with it.

In the Dominican Republic it is given a number of names: *guevedoces* ('penis-at-twelve'), *machihembra* ('male-female') or *guevotes* ('penis-and-eggs'). In interviews conducted with adults affected by the condition, most said that they were aware of their ambiguous status in childhood and embarrassed about having unusual genitals. They did not feel they were 'real girls'. After the biological changes in puberty most had chosen to be men in adulthood, since they saw it as more desirable. As men, for example, they could become heads of households. But not all individuals did so. One person who moved to live in the USA, for instance, came under family pressure to retain the female gender.

Studies conducted in Papua New Guinea found that experienced midwives there have developed the capacity to recognize the condition at birth (Herdt, 1990; Herdt and Davidson, 1988). When this happens, such children are reared as boys in anticipation of the biological changes that will occur at puberty. However, boys so assigned are generally seen as incapable of achieving full adult male status (since they will be sterile and have a small penis). Consequently they are not allowed to go through all the necessary rituals for becoming a man, and, as adults, tend to be treated as less than fully male and hence as of lower status.

But for children where the condition went unrecognized at birth and who were therefore reared as girls, the outcome is different. They usually retain their assignment as female into adolescence, and initially try to live as women. Since it is common to marry young in this culture, they often marry before their bodies have fully changed. When the change happens they are usually rejected by the men they marry. But then, when they try to live as men, they are socially ostracized. Since they have not undergone any of the rituals required for achieving manhood, they are accorded an identity as neither-male-nor-female: *kwolu-aatowol*. If they leave their villages they can 'pass' as men. Some did so and were able to live relatively 'normal' lives. But for those who stayed within their own communities, their gender was so 'damaged' that they are treated as social misfits.

These studies of the 5-alpha-reductase deficiency syndrome allow us to explore the relationship between the biological and socially constructed aspects of gender. Biology – in the sense of an individual's genetic make-up and hence physiology – is not open to change (not yet, anyway). Surgery and medication can be used to transform a person's physical appearance and produce an apparent sex change. A man can be given a fair approximation of a woman's body, and vice versa. But whether the sex change happens 'naturally' (through a syndrome leading to masculinization at puberty) or through human intervention, simply changing the physical body does not mean that a person's gender automatically changes. Gender is much more resistant to change than that.

While being born with 5-alpha-reductase deficiency is a 'biological fact', its *effects* are cultural and social. They depend upon the person's social and cultural location and circumstances:

- If the individual lived in the USA, for example, they could choose to undergo reconstructive surgery and to live as a woman. As long as she were able to behave as a woman, she could be accepted as an ordinary member of her community.

- In the Dominican Republic an individual seen as *guevedoces* can become a man, albeit one of low status relative to other men. He could become the head of a household, thereby gaining a more powerful social position than if he were a woman.

- An individual described as *kwolu-aatowol* living in the village of their birth in Papua New Guinea is seen as neither male nor female. They cannot perform the 'natural' role of a woman – and so cannot be a woman. But they also cannot be a man, since they are not allowed to acquire full manhood by performing the necessary rituals. Consequently they face lifelong ostracism and exclusion.

4.4 Gender matters

Looking at these anthropological examples shows us that not only does gender matter, but *how* it matters is strongly affected by when and where a child's childhood is located. Some theorists have taken the analysis a stage further, notably Judith Butler. It was Butler who claimed that it is gender that produces sex, not sex that produces gender. This argument led Butler into what may appear at first sight an even more radical one – that sex is a fiction: 'If gender is the social construction of sex, and if there is no access to this "sex" except by means of its construction, then it appears not only that sex is absorbed by gender, but that "sex" becomes something like a fiction' (Butler, 1993, p. 5).

Now, by the term 'fiction', Butler is not suggesting that sexual characteristics (such as having a penis) do not exist. Nor is she denying the very potent influence of sex – quite the opposite. She is saying that our understanding of it is – like that of a movie or a play or a novel – the product of human creativity and inventiveness. Its apparent powerful reality arises because human conduct and human knowledge about the world are so enmeshed in an understanding of what it means to be female or male that we cannot escape from seeing people as defined by their sex – their maleness or femaleness – and hence as 'gendered'.

Butler views genderedness (that is, having and being a gender) as a profoundly powerful feature of an individual's identity, both for them and for others. It is there in everything we feel, think and do; pervading all our experiences and perceptions (though often at an unconscious level). Moreover, she stresses that its presence is not just woven into individual thoughts and feelings: it permeates throughout culture. In the modern world it is there in the books people read, the films they watch, the clothes they wear and the commodities they buy. Even when people think they are ignoring it – responding as themselves and treating others in ways in which gender is irrelevant – it is, nevertheless, constantly there and always exerting an influence.

For this reason Butler argues that while people may have some degree of control over their gender, they cannot choose to have it or not, or how it will be manifested. However much an individual may want to avoid being gendered, they cannot. Social, cultural and historical forces are powerfully 'gendering'. Through the discourses that construct the worlds in which people live, they position people – adults and children alike – as 'gendered subjects', whether they like it or not.

4.5 Social constructionist research

Social constructionist research is conducted from a different standpoint from the scientific approach. An important element of what it sets out is 'deconstruction', which you were introduced to in Chapters 1 and 2.

Deconstruction involves analysing a standpoint or argument, looking to see what has been avoided or left out or covered up, the avenues which could have been taken (but were not), and the use of taken-for-granted concepts.

Usually attributed to the French philosopher Jaques Derrida (1972), deconstruction involves scrutinizing the ways in which something (such as gender) has been socially constructed and what its consequences are. Deconstruction can be applied to all sort of things – an image, a piece of talk or writing, a definition, or, say, a theory. Deconstruction is not about destroying something. Rather it's a very meticulous 'unpicking' or 'unfolding' (for example, of an argument), looking to see what has been avoided or left out or covered up, the avenues which could have been taken (but were not), and the use of taken-for-granted concepts. Deconstructive research seeks to break away from such taken-for-granted concepts, especially those which pair opposites (e.g. black–white, male–female). Such pairs can be called 'dualisms'. Research into gender is obviously a prime target, given the strength of its assumed dualistic nature.

READING

Turn now to the Reading, an abridged version of 'Children and gender: constructions of difference' by Barrie Thorne (1997). In it she argues that the traditional study of sex differences tends to reify gender and has biased our understanding of gender in childhood. To get a broader picture, research needs to be done in ways that deconstruct the dualistic nature of gender, which Thorne illustrates by referring to her own research in the US. She describes herself as an 'ethnographer', someone who uses close observation and systematic description to conduct research into social groups.

As you read, make notes in answer to the following:

1   According to Thorne, why do we tend to think about gender in childhood in terms of 'oppositional dualisms'?

2   What does she see as the shortcomings of such an attitude?

3   What does she think we should do to move outside of these shortcomings?

COMMENT

Thorne argues that the usual ways of studying children *set out* to discover *differences* (at either an individual or group level) between boys and girls. So it is hardly surprising that differences are what are found. Moreover, much of this work has been done by developmental psychologists using methods which require clear categories and the stripping away of social contexts. These are not suited to exploring the subtleties of social relations within and between the genders.

According to Thorne, the preoccupation with studying children's gender relations in terms of opposites also applies to studies of children's relationships which as a result fail to acknowledge the complex choreography of these relationships. Research portrays the worlds of boys and of girls as separate when they are far from being so. And thus it stereotypes the gendered nature of boys and girls. In so doing it ignores the boys and girls who are on the fringes of these worlds or outside of them.

SUMMARY OF SECTION 4

- Social constructionism argues that in all human societies gender is both taken-for-granted and so pervasive that people tend to assume it is natural. But, social constructionists claim, it is not: gender is constructed through the social and cultural practices whereby people live together.

- Judith Butler argues that it is not sex that produces gender, but gender that produces sex. Sex only matters because of the gendered worlds in which we live. If gender were unimportant and went unnoticed, a child's sex would not matter and child development would not include the acquisition of gender.

- The theory of discursive positioning states that people's gendered identities are not fixed but fluid. Different discourses position gender in different ways. They accord different levels and kinds of power and different means to exercise it. 'Doing gender' through an empowering discourse, for example, makes resistance possible.

- One social constructionist approach to research into gender in childhood seeks to deconstruct the assumed difference between boys and girls. Instead of assuming a simple, oppositional division between masculinity and femininity, it looks instead at the different ways in which masculinity and femininity are 'done'; at the complex relationships within and between genders, and at the effects of context and situation.

5 THE IMPACT OF GENDER ON CHILDHOOD

The last section should have helped you to recognize that boyhood and girlhood are not necessarily as distinctly separate as is often assumed. But this is not to deny that gender is not a construct, nor that it has a massive impact upon children. Indeed, a child's gender can have life-or-death consequences. In this section I will give a few examples of the impact of gender upon childhood.

5.1 A matter of life or death

In Africa, Europe and South America there are slightly more boys born than girls. This is common in other mammals and is seen to have a biological basis, since males tend to be more prone to genetic disorders and hence have a slightly higher death rate in infancy. However, in China, India, Bangladesh and West Asia the records of children's births show relatively much higher numbers of boys than girls. Let me give you a sense of how large the discrepancy is. It has been calculated that if the boy:girl ratios had been the same as in other parts of the world, in the 1980s there would be over 30 million more girls growing up in India and 38 million more girls in China than there actually were (Sen, 1990). So what happened to the missing girls?

The explanation given is that in such countries, sons are more valued than daughters for a variety of reasons, such as providing an heir. In China this is seen to have been exacerbated because of the 'one child' policy, which severely penalized parents if they had more than one child. The 'missing girls' are assumed to have been either aborted before birth or killed at birth.

In the past, there were similar practices in Europe (Johansson, 1984) which, indeed, were often far more extreme. Coleman, for example, by examining a tax census, found instances where there were nearly two-and-a-half times more men than women living in certain areas of France in the ninth century (Coleman, 1976). The selective infanticide of girls is generally attributed to the impact of poverty in times and societies where boys are believed to offer a net gain to the family (for instance, in their capacity to work) and girls a net loss (for example, in requiring a dowry). Gender in such circumstances can be, quite literally, a matter of life or death.

5.2 The consequences of gender

But other consequences, while not so extreme, can also be far reaching.

Allow about 20 minutes

ACTIVITY 6   **The consequences of gender**

What other consequences do you think gender can have for children?

First, make a list of some of the ways in which boys and girls in your community have:

(a) different experiences during childhood;

(b) different opportunities at various ages;

(c) different expectations of them by their families.

When you have done this, think about whether these are mainly due to 'nature' (i.e. biological differences between boys and girls) or to 'nurture' (i.e. social and cultural institutions and practices).

COMMENT

Your answers will depend, of course, on the community in which you live.

In terms of childhood experiences you may have mentioned different responsibilities, such as girls being more involved in domestic tasks such as cooking, fetching water, cleaning and child care than boys. You may have observed that boys and girls tend to play different sports, or that boys tend to spend more time outside the home whereas girls tend to spend more time indoors. Or you might have noted that boys in your community are much more likely than girls to take part in criminal activities.

These differences may show up in the opportunities offered to boys and girls. Perhaps you observed that it is harder for girls to join a football team than boys, but easier for them to take ballet classes. Perhaps boys in your community have better educational opportunities. Or, conversely, boys may be more likely to be excluded from school.

Perhaps you are aware of the way experiences and opportunities have changed since you were a child. The same applies to expectations. For example, during much of the last century in Britain, boys were typically expected to become the wage-earner for their family when they grew up, whereas girls were expected to become mothers who would stay at home bringing up children. By the beginning of the twenty-first century, these expectations had changed significantly, even if gender divisions remain in practice.

Some of these examples can be linked to biological differences. Only girls, for example, will be able to bear children. But I would argue that most of the other differences are predominantly due to social and cultural institutions and practices.

Experiences, opportunities and expectations are usually linked. In order to examine this interplay, let's look again at education. In many countries, girls tend to have fewer educational opportunities than boys. A major reason for this is the traditional expectation that a girl's natural role is to become a wife and a mother. Within this traditional discourse girls are seen not to have the same need for a formal education. Secondly, early marriage can curtail education, since going to school is not seen as compatible with performing the roles of wife and mother (remember Maya whom you met in Chapter 4).

The result is that in poor countries women's level of literacy is, on average, significantly lower than that of men (see Table 1). However, this is not just significant for the girls themselves (for example, in terms of reduced earning capacity). It has knock-on effects. Large-scale statistical studies show that educated women are less likely to die in childbirth and give birth to fewer

children. The children themselves are less likely to die during infancy, are better nourished and suffer less from illnesses (UNICEF, 1999, p. 52). Overall, it has been estimated that for the world's poorest countries, each additional year of schooling available to girls is linked to a 5 to 10 per cent reduction in rates of infant mortality (Schultz, 1993, p. 69). Explanations of why this is so include the benefits of education for a mother's ability to earn a higher income (hence increasing the income coming into the family), her capability to benefit from health education and her capacity to access health services. In response to these findings, increasing girls' and women's access to education has become a high priority in poorer countries – often seen as the most effective strategy for improving children's health.

Table 1 Literacy of men and women compared.

| | Adult literacy rate | | | |
| | 1980 | | 1995–99* | |
	male	female	male	female
Sub-Saharan Africa	50	29	64	46
Middle East and North Africa	57	28	74	53
South Asia	52	24	69	43
East Asia and Pacific	80	56	91	79
Latin America and Caribbean	82	78	89	87
CEE/CIS and Baltic States	-	-	99	95
Industrialized countries	99	97	-	-
Developing countries	68	46	81	66
Least developed countries	47	24	63	44
World	75	58	83	69

* Data refer to the most recent year available during this period.

Source: UNICEF, 2001, p. 93.

5.3 Equal opportunities?

Given the degree of social, historical and cultural diversity in the gender differences in childhood experiences, the expectations of boys and girls and the opportunities offered to them, it is clear that most aspects of gendered childhoods are open to change. And, as the data shown above demonstrate, there are good arguments for making changes. However, changes can be made not only in the years of schooling a girl can receive. Earlier in this chapter I mentioned the changes in girls' mathematics performance in Britain, said by some to be caused by a change in educational methods. These changes were not adopted to promote equal opportunities for girls. But it seems that this is the impact they have had – alongside other social changes such as in girls' aspirations. So now let's look at gender and educational performance in relation to work opportunities in adulthood.

In the UK girls have generally had equal access to schooling for a considerable time. Even so, up until the 1960s they tended to leave school earlier than boys, and to gain fewer qualifications. But since then there has been a gradual rise in girls' achievements in public examinations. In 2001, when I was writing this, girls significantly out-performed boys in terms both of passes and grades in A and AS level examinations in England and Wales. Even in the 1990s, this trend had raised concerns about the consequences for boys:

> Now it is boys who are suffering from low self-esteem, who are less ambitious, less willing to continue in education and more likely than girls to want to start a family. Boys' relative pessimism appears to be affecting their educational performance, setting in motion a vicious spiral as unemployment fuels low aspiration which in turn makes young men unemployable.

(Wilkinson, 1994, pp. 38–9)

However, as noted in an editorial in the *Guardian*, a British newspaper, headed 'Unequal and unfair: Girls beat boys but end up with less pay' (Friday 17 August 2001), girls' better exam achievements are not reflected in their pay when adult. At university young women are now outperforming young men (except in the proportion gaining first-class degrees – and here the gap is narrowing), but women in full-time jobs in the UK still earn 82 per cent of the average hourly pay of men in full-time jobs (Equal Opportunities Commission, 2001).

In other words, even when girls are given equal educational opportunities in childhood, and even where girls' academic performance in childhood is better than boys', their opportunities in adulthood – in the workplace and the boardroom – remain heavily curtailed by their gender.

Some argue that this discrimination should be removed and applaud the evidence that this is happening. Wilkinson (1994), for instance, has suggested that there is a 'genderquake' underway in the UK. She argued that as a result of young women's changing values (favouring their careers rather than roles as wives and mothers as the focus for their aspirations), of the 'feminization' of work and a shift from manufacturing to service industry, women will rapidly achieve parity in the world of work. Others are less sanguine. While they have advocated equal opportunities, they are less optimistic about outcomes, saying that gender discrimination is so deeply entrenched it will not be removed easily or quickly.

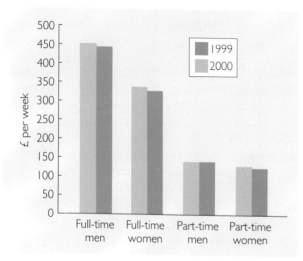

Figure 3 Male and female average gross weekly earnings in the UK, 1999 and 2000 (April of each year) (data from Office for National Statistics, 2000 and 2001).

SUMMARY OF SECTION 5

- A child's gender will have a significant impact on their experiences of childhood, their aspirations and expectations, and their opportunities. However, this impact will differ according to the child's social, cultural and economic location, their particular circumstances, and the child's own character and behaviour.

- Children's education is an example of how a child's gender influences their childhood. In the South, as a general trend, girls receive less education than boys. This not only limits their opportunities (for example in their access to employment), but can have a detrimental effect on *their* children, since the better educated a mother, the greater chance her children have of survival.

- In the North there is more equal access to education for girls. In the UK, there is a trend for girls to outperform boys at school. However, so far at least, this advantage does not result in greater earning capacity or equal access to the most powerful positions.

6 REVIEW

In this chapter you have seen that gender in childhood is a complex matter and that it has been theorized and researched in a variety of ways. Let us end by briefly reviewing these, and their implications for social policy and practice.

6.1 Scientific and social constructionist approaches

Scientific theory and research have provided extensive knowledge about the biological processes and mechanisms through which children are born male or female, and develop into men and women. It has also informed us about the social processes through which girls and boys acquire their gender, and learn about how to behave in gender-appropriate ways. Social constructionist theory and research have expanded our understanding by highlighting the fluidity, complexity and subtlety of gender, both within and between cultures, historical times and socio-economic settings.

6.2 Nature or nurture?

Most theorists acknowledge that a child's gender is moulded and shaped by both biology and socio-cultural influences. But they differ in which of these they consider most important. Biological theories view sex differences as mainly the product of *nature*. They see them as 'wired in' by the genes, and as manifested through physiology (e.g. the influence of hormones) and brain organization (e.g. the effects of lateralization).

Socio-cultural theories view gender as mainly a product of *nurture*. They view gender as something children acquire through the way they are nurtured and reared, and do in their social interactions, and through the influence of social, cultural and economic practices and institutions of the world in which they live.

Social constructionist theory sees the nature/nurture debate as misconceived. It views gender as constructed through the meaning-making that goes on at a social and cultural level as well as at an individual level. Gender is not something that is acquired passively, but something that people continually *do*. Gender is something all of us – adults and children – have to constantly 'work on'. At the same time, it constantly 'works on' us. From this perspective gender is thus neither a product of 'nature' nor 'nurture' but of discourse.

The theory of discursive positioning is used to explain how this happens. Everyone, it claims, lives in a discursive world wherein a number of competing discourses are continually in play. In different cultures different discourses operate, and their relative importance and dominance also vary from one culture to another. For example, in some cultures the traditional discourse is dominant; in others its influence is less.

By resorting to one discourse rather than another, people – including children – can achieve different outcomes and understandings of themselves. Each offers different strategies for exercising power and for resisting it. Social constructionist theorists argue that gender is always present in discourse, though it is not always the most salient feature. For this reason, while children can and do operate in gender-separated worlds, they don't always do so. Sometimes, for example, they live in worlds where the separation is between the adult world and the world of children.

6.3 Theories and explanations

As I said at the beginning of the chapter, examining the gendered nature of childhood involves considering different theoretical positions (scientific versus social constructionist) and different kinds of explanation (nature/nurture versus gender-as-constructed). The interplay between these is subtle and complex. Table 2 gives a simplified summary of some of the key elements.

6.4 Implications for policy and practice

The different explanations of gender, not surprisingly, are frequently linked to different views on what are strategies for child care, child rearing and the services (such as education) provided for children.

Those who see 'nurture' as the main influence on gender, or who view gender as socially constructed tend to downplay the differences between boys and girls, and to see them as malleable and open to change. They generally advocate the promotion of equal opportunities for, and treatment of, boys and girls, and for moving to an integration of boys' and girls' worlds.

Table 2 Theoretical positions and explanations of sex and gender.

Theoretical position	Sex and gender	Nature and nurture	Research methods	Example
Scientific	Sex is the biological basis upon which gender is overlaid	Sexual differences between males and females are mainly the products of nature	Experiments	Did Shaywitz et. al. (1995) find significant differences in the brains of men and women? p. 191
		Gender differences are mainly the products of nurture	Experiments	Lloyd and Duveen (1990) dressed both male and female babies in either pink or blue: p. 198
Social constructionist	Both sex and gender are socially constructed	To ask whether gender is the product of 'nature' or 'nurture' is to ask the wrong question. Rather we should be asking why gender matters to people and societies	Ethnography, discourse analysis and deconstruction	Thorne (1997) looked at shifting patterns of social interactions between boys and girls according to context and activity: p. 204

By contrast, biological explanations encourage the view that gender differences between boys and girls, men and women are 'natural' and hence largely fixed and subject only to minimal change. They advocate a 'separate worlds' approach to children. For instance, in terms of education and careers guidance, they contend that boys and girls need different treatment, tailored to their different capabilities, attributes and natural inclinations and aspirations. Table 3 summarizes these positions.

Table 3 Implications for policy and practice.

Standpoint	Position on whether gender is open to change	Implications for policy and practice
Theories that view gender as socially constructed	See gender differences as open to change	Policy and practice should be directed to promoting equal opportunities for girls and boys.
Scientific theories of gender as primarily a product of biology	See gender differences as largely unchangeable	'Separate worlds' approach, where policy and practice are directed to enabling girls and boys to have equal – but different – opportunities for optimal development.

The gendered nature of childhood is not in doubt. But how and why this is so is a matter of considerable controversy. I hope that the material covered in this chapter has given you more insight into the different viewpoints, and into their origins and their consequences.

REFERENCES

BANDURA, B. (1986) *Social Foundations of Thought and Action: a social cognitive theory*, Englewood Cliffs (NJ), Prentice-Hall.

BANDURA, B. and WALTERS, R. H. (1963) *Social Learning and Personality Development*, New York, Holt, Rineheart and Winston.

BRANNON, L. (1998) *Gender: Psychological Perspectives*, Boston, Allyn and Bacon.

BUTLER, J. (1993) *Bodies that Matter: on the discursive limits of 'sex'*, London, Routledge.

COLEMAN, E. (1976) 'Infanticide in the early middle ages' in STUARD, S. M. (ed.) *Women in Medieval Society*, Philadelphia, University of Pennsylvania Press.

DERRIDA, J. (1972) *Speech and Phenomena and Other Essays on Husserl's Theory of Signs* (translated by D. B. ALLISON), Evanston (Ill.), Northwest University Press.

DUNN, J. and KENDRICK, C. (1982) *Siblings: love, envy and understanding*, London, Grant McIntyre.

FAGOT, B. I. (1978) 'The influence of sex of child on parental reactions to toddler children', *Child Development*, **49**, pp. 459–65.

FRANCIS, B. (1998) *Power Plays: primary school children's constructions of gender, power and adult work*, Stoke-on-Trent, Trentham.

GESCHWIND, N. and GALABURDA, A. S. (1987) *Cerebral Lateralization*, Cambridge (MA), MIT Press.

HERDT, G. (1990) 'Mistaken gender: 5 (alpha)-reductase hermaphroditism and biological reductionism in sexual identity reconsidered', *American Anthropologist*, **92**, pp. 433–46

HERDT, G. and DAVIDSON, J. (1988) 'The Sambia "turnim-man": sociocultural and clinical aspects of gender formation in male pseudohermaphrodites with 5-alpha-reductase deficiency in Papua New Guinea', *Archives of Sexual Behaviour*, **17**, pp. 33–56.

HYDE, J. S (1981) 'How large are cognitive gender differences: A meta-analysis using ω and d', *American Psychologist*, **36**, pp. 892–901.

JOHANSSON, S. R. (1984) 'Deferred infanticide: excess female mortality during childhood' in HAUSFATER, G. and HARDY, S. B. (eds) *Infanticide: Comparative and Evolutionary Perspectives*, Aldine: New York.

KIMURA,D. (1992) 'Sex differences in the brain', *Scientific American*,September, pp. 119–25.

LEGUIN, U. K. (1969) *The Left Hand of Darkness*, London, Macdonald and Co. Ltd.

LLOYD, B. and DUVEEN, G. (1990) 'A semiotic analysis of the development of social representations of gender' in LLOYD, B. and DUVEEN, G. (eds) *Social Representations and the Development of Knowledge*, Cambridge, Cambridge University Press.

LORBER, J. (1994) *Paradoxes of Gender*, New Haven, Yale University Press.

MACCOBY, E. E. and JACKLIN, C. N. (1974) *The Psychology of Sex Differences*, Stanford (CA), Stanford University Press.

MASON, M. (1992) 'The Integration Alliance: background and manifesto' in BOOTH, T., SWANN, W., MASTERTON, M. and POTTS, P. (eds) (1992) *Learning for All 2: policies for diversity in education*, London, Routledge/The Open University.

MIELL, D. (1995) 'Developing a sense of self' in BARNES, P. (ed.) *Personal, Social and Emotional Development of Children*, Oxford, Blackwell/The Open University.

MOIR, A. and MOIR, B. (1998) *Why Men Don't Iron: the real science of gender studies*, London, HarperCollins.

NSAMENANG, A. B. and LAMB, M. E. (1998) 'Socialization of Nso children in the Bamenda Grassfields of North Cameroon' in WOODHEAD, M., FAULKNER, D. and LITTLETON, K. (eds) *Cultural Worlds of Early Childhood*, London, Routledge/The Open University.

OFFICE FOR NATIONAL STATISTICS (2000 and 2001) *New Earnings Survey 1999* and *New Earnings Survey 2000*, London, National Statistics.

PIERCY, M. (1976) *Woman on the Edge of Time*, New York, Knopf.

RICHARDS, M. P. M. (ed.) (1974) *The Integration of a Child into a Social World*, Cambridge, Cambridge University Press.

SCHULTZ, T. P. (1993) 'Returns to women's education' in KING, E. M. and HILL, M. A. (eds) *Women's Education in Developing Countries*, Baltimore, John Hopkins University Press (for the World Bank).

SEN, A. K. (1990) 'Gender and co-operative conflicts' in TINKER, I. (ed.) *Persistent Inequalities: women and world development*, Oxford, Oxford University Press.

SHAYWITZ, B. A., Shaywitz, S. E., Pugh, K. R. *et al.* (1995) 'Sex differences in the functional organization of the brain for language', *Nature*, **373**, pp. 607–9.

SPRINGER, S. P. and DEUTSCH, G. (1989, 3rd edn) *Left Brain, Right Brain*, New York, W. H. Freeman.

STANGOR, C. and RUBLE, D. N. (1987) 'Development of gender-role knowledge and gender constancy' in LIBEN, L. S. and SIGNORELLA, M. L. (eds) *Children's Gender Schemata*, San Francisco, Jossey-Bass.

THORNE, B. (1997) 'Children and gender: constructions of difference' in GERGEN, M. M. and DAVIS, S. N. (eds) *Towards a New Psychology of Gender*, New York, Routledge.

UNITED NATIONS CHILDREN'S FUND (UNICEF) (1999) *The State of the World's Children: Education*, New York, UNICEF.

UNITED NATIONS CHILDREN'S FUND (UNICEF) (2001) *The State of the World's Children*, New York, UNICEF.

UNITED NATIONS DEVELOPMENT PROGRAMME (UNDP) (1990) *Human Development Report*, New York, United Nations.

WABER, D. (1976) 'Sex differences in cognition: a function of maturation rate?' *Science*, **192**, pp. 572–3.

WALKERDINE, V. (1998) *The Mastery of Reason*, London, Routledge.

WILKINSON, H. (1994) *No Turning Back: generations and the genderquake*, London, Demos.

WILLIS, P. (1977) *Learning to Labour*, London, Saxon House.

Children and gender: constructions of difference

Barrie Thorne

When I first began observing in elementary schools as an ethnographer with gender on my mind, events like the following drew me and my note-taking like a magnet:

> On the playground, a cluster of children played 'girls-chase-the-boys' or 'boys-chase-the-girls' (they used both names). Boys and girls were by definition on different sides. In the back-and-forth of chasing and being chased, they used gender terms ('I'm gonna get that girl'; 'let's go after those boys') rather than individual names for members of the other side. In a combined fourth- and fifth-grade classroom the teacher introduced a math game organized as girls against boys; she would write addition and subtraction problems on the board, and a member of each team would race to be the first to write the correct answer. As the teacher wrote two scorekeeping columns headed 'Beastly Boys' and 'Gossipy Girls', several boys yelled out, 'Noisy girls! Gruesome girls!' while some of the girls laughed. As the game proceeded, the girls sat in a row on top of their desks; sometimes they moved collectively, pushing their hips or whispering, 'Pass it on.' The boys stood along the wall, several reclining against desks ...

On such occasions – when gender divisions were highlighted and 'the girls' and 'the boys' were defined as separate, opposing groups – I felt I was at the heart of the children's gender relations. But these moments are not the whole of social life in elementary schools; at other times boys and girls interacted in relaxed rather than bounded and antagonistic ways. An example from the same fourth- and fifth-grade classroom:

A student teacher had listed various activities on the board and asked students to choose one and sign up for it. Three boys and two girls had chosen to tape record a radio play. The teacher told them they could rehearse in the back of the room. They moved from their desks, settled in chairs at a round table (seated girl-boy-girl-boy-boy), and took turns leaning into the microphone and reading from the script. Now and then they stopped to talk and argue as a group.

I had to press myself to record the details of this situation; it seemed less juicy, less ripe for gendered analysis than the chasing sequence, the math game, or a same-gender group. This disparity in my perception of its relevance led me to ponder our frameworks for thinking about children and gender. These frameworks, which emphasize oppositional dichotomies, neatly fit situations in which boys and girls are organized as separate, bounded groups, and they obscure more relaxed, mixed-gender encounters. What kinds of frameworks can more fully account for the complexity of children's gender relations?

In the last two decades our frameworks for thinking about adults and gender have moved beyond unexamined dualisms toward greater complexity. But when we focus on children, we tend to think in more simplistic terms – perhaps one reason for the lingering power of dualisms (Rosaldo, 1980).

The dualistic model of sex differences

Most of the research on children and gender involves a search either for individual or for group sex differences. Both approaches conceptualize gender in terms of dualisms.

Studies in the 'individual sex differences' tradition typically set out to explore possible statistical correlations between individual sex/gender (usually understood as an unproblematic male/female dichotomy) and a specific piece of behavior or measure of personality. The pieces that have been studied range widely, including such personality traits as self-esteem, intellectual aptitudes like verbal or spatial ability, such motivational structure as need for affiliation, and specific behaviour, for example, the amount of time spent in rough-and-tumble play. Extensive research has studied whether parents and teachers interact (for example, touch or talk) differently with girls and boys. Sex difference studies specify and gauge behaviour (for example, with tests of spatial ability or measures of time spent in rough-and-tumble play or talking with a teacher), aggregate across many individuals, and then look for statistically significant correlations by sex [for reviews of some of the research on sex differences see Maccoby and Jacklin, 1974; Brophy and Good, 1974] ...

But dichotomous portrayals may be unavoidable when one's basic strategy is to compare males and females. Individual sex categories – female/male, women/man, girl/boy – divide the population in half and are marked and sustained by daily social practices of gender display and attribution [see, for example, Kessler and Mckenna, 1978; West and Zimmerman, 1987]. Sex difference research treats these categories as relatively unproblematic and continues binary framing with distinctions like similarity versus difference. Recent proposals to use phrases like 'sex similarities and differences' or 'sex-related differences' provide at best awkward and ambiguous tools for grasping the complexities of gender.

Although the situation is gradually beginning to change, sociologists and anthropologists have largely ceded the study of children to psychologists, who in turn have relegated the study of children to specialists in child development. The social science literature on children and gender reflects this division of labor. The focus has been more on individuals than on social relations, and the favored methods – laboratory experiments, observations organized around preset categories – strip human conduct from the contexts in which it is given meaning...

When psychologists, sociologists, and anthropologists of gender have studied the social relations of children, they have primarily relied on a model of group differences that is founded on the prevalence of gender separation in children's friendships and daily encounters. Every observational study of children's interactions in preschools, elementary schools, and junior high schools in the United States has found a high degree of gender separation in seating choices and in the groups that children form. In a study of sixth- and seventh-graders in a middle school whose enrolment was half Black and half white, Schofield found that while racial separation among the students was extensive, gender separation was even greater [Schofield, 1982].

After documenting widespread gender separation in children's social relations, most researchers have compared the separate worlds of boys and girls. The result is a by now familiar litany of generalized contrasts, usually framed as a series of dualisms: boys' groups are larger, and girls' groups are smaller ('buddies' versus 'best friends'); boys play more often in public, and girls in more private places; boys engage in more rough-and-tumble play, physical fighting, and overt physical conflict than do girls; boys play more organized team sports, and girls engage in more turn-taking play; within same gender groups, boys continually maintain and display hierarchies, while girls organize themselves into shifting alliances.

There are problems with this separate worlds approach ... [First, g]ender separation among children is not so total as the separate worlds rendering suggests, and the amount of separation varies by situation ... Girls and boys interact frequently in most elementary school classrooms, since adults organize much of the activity and usually rely on criteria other than gender. Children often report engaging in more cross-gender play in neighborhoods and in families than they do on school playgrounds; in these less populous situations they may have to cross gender and age categories to find playmates, and there are fewer witnesses to tease girls and boys who choose to be together [Harness Goodwin, in press].

... [Secondly], comparing groups of girls with groups of boys not only neglects the occasions when they are together but also ignores the complex choreography of separation and integration in children's daily interactions. Frequency counts provide snapshots of single moments, but they cannot teach us about the social processes by which gender is used – or overridden or ignored – as a basis for group formation [Thorne, 1983].

Finally, in relying on a series of contrasts to depict the whole, the separate worlds approach exaggerates the coherence of same-gender interaction and glosses extensive variation among boys and among girls. Characterizations of the 'boys' world' suffer from a distortion akin to the 'Big Man Bias' in anthropological ethnographies in which male elites are equated with men in general. Larger, bonded groups of boys figure prominently in Joffe's [1974] ethnographic description of the 'male subculture' of a pre-school, Best's [1983] description of boys in an elementary school, Everhart's [1983] ethnography of a junior high and Cusick's [1973] of a high school, and Willis' [1977] study of working class 'lads' in a vocational secondary school in England. Other less popular, disruptive, dominant, or socially visible boys – and girls (who remain invisible in the majority of school ethnographies) – appear at the edges of these portrayals, but their standpoints and experiences are voiced only indirectly ...

In the fourth- and fifth-grade class in which I was a participant observer, a relatively stable group of four to six boys (often joined by a girl who successfully crossed gender boundaries) sat together in the classroom and the lunchroom and moved around the playground as a group, playing the team sports of every season. Because of the group's size, physicality, and the social dominance, it *seemed* to be the core of the 'boys' world' in that classroom ... But other fourth- and fifth-grade boys did not fit the model. Three of them were loners who avoided sports, preferred to stay indoors, and hung out at the edges of the playground. Three more were involved in an intense dyad-into-triad-pattern similar to the social organization often generalized as typical of girls' friendships. Two boys were recent immigrants from Mexico, spoke little English, were marginal in most classroom interaction, and on the playground often joined six to ten other Spanish-speaking, non-bilingual children in an ongoing game of dodgeball that was more mixed in gender and age than any other recurring playground group.

Depictions of girls' social relations have also masked considerable variation. While the fourth- and fifth-grade girls I observed often used a language of 'best friends' (dyads and triads did figure centrally in their social relationships), they also regularly organized into groups of five to seven doing 'tricks' on the bars or playing jump rope. ... Girls' social relations are usually depicted as more cooperative than those of boys, but ethnographers have documented patterns of dispute and competition in girls' interactions with one another, including ritual insults that are often said to be typical of boys [Harness Goodwin and Goodwin, 1988]. Boys' social relations are usually claimed to be more hierarchical than girls', but type of activity affects mode of interaction. The group of neighborhood girls Goodwin studied constructed hierarchies when they played house [Harness Goodwin, in press]. But when the girls engaged in a task activity like making rings from the rims of glass bottles, their interactions were more collaborative and egalitarian.

[...]

Social contexts and the relative salience of gender

[...] A different perspective emerges when one shifts from individuals to group life, with close attention to social contexts. ... When children play 'boys-chase-the-girls', gender is basic to the organization and symbolism of the encounter. Group gender boundaries are charged with titillating ambiguity and danger, and girls and boys become by definition separate teams or sides.

[...]

Gender-marked moments seem to express core truths: that boys and girls are separate and fundamentally different as individuals and as groups. They help sustain a sense of dualism in the face of enormous variation and complex circumstances. But the complexities are also part of the story. In daily school life many situations are organized along lines other than gender, and girls and boys interact in relaxed and non-gender-marked ways. For example, children often play handball and dodgeball in mixed groups; girls and boys sometimes sit together and converse in a relaxed way in classrooms, the cafeteria, or the library. Collective projects, like the radio play described earlier, often draw girls and boys together and diminish the salience of gender.

Children's gender relations can be understood only if we map the full array of their interactions – occasions when boys and girls are together as well as those when they separate ... To grasp the fluctuating significance of gender in social life, we must examine encounters where gender seems largely irrelevant as well as those where it is symbolically and organizationally central.

[...]

Multiple standpoints

Exploring varied standpoints on a given set of gender relations is another strategy for deconstructing a too coherent, dichotomous portrayal of girls' groups versus boys' groups and for developing a more complex understanding of gender relations. Children who are popular or marginal, those defined as troublemakers or good students, and those who are more or less likely to cross gender boundaries have different experiences of the same situations. Their varied experiences – intricately constructed by and helping to construct gender, social class, ethnicity, age and individual characteristics – provide multiple vantage points on the complexity of children's social worlds.

An array of social types, including the bully, the troublemaker, the sissy, the tomboy, and the isolate populates both fictional and social science literature on children in schools. If we shift from types to processes, we can get a better hold on the experiences these terms convey. For example, the terms tomboy and sissy take complicated social processes – changing gender boundaries and a continuum of crossing – and reify them into individual essences or conditions (for example, 'tomboyism'). Crossing involves definition, activity, and the extent to which a child has a regular place in the other gender's social networks. Boys who frequently seek access to predominately female groups and activities ('sissies') are more often harassed and teased by both boys and girls. But girls who frequently play with boys ('tomboys') are much less often stigmatized, and they continue to maintain ties with girls, a probable reason that, especially in the later years of elementary school, crossing by girls is far more frequent than crossing by boys.

[...] Unitary notions like the girls' world and girls versus boys are inadequate for this sort of analysis. Instead, one must grapple with multiple standpoints, complex and even contradictory meanings, and the varying salience of gender.

References

BARTH, F. (1969) *Ethnic Groups and Boundaries*, Boston, Little Brown.

BEST, R. (1983) *We've All Got Scars*, Bloomington, Indiana University Press

BROPHY, J. E. and GOOD, T. L. (1974) *Teacher, Student Relations*, New York, Holt, Rinehart.

CUSICK, P. A. (1973) *Inside High School*, New York, Holt, Rhinehart and Winston.

EVERHART, R. B. (1983) *Reading, Writing and Resistance,* Boston, Routledge & Kegan Paul.

HARNESS GOODWIN, M. (in press) *Conversational Practices in a Peer Group of Urban Black Children*, Bloomington, Indiana University Press.

HARNESS GOODWIN and GOODWIN, C. (1988) 'Children's arguing' in PHILIPS, S., STEELE, S. and TANZ, C. (eds) *Language, Gender and Sex in Comparative Perspective*, Cambridge, Cambridge University Press.

JOFFE, C. (1974) 'As the twig is bent ' in STACEY, J., BEREAUD, S and DANIEL, J. (eds) *And Jill came Tumbling After*, New York, Dell, pp. 79–90.

KESSLER, S. J. and MCKENNA, W. (1978) *Gender: an ethnomethodological approach*, New York, John Wiley.

MACCOBY, E. and JACKLIN, C. (1974) *The Psychology of Sex Differences*, Stanford, Stanford University Press

ROSALDO, M. S. (1980) 'The use and abuse of anthropology: reflections on feminism and cross cultural understanding', *Signs*, **5**, pp. 389–417.

SCHOFIELD, J. (1982) *Black and White in School*, New York, Praeger.

THORNE, B. (1983) 'An analysis of gender and social groupings' in RICHARDSON, L. and TAYLOR, V. (eds) *Feminist Frontiers*, Reading (Mass.), Addison-Wesley, pp. 61–63.

THORNE, B. (1985) 'Crossing the gender divide: what "tomboys" can teach us about processes of gender separation among children', unpublished paper presented at 1985 meeting of the society for research on Child Development, Toronto.

WEST, C. and ZINNERMAN, D. (1987) 'Doing gender', *Gender and Society*, **1**, pp. 125–51.

WILLIS, P. (1977) *Learning to Labour*, New York, Columbia University Press.

Source

THORNE, B. (1997) 'Children and gender: constructions of difference' in GERGEN, M. M. and DAVIS, S. N. (eds) *Towards a New Psychology of Gender*, New York, Routledge, pp. 185–202.

Chapter 6

Innocence and Experience

Mary Jane Kehily and Heather Montgomery

CONTENTS

When you have studied this chapter, you should be able to:

1   Discuss the concept of childhood innocence and some of the ways in which this concept is evident in textual and visual representations of children.

2   Develop ways of reading and analysing representations of children.

3   Explore, and gain insight into, some of the practical consequences for children of the ways in which they are presumed to be innocent.

4   Understand the negotiation that goes on between adults and children over constructions of innocence, especially in relation to sexuality.

5   Discuss the relationship between innocence and evil in relation to children.

I CHILDHOOD AS A TIME OF INNOCENCE?

In the preceding chapters of this book you have been asked to look at childhood from different and contrasting perspectives. You have also been introduced to children in different parts of the world and have been asked to reflect upon the fundamental question, 'What is a child?' One of the underlying themes of the book has been about how far innocence is a defining feature of childhood. In other words, how far are children seen as immature, developing human beings who need protection, or as competent, participating social actors? Chapter 2 described the origin of discourses around children's innocence, through the work of Jean-Jacques Rousseau and looked also at conflicting discourses which view children as naturally evil (exemplified in the work of Thomas Hobbes). It also looked at the tension in Judaeo-Christian theology concerning the issue of whether children were naturally innocent or born in original sin.

In this chapter we will examine the idea of children and innocence in more detail, arguing that innocence is a problematic term with several different meanings. The idea of childhood innocence is further complicated by the range of childhoods that exist. Obviously, not all children under eighteen are seen as innocent; a group of seventeen year olds may well appear as threatening rather than innocent, and age, ethnicity, gender and class all influence ideas of childhood innocence. We will look at how far children can indeed be seen as innocent and, in contrast, what happens when children 'lose' their innocence. In particular, we will focus on British and North American images and representations of childhood innocence and examine what they say about childhood. We will draw our examples from, among other things, advertisements, fiction and newspapers. Our focus on these forms aims to encourage you to read representations as *texts* – cultural products such as advertisements that construct children in particular ways. Innocence and evil can be seen as powerful themes within representations of children that have a bearing on the way people think about childhood more generally.

1.1 Approaches to innocence

By focusing on images and representations, this chapter emphasizes social constructionist approaches, but it should be remembered that these images have important social implications. Earlier in this book, you were introduced to three different ways of approaching childhood: through a scientific study of children's development, as a social construction or through policy. All three of these standpoints influence ideas about childhood innocence. The three positions can be summarized in the following way:

1   The scientific approach looks at the ways that science informs and revises beliefs and practices through theories and evidence about children's 'actual' innocence and understanding about morality and sexuality. This approach was illustrated by developmental research into children's cognitive development, and moral and social understanding in Chapters 1 and 3.

2   There are powerful cultural representations that inform the way adults think, write about, represent and challenge notions of children's innocence. This social constructionist approach was introduced in Chapter 1, elaborated in Chapter 2 and it is the main emphasis of this chapter.

3   A policy approach examines how beliefs about childhood innocence shape the regulation of children's lives through laws and practices. Chapter 1 introduced this theme in relation to the age of criminal responsibility, and Chapter 4 touched on similar themes in contrasting protectionist versus participatory approaches to children's rights. In this chapter, we will refer to another way children's lives are regulated through age of consent legislation.

In short, the emphasis of this chapter is mainly on social constructionist approaches to the study of images and representations of childhood innocence. The chapter will inevitably raise sensitive issues, especially around children's sexuality and protection from abuse. Detailed discussion of policies and practice in child protection are beyond the scope of this chapter (but see, for example, Stainton Rogers *et al.*, 1992).

1.2 What is innocence?

Allow about 10 minutes | ACTIVITY 1   **What do you understand by innocence?**

Think about what innocence means to you in relation to children. Write down as many different associations as you can think of. It might be worth comparing your responses with someone from a different generation. For example, were your parents' experiences as children different from your own? If you are a parent, do you think your views on protecting children's innocence are different from your parents'?

COMMENT

There are several ways of looking at innocence. You may view innocence as the opposite of evil or (in Judaeo-Christian terms) as a lack of sin. You might understand it as the opposite of guilty. You may see innocence as a lack of certain forms of knowledge, as a form of ignorance of things that children should not know about, such as drugs or sex or difficult emotions such as hatred or grief. You may have considered innocence as a guileless form of naivety, a lack of knowledge that is difficult to protect and impossible to maintain. You may see innocence as synonymous with purity and virtue and, in particular, with sexual purity. You may see innocence as the natural, universal state of children, or conversely as a social construct. Innocence might be something that you see as applicable to all children, or only to some children in certain circumstances.

If you managed to ask people of a different generation the same question, you might have noticed very different attitudes. Older generations in Britain frequently talk about how much more innocent they were than today's children, especially where sexual knowledge and experience is concerned. But in other respects they may feel they were less innocent and more worldly-wise, for example if they had to cope with hardships associated with poverty or if they experienced war.

It is important to emphasize here that there are no right answers to the question 'What is innocence?' Instead, there are competing norms, values and experiences linked, for example, not only to age but also to social class, religious beliefs and many other influences that shape people's beliefs about childhood.

Activity 1 illustrated ways in which innocence is a problematic category that conveys a range of different and sometimes ambiguous meanings. This chapter explores some of these different meanings, as well as some ambiguities and contradictions in the way the concept is applied. In later sections we explore two aspects of innocence in some detail, in relation to child sexuality (Section 3) and child crime (Section 4). But first we explore some broader connotations of innocence (and experience) and look at the ways these influence the way children are treated. For example we asked two mothers of four year olds in a small, English market town, what innocence meant to them. Their replies show how concerns about violence and about the negative images purveyed by television, affect their views of children's innocence.

Elaine, mother of twins Rachel and Camilla:

'I'd like to bring the children up in a safe environment, and try and protect them from certain things. I got very concerned about the television, and what they were watching and felt that I didn't want them to be associated with violent acts, that I felt they were acting out. So I've stopped that. [Children] are bothered about fashion, and I do see some children who are obviously wearing high heels when they're younger and things, and I don't want [my children] to go down that line.'

Amanda, mother of Max:

'I don't think children are children for as long as they were when I was young. They're far too knowing.'

(The Open University, 2003)

There are also, of course, many different views on what constitutes a threat to innocence. Some parents might think that news reports of suffering or death damage their children's innocence and will try to protect their children from seeing them, while others may wish their children to be informed about world events. Others may encourage their children to learn about sex through sex education but might be worried about violence on TV. Innocence is a complex concept with multiple interpretations.

1.3 Historical representations of childhood innocence

This chapter takes its title from William Blake's series of poems, *Songs of Innocence and Experience*. The poems below, written in 1789 and 1793 respectively, present two contrasting images of the child: the child of joy and the child of sorrow.

Infant Joy

'I have no name –
I am but two days old .'
What shall I call thee?
'I happy am,
Joy is my name.'
Sweet joy befall thee!

Pretty joy!
Sweet joy but two days old –
Sweet joy I call thee.
Thou dost smile,
I sing the while –
Sweet joy befall thee!

Infant Sorrow

My mother groaned, my father wept –
Into the dangerous world I leapt,
Helpless, naked, piping loud,
Like a fiend hid in a cloud.

Struggling in my father's hands,
Striving against my swaddling bands,
Bound and weary, I thought best
To sulk upon my mother's breast.

In both poems the child is being used to represent and comment upon broader ideas about society and human nature. Like the philosophers discussed in Chapter 2, Blake wrote about what he regarded as universal

Infant Joy

I have no name
I am but two days old .—
What shall I call thee ?
I happy am
Joy is my name ,—
Sweet joy befall thee !

Pretty joy !
Sweet joy but two days old.
Sweet joy I call thee;
Thou dost smile.
I sing the while
Sweet joy befall thee.

William Blake's own illustration of his poem, 'Infant Joy'.

attributes of human beings, in particular on the contradictions of the human soul. The child of the poems can be seen symbolically as a manifestation of opposing ideas, such as: good/bad; light/dark; happiness/misery; innocence/experience. The pretty, smiling child, giving and receiving joy can be contrasted with the 'fiend' in swaddling bands, struggling into a world full of danger. Reading the two poems together, 'Infant Joy' and 'Infant Sorrow' creatively suggest that childhood innocence exists in relation to its opposite, experience or lack of innocence.

INFANT SORROW

My mother groand! my father wept,
Into the dangerous world I leapt:
Helpless, naked, piping loud:
Like a fiend hid in a cloud.

Struggling in my fathers hands:
Striving against my swaddling bands
Bound and weary I thought best
To sulk upon my mothers breast

William Blake's own illustration of his poem, 'Infant Sorrow'.

Blake called his 1789 poems (from which 'Infant Joy' is taken) *Songs of Innocence* and his 1793 set *Songs of Experience*, suggesting that innocence gives way to often bitter experience during a person's life. This theme is powerfully illustrated in the quote below, taken from *London Labour and the London Poor*, written by Henry Mayhew and published in 1861. Mayhew was a social commentator who observed at first hand the lives of working class people in London. His detailed descriptions provide us with a rich social history of life and conditions in nineteenth century England.

Watercress girl

The little watercress girl who gave me the following statement, although only eight years of age, had entirely lost all childish ways, and was, indeed, in thoughts and manner, a woman. There was something cruelly pathetic in hearing this infant, so young that her features had scarcely formed themselves, talking of the bitterest struggles of life, with the calm earnestness of one who had endured them all. I did not know how to talk with her. At first I treated her as a child, speaking on childish subjects; so that I might, by being familiar with her, remove all shyness, and get her to narrate her life freely. I asked her about her toys and her games and her companions; but the look of amazement that answered me soon put an end to any attempt at fun on my part. I then talked to her about the parks, and whether she ever went to them. 'The parks!' she replied in wonder, 'where are they?' I explained to her, telling her they were large open places with green grass and tall trees, where beautiful carriages drove about, and people walked for pleasure, and children played. Her eyes brightened up a little as I spoke; and she asked, half doubtingly, 'Would they let such as me go there – just to look?' All her knowledge seemed to begin and end with watercresses, and what they fetched. She knew no more of London than that part she had seen on her rounds ... Her little face, pale and thin with privation, was wrinkled where the dimples ought to have been, and she would sigh frequently. [...] 'I go about the streets with water-creases, crying, "Four bunches a penny, water-creases." ... On and off, I've been very near a twelvemonth in the streets.'

(Mayhew, 1861, p. 151)

Henry Mayhew's description of the watercress girl expresses his sense of surprise that a child of eight has 'lost all childish ways'. Mayhew begins by positioning her as a child and speaking to her about 'childish subjects' such as playing with toys, playing with friends and going to the park. The watercress girl, however, is not familiar with this aspect of childhood and has no experience of playing for pleasure. Mayhew then draws our attention to the material circumstances of the girl's existence: she is unhealthy, under-nourished and barely educated and she has become accustomed to a life of hardship. Mayhew is moved by the child's description of her life to the point where he finds her account 'cruelly pathetic'. From this description we can deduce something of what Mayhew's expectations of childhood may be. It would be reasonable to suggest that Mayhew views childhood as a period of life where innocence is protected, where play and carefree pleasure are indulged, where the child is protected from adult experiences such as work and where she is cared for, kept warm and well fed. The watercress girl challenges Mayhew's concept of childhood and disturbs his notion of what a child is and how a child behaves. Hence his difficulty seeing someone so young, talking to her as a child, while simultaneously recognizing that she is not child-like and in fact is 'in thoughts and manner, a woman'. The account can also be seen and understood in terms of social class. Mayhew's description of the watercress girl implies that, in his eyes, she has been deprived of her childhood. Her innocence is lost through work, hardship and knowledge and experience of the adult world.

Images of childhood innocence are not just conveyed through contrast with the corrupting effect of experience. In Western culture, romantic images of childhood innocence sit alongside equally compelling images of childhood wickedness and sin. We introduced this contrast in Chapters 1 and 2, and it is developed further in the next reading.

READING

Now read Reading A. In this, Marina Warner discusses the contradictory notions of children as evil and children as innocent and applies them to representations of children in European literature.

There is much to absorb from this reading. Warner draws on a wide range of literary examples and her own language is quite poetic in places. (She sometimes presents assertions that she does not give evidence for and with which you may disagree.) Warner is trying to convey the complex and contested nature of childhood innocence, and she explores many different aspects of the theme.

As you read, make a note of these different aspects of innocence.

COMMENT

As Warner points out, discourses around childhood innocence are complex and inconsistent. She points to at least six distinct areas that inform understandings of childhood innocence and experience.

Children as 'innocents':

Children are naturally innocent, pure and virtuous. They are uncontaminated by the adult world of corruption that exists beyond their immediate experience and poses an ever-present danger to their young minds and bodies.

Children as blank slates:

Children are innocent because they are blank slates. Like Casper Hauser, they have no knowledge, no experience and no wickedness or indeed any sense that others might wish them harm.

Children as agents of redemption:

Children's innocence is redemptive. Children, as seen in characters such as Peter Pan, the boy who never grew up, will always have the innocence, the lack of cynicism and the childish wonder that adults have discarded.

Childhood as the basis of adult identity (psychoanalytical understandings of the child):

Psychoanalytical theories emphasize the links between the child and the adult. Childhood is the key to an adult's identity. The child's experiences shape the adult psyche. Any psychological injury done to a child will lead to a damaged adult.

Childhood as a separate state:

Children are innocent because they are outside society. They have no knowledge of life or of social organization. They exist in a special uncorrupted state, separate from the adult world.

Children as consumers:

Children's innocence is being lost by pushing them into the economic market place as consumers. Modern Western societies position them as economic consumers 'pestering' their parents to buy them goods that advertisers market directly to them.

Warner's article briefly mentions all these ways of looking at childhood innocence and, of course, many of these ideas are linked and interrelated at particular moments. You may well be able to think of several more and you may not agree with the ones she has used. However, she is undoubtedly right to point to the tensions and unease that ideas about children's innocence raise.

In the remaining sections of this chapter we will focus upon the ways in which aspects of childhood innocence in the contemporary era can be disrupted by dangerous knowledge and unlawful action. We will look specifically at childhood innocence as a contested area that is challenged by issues of sexuality and violence.

SUMMARY OF SECTION I

- Ideas about children's innocence are difficult and sometimes contradictory.
- Innocence has several connotations and is a contested concept.
- There are several ways of seeing innocence; it can be seen as:
    - a lack of knowledge, particularly of sex and violence;
    - a lack of experience of the adult world, especially in relation to issues such as sex, money, work, grief or hatred;
    - a lack of evil or sin;
    - synonymous with purity and virtue;
    - related to lack of knowledge of economics and consumerism;
    - inherent to children.

2 IMAGES OF INNOCENCE AND EXPERIENCE

ACTIVITY 2   Children and advertisements

Allow about 20 minutes

The three images of children on the page opposite are taken from recent television advertisements, screened in the UK. Make notes on whether you think the children are portrayed as innocent, and in what sense.

COMMENT

These images are all from advertisements; therefore they are trying to elicit particular responses and to sell a product. Associations of innocence are thus being utilized for profit. In the Peugeot advertsiement, innocence is associated with vulnerability, with an adult's fantasy of rescuing an innocent child – a helpless, unprotected girl. Although the association with childhood innocence may seem tenuous, this image would not have been so powerful if it involved an adult rescuing another adult. It is the innocence of the child and the need to protect her from the dangers of the outside world that reinforces ideas of innocence. In the Evian advertisement, innocence is directly related to purity. There is nothing more pure, this advertisement states, than a newborn child. These children are innocent because they are pure; they lack knowledge, experience, and any idea of wrongdoing. Their bodies are also pure because of their diet. These are not children who have eaten junk food, alcohol, coffee or any of the things that adults eat and drink and whose effects they attempt to ameliorate by drinking pure Evian water. In the Gap advertisement, children are represented differently again. They are older, dressed in the latest fashions but they are still pre-sexual. The clothing company has been careful to present the children as energetic and fun-loving rather than sexy or seductive. They are acknowledging that these children have some knowledge of adult concerns and the affairs of the wider world, in this case, fashion and music, but the dangerous world of sex is not one they participate in.

'Search for the hero inside yourself.'
(Advertisement for Peugeot cars.)

Gap girl sings, 'I saw momma kissing Santa.'
(Advertisement for Gap clothes.)

'L'Evian. Live young.' (Advertisement for Evian mineral water.)

2.1 Contemporary images of childhood innocence

Images of children in advertisements are not always employed to sell a product. They are also widely used in charity campaigns in order to comment on the concept of childhood, sometimes in overtly ideological ways. Barnardo's is a leading children's charity based in the UK. Originally set up to run orphanages, Barnardo's remit is now significantly different. Barnardo's no longer run children's homes but they continue to be involved in many charitable projects to support children and young people. Barnardo's describe their approach to caring for children in the twenty-first century in the following way:

> Children have only one chance of a childhood. They deserve to be protected from harm, to enjoy good emotional, mental and physical health and to feel that they belong in their home and community.
>
> Sadly, for many children, the reality is very different. But Barnardo's believes that it is never too early or late to offer a helping hand – and to give the most disadvantaged youngsters the chance of a better childhood and happier future.
>
> (*Giving children back their future*, Barnardo's, 1999)

Like other charities Barnardo's rely upon donations from the public and are constantly engaged in fund-raising ventures to support their work and promote the public profile of the organization. In October 1999 Barnardo's launched an advertising campaign in newspapers and magazines to raise awareness of their work with children. The series of advertisements portrayed children in a variety of 'adult' situations: homelessness, drug and alcohol abuse, prostitution, suicide and prison.

Allow about 20 minutes

ACTIVITY 3   **Damaged children**

The images on pages 233 and 234 are taken from the Barnardo's advertising campaign discussed above. Look at the advertisements and complete the following tasks:

1   Make a note of your responses to each advertisement. Include initial reactions and thoughts that may occur to you when you have had a little time to reflect upon the image.

2   Try to suggest some reasons for your responses.

3   What do the Barnardo's advertisements suggest about the link between childhood and adulthood?

COMMENT

Your responses to the advertisements may have included initial feelings of shock and revulsion. The Barnardo's advertising campaign, particularly the image of a baby injecting drugs, aroused a great deal of controversy. In the face of public protest Barnardo's replaced the image with one of a happier baby without the syringe and tourniquet. But why is the image such a shocking one? It could be argued that the power of the image lies in the fact that it deliberately and self-consciously transgresses boundaries. While

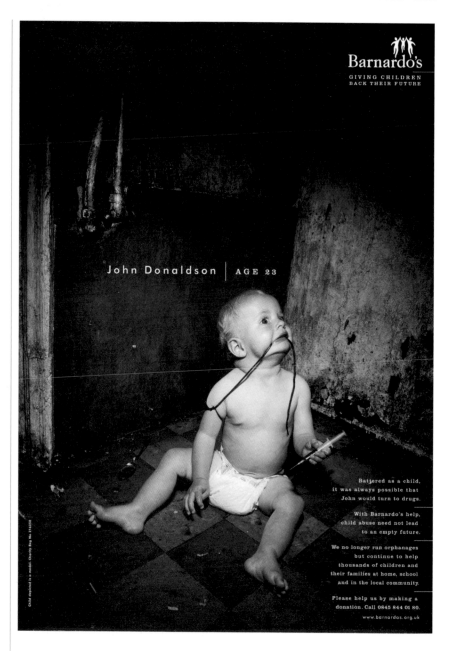

'Battered as a child, it was always possible that John would turn to drugs. With Barnardo's help, child abuse need not lead to an empty future.'

it is generally accepted that adults have knowledge of the world of drug use, it is usually assumed that children should be protected from such knowledge. To see a baby who is not only exposed to the reality of drug use but actually participating in it, can be seen as a violation of generally held sensibilities about appropriate knowledge and behaviour. Yet all drug users were, of course, once babies. And this is the point that the Barnardo's advertisement makes very forcefully; that children's environment and experiences have a bearing on their adult life.

From the perspective of the charity, the link between abused childhood and troubled adulthood calls for intervention and change summarized

'Neglected as a child, it was always possible Kim would be an easy victim for pimps. With Barnardo's help, an unhappy childhood need not mean an empty future.'

in the Barnardo's logo, 'Giving children back their future'. The Barnardo's advertisements suggest several things: that children deserve to have a future and that they represent the future; that childhood should be a time of innocence where children are protected from harmful knowledge such as drugs and sex; that these children exist in a cycle of abuse, which suggests that damaged children lead to damaged adults who may, in turn, damage their own children.

This campaign also draws upon the three ways of looking at childhood that this book has introduced to you. These posters claim that:

1   Children are not intrinsically innocent but have been constructed as such by adults who have chosen to see them as innocent (a social constructionist claim) despite evidence that children are taking drugs.

2   Children are unknowing and naive (a scientific claim), so they must be protected from the harsh world of drugs.

3   Children must be protected (a policy claim) because if children's innocence is abused this will lead to severe problems for themselves and for society as they grow up.

The age issue here is crucial. One of the reasons that these images are so effective is that while an adult may turn to drink, drugs or prostitution, the images in conjunction with childhood violate notions of what childhood should be about.

Allow about 10 minutes

ACTIVITY 4   Damaged youth

Look at the pictures again and imagine a teenage 'John Donaldson' rather than a one-year-old or a sixteen-year-old Kim rather than a six-year-old. What would be the impact of such photos on you? Would they have been less dramatic? Would your sympathy for the child be less? If so, why?

COMMENT

Barnardo's obviously chose images that delivered the greatest possible impact. The contrast between the innocent child and the damaged adult that these children might become lies at their heart. By substituting the images of young children for older ones, it becomes clear that the age difference is very significant. Although innocence is associated with children, children become less innocent and less dependent as they grow up. Adolescence in particular is not constructed as a period of innocence – indeed it could be characterized as a period of 'guilty knowledge' of sex, drugs and rebellion. Small children (in this case a one year old and a six year old) are vulnerable, needing adult protection and are innocent of the consequences of their actions. A one-year-old toddler would not knowingly inject heroin. Teenagers however, are more problematic; they may well choose to take heroin, and a picture of a teenager with a needle in his arm may well elicit disgust and fear rather than sympathy. Both a one year old and a sixteen year old are children but innocence is more likely to be associated with the toddler than the teenager.

SUMMARY OF SECTION 2

- Images of innocence are used by advertising companies and charities such as Barnardo's. Commercial advertising tends to emphasize the uncorrupted innocence of children to sell products, whereas groups like Barnardo's stress the catastrophic effects of knowledge and experience on children.

- Innocence is also graded. Children become less innocent as they become older and innocence tends to be associated with younger, more dependent and more vulnerable children.

3 CHILDHOOD AND SEXUALITY

In this section we will look more closely at issues of childhood innocence and awareness in relation to sexuality. We will examine the ways in which issues of sexuality have the power to disrupt adult conceptualizations of childhood and to challenge notions about childhood. Following on from the previous chapter, which looked at the ways in which children are gendered and the relationship between sex and gender, we will also examine how ideas about sexuality are related to ideas about gender. Discussions of children's sexual innocence are shaped not only by the age of a child, but also by whether the child is a girl or a boy.

In the British context, sociologist Stevi Jackson (1982) has commented on the way in which discussions of children and sex remain controversial. Her analysis suggests that children are defined by adults as a 'special category of people' deserving of our sympathy and protection. At the same time sexuality is usually defined as a 'special area of life' that is the preserve of adults. Hence, Jackson points to the formation of a powerful social taboo – that children and sex should be kept apart:

> Our feelings about children and sex are not a natural response to people of a particular age but result from the way childhood is defined within our society.

(Jackson, 1982, p. 22)

Western ideas about sexuality are entrenched in the notion of 'naturalness'. Human sexuality is commonly seen as inherent and biological, driven by instincts that parallel the animal world. However sex is a social behaviour that only makes sense to people within a specific context and with a specific intent. The ways in which sexuality varies and changes across cultures and across time refute the notion of a biologically defined sexuality. Consequently what people may understand and experience as erotic may be different in different societies. It is not possible therefore to make universal statements about the nature of children's sexual awareness as every society draws on different (and often contested) discourses concerning appropriate expressions of children's sexuality and behaviour.

Individual parental practices also reflect beliefs about what is natural, normal and healthy and this in turn shapes children's awareness or innocence. Attitudes towards, for example, children's masturbation depend on the gender of the child, class, epoch and culture and show the difficulties of talking about children's expression of sexuality as if this were a natural, biological fact. The varieties of injunctions and instruments used by Victorian middle class parents to control children's masturbation has been well documented, from devices to ensure that children could not reach their genitals to warnings that it caused blindness and insanity. Today, many Western parents may implicitly recognize that their children masturbate but social taboos against its revelation still exist.

Other societies have profoundly different attitudes towards children and sex, and in some societies, children are encouraged to have early sexual experience. Amongst the Canela, an Amerindian community living in

Brazil, it is considered necessary and desirable for a girl to have multiple sexual partners from a young age (around 9 or 10) both before her marriage (which takes place around 11) and after (Crocker and Crocker, 1994). This is a society without a word for innocence, especially sexual innocence. This might seem unusual or unnatural to an audience outside this community but it shows that sexual behaviour is not a natural, biological, universal process but is interpreted by societies in different ways. In other societies, such as those of the Mediterranean or the Middle East, concepts and values of honour, shame and innocence do exist and are strongly upheld, especially in relation to girls' sexual behaviour (Peristiany, 1966). In such societies, the honour of the men is dependent on their ability to control the sexual behaviour of their daughters, sisters and wives.

Sexual acts vary between cultures, as do the meanings ascribed to them. For instance, in some parts of rural Thailand, and in many parts of the Middle East, a crying baby boy is comforted by his mother playing with or sucking his genitals, an activity known as gentling. This soothes the child and helps him to sleep and is considered a normal and totally asexual part of caring for a child. A mother doing the same in Britain or America might be prosecuted for child abuse. The act itself is the same but the intention behind it is very different. We must be very wary therefore about making cross-cultural generalizations about universal or natural sexual behaviours. However, in most cultures sexuality is marked by the creation of moral and symbolic boundaries which have implications for children. Similarly most societies construct differences between appropriate and acceptable forms of sexuality for boys and girls.

Sigmund Freud challenged conventional views on child sexuality.

Of course, beliefs about child sexuality are not static. Conventional views in Western societies were strongly challenged by Sigmund Freud (1856–1939), the originator of psychoanalysis. Freud popularized the notion of the innately sexual child and viewed sexuality in childhood as part of the natural developmental process. Although Freud's work has been heavily criticized since (especially by feminist writers who argue that Freud ignored evidence of actual child sexual abuse because he would not, and could not, believe in it), it is important to look at his work because so many of his concepts, such as the Oedipus complex, the death wish and penis envy, are well known, even by those who have not read him. It is his views on infantile sexuality (concerning children under the age of four) which are most pertinent here and which tie discussions of children's innocence to the developmental perspective discussed in Chapter 3. Freud wrote:

> It is a part of popular belief about the sexual impulse that it is absent in childhood and that it first appears in the period of life known as puberty. This, though an obvious error, is a serious one in its consequences and is chiefly due to our present ignorance of the fundamental principles of the sexual life. [...] No author has to my knowledge recognized the lawfulness of the sexual impulse in childhood, and in the numerous writings on the development of the child the chapter on 'Sexual Development' is usually passed over.

(Freud, 1909, cited in Kessen, 1965, pp. 247–8)

In Freud's view children are innately sexual from birth and puberty is not the beginning of sexual feelings and activity. Freud believed that childhood activities such as thumb sucking or touching of the genitals (in both boys and girls) should be seen in their sexual context, as part of a child's growing sexual nature which the adult world aims to bring under control and repress. Freud viewed childhood sexuality as biologically given and not as a social construct.

There is, however, a problem inherent in Freud's work in that he does not look at the issue of intention. Young children may know that playing with their genitals gives them pleasure but do they know that it is sexual pleasure? If they are unaware of the sexual meaning of the act, then to label it as sexual is very problematic. It would be very easy to argue that children may be aware of sexual sensation but still be sexually innocent. There is no clear answer of course as to when children do become sexually aware as it is conditioned by multiple factors such as upbringing, cultural and historical context.

The issue of when children become aware that their feelings and sensations are sexual and label them as such is ambiguous. This is exemplified in the writing of Australian novelist, Patrick White, who writes an account of boyhood friends in Sydney:

> We saw a lot of each other as young boys. Hilary was welcome at our house, after school, and for week-ends. We cut up a frog in the bath to watch its heart movement, we smoked a cheroot under the buhl [brass and tortoiseshell] table in the hall, and we masturbated together in bed. We were quick to tidy up and it seemed to me at the time my parents were unaware of any of these activities. They must have been. For the friendship was brought to an abrupt end. It filtered back to me through maids' chatter and innuendo from the masters that my friend was an unhealthy influence ...

(White, 1986, p. 11)

Reactions to these boys will be strongly conditioned by their ages. This piece itself is ambiguous; it starts by referring to young boys but cheroots and shared masturbation sounds more like pubertal boys. Yet what follows suggests older boys because they are self consciously aware that their activity is sexual. In this recollection masturbation is mentioned casually alongside other boyish activities such as smoking and cutting up frogs. The boys' speed to tidy up suggests that they were aware that they were breaking a number of taboos, of which the most serious were masturbation and homosexuality. They are clearly aware that their actions would be considered sexual by their parents and understand their behaviour in the light of the social constructions of sexuality around them. This short passage also illustrates a further point about children's innocence; that it is not simply something that adults project onto children. Children themselves are part of the process, especially adolescents, protecting their parents from knowledge about their sexuality. Children too, share discourses of what is natural or taboo.

READING

At this point you should read Reading B. This reading concerns girls of around twelve who are sexually aware and knowing and the way in which they manipulate a man's sexuality. It is written by a contemporary novelist, Oonya Kempadoo, and is set in Guyana. Note that it is written in a Caribbean dialect and some of the words and spellings may be unfamiliar.

COMMENT

Oonya Kempadoo captures a sense of the girls' sexual awareness through a description of their lives and activities as told by the central character. The girls are alert and knowledgeable in many ways; they know all the secrets of the house and all the particularities of their neighbourhood. They know that Uncle Joe is always willing to help and eager to please. Finding him asleep, the girls indulge in a rush of curiosity to see his genitals. The mixture of excitement and repulsion they feel produces hilarity among the girls – an outpouring of laughter that can be seen as a celebration of their playfulness, naughtiness and sexual daring. Inspired by their success, the girls taunt Joe about Miss Ann. Their mixture of questions, suggestions and provocations points to an acute awareness of the dynamics of sexual attraction, arousal and sexual intercourse. Seeing Uncle Joe's penis is a moment of triumph, wonder and scrutiny. They note its size, colour and texture as a matter of intense interest. It is also interesting to note that it is Uncle Joe who is embarrassed and uneasy rather than the girls. This fictional example offers us a reversal of commonplace understandings about childhood innocence and gives us an insight into one particular group of girls and their relationship to, and understanding of, sexual behaviour.

The extract by White and the reading by Kempadoo both convey an image of children as sexually aware and experienced, even without fully understanding what they are doing. They show the complex relationship between children's agency and awareness of sex. They also show the struggles between adults' views of appropriate sexual expression for children and children's own reality; struggles that depend on many factors such as cultural context or the age and gender of the child. There are of course competing norms within societies as well as cross-culturally.

3.1 Protection and control of children's sexuality

The main emphasis of this chapter is on exploring cultural representations of innocence as revealed through the study of literature, advertising and popular beliefs about childhood. But beliefs about innocence are also expressed through the way societies regulate children's sexual activity, and seek to protect them from abuse. While issues in child protection are beyond the scope of this chapter (as we noted at the outset), we want briefly to draw attention to some of the complexities inherent in the way societies treat this topic, especially as revealed in laws about age of consent.

Beliefs about childhood innocence are closely associated with expectations of sexual ignorance. According to this view, children should not know about sex, and if they do, it is often assumed that there is something wrong. One of the reasons sexual abuse is seen as so damaging to children is because it is an attack on their innocence, which once lost can never be regained. However, there are contradictions in the way societies protect children's innocence. The supposed sexual innocence of children is balanced by the controls that adults place on children's sexual behaviour, especially through laws prohibiting sexual activity before a certain age. If children are sexually innocent and ignorant, then why is children's sexuality controlled and protected? Raising this issue opens up a whole series of further questions.

For example, the age of consent in the UK is sixteen. If it is acknowledged that some children are sexually active before then, what is the reason for a law that forbids children to have sex before this age? Furthermore, why should it be sixteen? In Holland, for instance, it is twelve, in China it is twenty. There is some link between the age of consent and the age of puberty and physical maturation, but this is very tenuous. The age of puberty for young women (in terms of first menstruation) has been falling for over a hundred years and now it is rare for a girl not to have had her first period by the age of sixteen. The age of consent was also much lower 150 years ago. Until 1886, it was twelve in Britain but this was changed after campaigns by early women's groups who were concerned about vulnerable young women being seduced by older men in higher social classes.

To understand these complexities, we must return to the two issues discussed in relation to children's rights in Chapter 4: protection and participation. A person taking a protectionist stance towards children's sexual activity would argue that children might be sexually aware and physically mature before the age of consent but they are not emotionally or mentally ready to make an informed decision about whether or not to have sex. There is also a concern that older people may take advantage of their ignorance and force or cajole them into having sex before they are ready to. Age of consent legislation is necessary to protect children from predatory adults and from the consequences of sexual experience.

A person taking a participatory approach to this might argue that a protectionist stance places sex in a very special position to childhood. Girls and boys of fourteen and fifteen (and sometimes as young as ten) are made to take legal responsibility for their actions, as we will see later in this chapter. They are expected, before the age of sixteen, to make an informed decision about the difference between right and wrong. In the case of sex however, they are not allowed to do so and sex remains unlawful for them. They do not have the right to participate in decisions about sexual activity before the age of sixteen and sex remains forbidden to them.

Age of consent legislation has a strong developmental aspect to it and is based on understandings of how emotionally and intellectually developed children are at certain ages. However a scientific approach cannot fully answer these questions and there is little consensus on what children are able to understand and cope with at what ages. Those who argue that children should be empowered through knowledge, for example through sex education, often face accusations that they are encroaching on childhood, telling children things that they do not need to know as yet and do not have the experience or understanding to cope with. This is countered by writers such as Jenny Kitzinger who argue that 'The twin concepts of innocence and ignorance are vehicles for adult double-standards: a child is ignorant if she doesn't know what adults want her to know, but innocent if she doesn't know what adults don't want her to know' (1997, p. 169).

The issue of sexuality and control has been further taken up by French philosopher Michel Foucault (1926–84). His book, *The History of Sexuality* (1976), argues against the Freudian idea that sex is repressed by adults and by societal structures more generally. His work is important because it highlights the issue of power and sexuality, in particular who controls the sexuality of others. In *The History of Sexuality*, Foucault argues that the control of children's sexuality was a key feature in the development of educational provision and social policy in western Europe. Children's sexuality, in his view, has been constantly monitored since the eighteenth century and children have been kept under surveillance and their bodies regulated. He argues that schools, educationalists, the Church and writers about childhood have paid almost obsessive attention to children's sexuality and are constantly trying to regulate it. The effects of all these attempts at regulation have done nothing to restrict or confine children's sexuality. On the contrary, the proliferation of discourses around sex and, specifically, the sexuality of adolescents, can be seen to increase awareness of sexual matters and thereby serve as a further incentive to talk about sex. Foucault refers to this as a 'discursive explosion'.

3.2 The eroticization of girls

Eroticization means the tendency to sexualise and make desirable persons or things that may not in themselves be sexual.

So far we have discussed the relationship between children and sexuality in fairly general terms, with little acknowledgement of the significance of gender. Beliefs about protecting children's sexual innocence vary immensely according to whether the child is a girl or a boy, and the extent of differentiation between genders is also highly variable, as Chapter 5 made clear. Discussions of children's sexuality are often focused on the ways that girls are represented and eroticized in Western culture. This topic offers particularly powerful evidence of contradictions inherent in the concept of innocence. It also draws attention to the relationship between how images of childhood are represented, how they are perceived, and by whom.

Despite a horror of child abuse and an ideal of sexual innocence for children, girls are often represented in a titillating and sexualized way. The social construction of girls' sexuality is particularly difficult and complex in Western societies as it problematizes ideas about sexual purity and challenges the precarious boundary between a charming, flirtatious and innocent *child* and a sexualized, alluring adolescent. Patricia Holland analyses the eroticization of girls in Western cultures:

> As a child, sexuality is forbidden to her, and it is that very ignorance that makes her the most perfect object of men's desire, the inexperienced woman. Thus the fascinating exchange between knowledge and ignorance reaches beyond the boundary between girl and woman and towards the forbidden attraction of innocence itself ...

(Holland, 1992, p. 127)

In Holland's argument, it is the boundary between sexual innocence and sexual knowledge that is so titillating and which eroticizes girls. This is a difficult and problematic area to deal with as the issue of sexual abuse is not far from the surface. This is evident in the unease many people now feel when looking at Lewis Carroll's suggestive and provocative, and sometimes semi-naked, pictures of young girls (photographed around 1859), including Alice Liddell (his model for *Alice in Wonderland*), which is reproduced as part of Activity 5 below. We cannot know the exact nature of the relationship between Carroll and the girls who posed for him so why are they so unsettling?

Allow about 10 minutes

ACTIVITY 5   Erotic or innocent?

Examine the photographs opposite. Write short notes on all three, commenting on whether you feel the girls in these pictures are eroticized or not. What is it about their clothes, posture and the way they look at the camera that influences you?

COMMENT

In Carroll's picture of Alice Liddell as an urchin, she is posed in a suggestive manner. Her shoulders are bare and her head is tilted coquettishly to one side. It is impossible to say if, in this picture, she is depicted as innocent or not. Although, in no way pornographic, it is suggestive of sexual knowledge and certainly the potential to see this as a seductive image is there. Evelyn Hatch, in the top photograph, is naked and positioned as an adult woman, reclining alluringly on a *chaise longue*. She looks straight at the camera with no hint of demureness or reticence. There is nothing intrinsically pornographic in her pose but a naked child displayed in this way does disturb many people. The picture is ambiguous and any interpretation of it will depend on your own views of what you consider seductive and your ideas about children's sexuality and adults' portrayal of that. In the third picture, Shirley Temple is dressed and there is nothing overtly sexual about the picture. But she is made up, wearing lipstick and could be seen as sexually enticing.

How can we make sense of these issues? One possibility is that the key to understanding childhood innocence lies in the eye of the beholder. You may recall the point in Reading A where Marina Warner says 'It's we who have lost innocent eyes ...' and she notes that Lewis Carroll's friends were undisturbed by semi-naked images of their children. According to this view, what adults view as innocent says very much more about adults than it reveals about childhood. All these pictures are ambiguous and it could be claimed that in all of them the girls are eroticized. The question is, however, by whom, the photographer or the viewer? It is interesting to note that in 1937, the novelist Graham Greene was prosecuted for libel by the child star, Shirley Temple, after he published an article entitled 'Sex and Shirley Temple?' Shirley Temple was a nine-year-old child actress who was golden haired, very cute and the personification of wholesomeness. Greene suggested that the film studio she worked for deliberately promoted her erotic appeal. He was subsequently sued for damages and denounced in court as having committed a 'gross outrage'. Although such a suggestion is

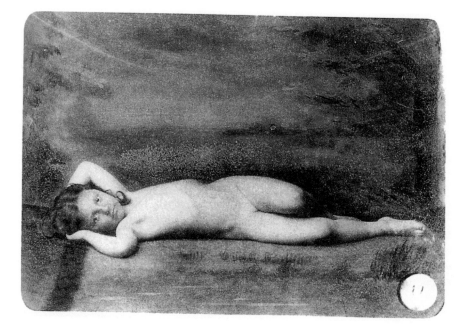

Evelyn Hatch.

Alice Liddell.

Shirley Temple.

not as shocking today, it emphasizes the fine line that exists between innocent children and sexualized older girls. As Patricia Holland pointed out, often this very quality of innocence is seen as erotic.

The most famous (or notorious) example of the eroticization of innocence is Vladimir Nabokov's novel *Lolita*. Some people find this book distasteful in that it represents a relationship between a man in his fifties and a girl of twelve without dealing with the question of abuse. An extract from it has been included here as Reading 3.

Since its publication in 1955, the word 'Lolita' has become synonymous with the eroticization of young girls and specifically the sexual potential of girls and the desires of older men. The term Lolita has been so widely used that it has come to mean a sexually precocious adolescent – a temptress who is in control of her own sexuality and who is the sexual predator. However, while many people know the word Lolita, fewer have read the novel on which it is based. The book is told in the first person by Humbert Humbert, a European professor living in America who has an obsession with pubescent girls whom he calls 'nymphets'. The story concerns his obsession with, and eventual seduction of Dolores 'Lolita' Haze, the twelve-year-old daughter of his landlady, who he later marries in order to be near Lolita. When her mother dies, he becomes Lolita's legal guardian.

READING

Now read the extract from *Lolita* by Vladimir Nabokov. As you are reading it, note the ways in which Humbert eroticizes Lolita.

COMMENT

The book has always been extremely controversial and you may have reacted to it in a number of different ways. One critic called it 'a fusion of the pornographic, the comic and the ironic' (Couturier 1996). Others have seen the book as a glorification of child abuse. On publication, critic Lionel Trilling argued 'in the course of reading the novel, we have come virtually to condone the violation it presents' (Trilling, 1958 cited in Podhoretz 1997, p. 30). Others have been even more explicit '[there is] the possibility that (the book) *Lolita* bears at least some share of the blame for the plague of pedophilia that has been raging through this country' (Podhoretz 1997, p. 35).

Humbert is the classic unreliable narrator. He purportedly writes his book from prison where he is on trial for murdering Lolita's later lover. His speeches are full of self justifications and black humour. However, Lolita is only twelve in this book. Despite Humbert's description of her as a nymphet and therefore inherently sexual, this is an adult projection from a much older man. The contrast between childhood innocence and experience is described by Humbert in the following way:

> Humbert Humbert tried hard to be good. Really and truly, he did. He had the utmost respect for ordinary children, with their purity and vulnerability, and under no circumstances would he have interfered with the innocence of a child, if there was the least risk of a row. But how his heart beat when, among the innocent throng,

he espied a demon child, '*enfant charmante et fourbe*,' dim eyes, bright lips, ten years in jail if you only show her you are looking at her. So life went.

(Nabokov, 1955, pp.19–20)

One of the reasons that a novel such as *Lolita* is so unsettling is that the issue of abuse is never fully articulated. Humbert sees Lolita as sexualized and indeed sexually aware. She is constructed as sexual by Humbert, he chooses to interpret her attitudes and behaviour as sexual whether they are or not. However, she is also legally still a child and possibly in need of protection from an older man's fantasy about her sexuality.

In everyday language, the term Lolita has come to mean a sexually experienced girl (sometimes even called 'jail bait' implying that her sexuality is so tempting to older men, that they are her victims rather than the other way round). It is of course dangerous to draw any conclusions about children from fiction but this example has been included for two reasons. Firstly, it has been included because the word Lolita exists above and beyond this book (although its meaning in the wider world is not necessarily consistent with the story of the book) and secondly, because it points to the unstable boundaries between sexual innocence and sexual experience. For Humbert, the gestures and behaviour of young girls manage to be innocent and erotic at the same time. In the novel, he constantly notices details of clothing and manner that draw his attention to the prepubescent body of such girls. Their child-like femininity fuels Humbert's desire and in different moments he refers to these girls as 'nymphets', 'demons' and 'darlings'.

Lolita from the 1997 film *Lolita* directed by Adrian Lyne.

This section has focused on childhood innocence in relation to issues of sexuality. The discussions you have been asked to engage with have raised many troubling questions about innocence, experience and sexual awareness. We have suggested that childhood innocence is not inherent to children. Rather, it is adults who link children with ideas of innocence. Adult views and interpretations of childhood innocence form powerful notions that shape and define what is appropriate for children to know and do. In the next section we will discuss some other challenging issues that also call into question children's innocence. In particular we will look at children's involvement in acts of criminality.

SUMMARY OF SECTION 3

- Children's awareness and experience of sex are conditioned by age, culture, gender and parental expectation.
- Freud argued that all children are inherently sexual and that this sexuality was repressed by their society.
- Critics of Freud claim that different forms and expressions of sexuality are culturally specific.
- Foucault argued that attempts to repress sexuality have had the opposite effect. He suggests that since the eighteenth century societies have developed new ways of talking about sex, categorizing sexual activity and defining people in terms of their sexual identity. All of these developments produce new forms of control and regulation.
- In relation to the sexuality of girls, some commentators point to the eroticization of pubescent girls in Western cultures and the unstable boundary between innocence and experience. This is exemplified in the novel, *Lolita*.
- The eye of the beholder is responsible for making associations and interpretations and this is done within specific cultural and historical contexts.

4 CHILDHOOD AND CRIME

The dominant assumption discussed in the early part of this chapter is that children are in need of protection from the dangers of the adult world. The Barnardo's advertisement of John Donaldson provides an arresting image to suggest that children should be shielded from the world of drug-use for their own protection and for their future well-being. The discussion of age of consent legislation suggested a similar need for children to be protected from sex. What, then, happens to the concept of childhood innocence when children actively engage in crime? In this final section, we return to the topic introduced in Chapter 1, about the way competing discourses of childhood shape the treatment of children who offend, especially when children commit very serious crimes like murder. In the same way that dominant images of childhood innocence are challenged by the eroticized child, they are also challenged by images of the criminal child. But in this case, alternative discourses of childhood are available, notably the 'little devils', 'little monsters' and 'little beasts' mentioned by Marina Warner in Reading A and discussed more fully in Chapter 2. Whereas girls are the main focus of concern about sexual innocence, boys are most often the focus of concern in relation to child crime.

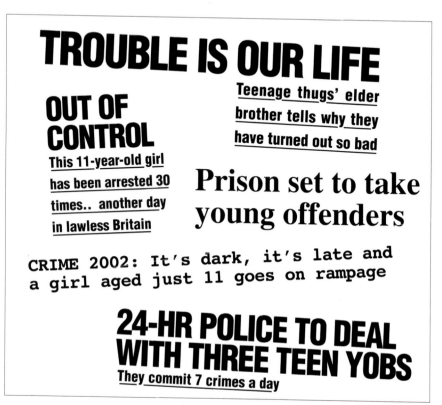

Headlines about child criminals.

The following examples are taken from a broadsheet newspaper in the UK. The headlines read:

Kinder Surprise kid, 14, who ran drugs empire

Court hears how prolific dealer in heroin and crack cocaine was a boy who stashed wares in chocolate treat.

(*Guardian G2*, 4 August 2001, p. 2)

Chronicle of a death foretold

In 1993 an 11-year-old crashed a stolen car through a neighbour's fence. When he later appeared on television cavorting in a black ski mask he became Balaclava Boy – Britain's most delinquent child. Seven years and 40 convictions later, he died after a suspected drugs overdose while in police custody.

(*Guardian G2*, 15 May 2000, p. 2)

The first point to note in relation to children and crime is that children who participate in acts of criminality become newsworthy. Their behaviour and their lives become the subject of media interest and scrutiny. In the examples above the individuals themselves acquire nicknames; the Kinder Surprise Kid and Balaclava Boy become epithets that attempt to characterize both who they are and what they do. Interestingly their names conjure up boy heroes of the fictional kind – Wonder-Boy, the Milky Bar Kid, the Boy Robin. The boys in the *Guardian* reports, however, neatly invert the boy-hero stereotype by becoming anti-heroes for a brief, inglorious moment. Secondly, there is an element of shock and surprise that children behave in this way. The ingenuity of the Kinder Surprise Kid and the energy of Balaclava Boy exist as examples of aberrant, unchild-like behaviour.

Allow about 20 minutes

ACTIVITY 6   Children and crime

Read the following extract from the newspaper report on Balaclava Boy cited above. Complete the following tasks:

1   List the ways in which Balaclava Boy unsettles contemporary notions of childhood innocence.

2   Suggest some ways in which the actions of the boy can be understood.

Chronicle of a death foretold

Gareth Brogden came to the nation's attention in February 1993 and was promptly adopted as a symbol of everything wrong with it. He was 11, the fourth child of one of the West View estate's large, criminal families. Harry Brogden Snr owns a roofing business and most recently went to jail for defrauding a customer; his brother-in-law is a veteran offender and his oldest son is serving a five-year sentence for heroin dealing. When Gareth made his criminal debut by crashing a stolen Vauxhall Astra through a neighbour's fence, no one was surprised.

It was what happened when a television crew from Tyne Tees turned up that made Gareth's name. He and his cronies pulled on black ski masks and capered about in front of the cameras. 'It was the police's fault,' he yelled. 'They rammed me and I'm only 11.' He stuck up two fingers and boasted that the authorities couldn't touch him. Within the week, Gareth's stunt had made the national news and was being held up in the House of Commons as a symbol of the Tory government's failure to deal with juvenile delinquency. Within a month, the image of Gareth sticking two fingers up to the world was on flyers for a local rock band, the White Negroes, and he was well on his way to becoming that dangerous thing, a decontextualized icon.

Rat Boy, Spider Boy, Homing Pigeon Boy: all have emerged from the housing estates of the north east [of England] and knocked around the news reports until their infamy burned out. Balaclava Boy produced a more enduring outrage. 'This is behaviour that scars the very fabric of our society,' said Tony Blair, then shadow home secretary, appropriating Gareth as a benchmark of delinquency that made all his future offences interesting to the press.

[...]

... Gareth's delinquency was initially tolerated because, like his father, he had charm ...

He was 'into everything', say friends, to the extent that, before the incident with the cameras, Gareth would intersperse his ruffian habits with sudden flights of Boy Scout goodness. 'He could be a little thug, nicking money off other kids,' says a West View resident who has lived there for the past 20 years. 'But then he would come to you and say, "Have you got some water?" and the next thing you knew he was washing your car. And he didn't want money for it. He could be like two different people.'

If he was trying out different shades of his personality, he hit upon the most comfortable one at the age of 11 when, having been excluded from school for poor attendance, he started joyriding and hanging out in a gang. His family has portrayed him as a gopher, led astray by older boys, but residents remember him more as the cocky, mouthy kid at the centre of trouble. 'Before he became Balaclava Boy, he was just a naughty kid,' says one. 'Afterwards, he was a criminal with something to live up to.'

[...]

One night in February, there was a knock at his mother's door and Gareth was taken into police custody on suspected drugs charges. Before he could be charged, he started experiencing breathing difficulties. Police say he had swallowed the drugs in his possession. Gareth slipped into a coma and died at the hospital he was born in, two weeks later.

(Brockes, 2000, pp. 2–3)

COMMENT

Like the two Blake poems at the beginning of this chapter, Gareth Brogden can be seen as a child born of joy and sorrow. The biographical details outlined in the newspaper report suggest that he lived and played out aspects of innocence and experience, goodness and evil, during his 18-year life. The charming boy who helped neighbours was also the joyrider, juvenile delinquent and drug user. The newspaper report indicates that one way of understanding Gareth's behaviour is to place him within the context of his immediate environment. Gareth grew up on a working class housing estate in an area of England that was once famous for its industrial enterprise and is now associated with post industrial decline, urban decay and social problems. The heritage of the locality is reflected in Gareth's family history: he was born into a large family that is known for their involvement in criminal activities. Put in these terms, it would be easy to pathologize Gareth, to see him as a product of his circumstances and, simultaneously, as a victim of his circumstances. However, the newspaper report suggests that the narrative of Gareth's life has a troubling twist that hinges around the involvement of the media. It is suggested that media coverage of the joyriding incident when Gareth was 11, turned a naughty kid into Balaclava Boy – a symbol of delinquency that gave him an image and a reputation to live up to.

To pathologize means a tendency to see individuals as inherently culpable, blameworthy and deviant.

4.1 Children who kill

So far we have looked at one contemporary example of a child who is involved in criminal activities. In this section we will explore these ideas a little further by taking the most extreme challenge to the idea that children are innocent – when children kill. In such cases the concept of childhood innocence carries some different connotations. A suspect is 'innocent' until they are proved 'guilty'. How does guilty as opposed to innocent apply to a child? Is it right to talk about a child being innocent even if they have also been found guilty of a serious crime? How far is it a question of 'innocence' versus 'experience'? The key issue we wish to emphasize here concerns children's knowledge. How much can adults expect children to know about the consequences of their actions, about morality or even about the finality of death? This raises other important questions about how adults respond to children who are not seen as innocent. Should the transgressing sexual innocent (who needs protection) be treated differently from the transgressing moral innocent (who needs to be punished)?

To explore these questions we will discuss two murders committed by children in Britain and Norway and compare the responses of the public, the authorities and the media to them. The Bulger case in Britain has already been mentioned in Chapter 1, along with the Raedergard case in Norway. There are differences between them in the age of the killers and the premeditation involved, and the aim is not to view them as identical. Nor is it the aim of this section to take sides or to suggest that one way of dealing with children and viewing children is better than others. However, a comparison of these two cases illustrates the point that childhood innocence is a construct of an adult society rather than an intrinsic and natural part of childhood. It also makes the point that there is no one age or developmental stage when children can be said to understand moral reasoning and that the ways in which children's capability to understand the consequences of their actions are measured depend on the society into which they are born. Consequently, the ways in which childhood capacities are enshrined in law and social policy have profound effects on the way children are treated (see Chapters 1, 4 and 5).

Liverpool, UK: the Bulger case

The murder of James Bulger, including its aftermath and repercussions, was a key event in Britain in the 1990s. It led to many newspaper editorials and commentaries on the nature of childhood, even though the case itself was remarkable for its very rarity. (The number of children killed by other children over the last 150 years has remained extremely low and totally constant: Smith, 1994). In 1993 James Bulger, a two-year-old boy, was shopping with his mother in Liverpool and wandered off. He was found and led away by two ten-year-old boys, Jon Venables and Robert Thompson, who subsequently assaulted and killed him and left his body on a railway line. The case appalled people in Britain for many reasons: the age of the murderers, the fact that they were caught on close-circuit television camera and images of them abducting James were broadcast on national television, and the indifference of passers-by who seeing James in distress being led away by his killers did nothing to help. The case opened up a public debate over the nature of children and childhood and the contrasting representations of children, with children such as James representing pure innocence and his killers, pure evil. The case continues to be bitterly contested and the release of the killers in June 2001 was extremely controversial.

Sections of the British public and media reacted to the two killers in an emotive and savage way. As the boys were taken to court a mob gathered outside the courtroom screaming for them to be given the death penalty. The courts decided that they should be tried as adults, in an adult court with none of the privileges usually accorded to children in such circumstances. They were found guilty and sentenced by the judge, Mr Justice Morland, to be detained 'for very, very many years, until the Home Secretary is satisfied that you have matured and are fully rehabilitated and are no longer a danger to others' (quoted in Morrison, 1998). In the words of the judge, 'The killing of James Bulger was an act of unparalleled evil and barbarity', while one police officer was quoted as saying, 'I truly believe they are just evil'. A colleague of his reinforced this with the words: 'You should not compare these boys with other boys. They were evil.' (All quoted in Morrison, 1998.) The newspapers weighed in: the *Sun's* headline read 'The Devil Himself Couldn't Have Made A Better Job Of Two Fiends', the *Mirror* called them 'Freaks of Nature' noting that although they had 'the faces of normal boys ... they had hearts of unparalleled evil' and the *Daily Star* said simply 'How Do You Feel Now You Little Bastards?' (quoted in Davis and Bourhill, 1997, p. 47).

The age of the killers was crucial and the laws of criminal responsibility in England and Wales are worth considering in more detail. As discussed in Chapters 1 and 4, there is no fixed age for moving into adulthood in England and Wales, despite the fact that for most administrative and state purposes (such as marriage or voting), the age of majority is eighteen. For legal purposes however, the issue concerned *doli incapax*, the idea that children cannot be held responsible for actions that they were too young to *knowingly* commit. (As discussed in Chapter 3, theories based on research by developmental psychologists about when a child is capable of mature reasoning and moral judgement are important here.) Until 1998, English law stated that under the age of ten, no child could be held criminally responsible. Over the age of fourteen, they were held accountable for their crimes although usually tried in a juvenile court. Between the age of ten and fourteen, however, the notion of *doli incapax* came into play. Children could be held responsible for their crimes, if it was proved that they knew what they were doing. In 1998, the Crime and Disorder Act abolished this distinction making all children over the age of ten responsible for the crimes they commit. However Thompson and Venables were tried before this act came into force and therefore, in their case, the question of *doli incapax* became important. Psychiatrists evaluated Venables and Thompson and decided that they were of 'normal intelligence'. They also said that any reasonable ten-year-old could distinguish between right and wrong and that consequently Venables and Thompson should be tried for murder in an adult court.

ACTIVITY 7   Guilt and knowledge

Read the passage by Blake Morrison below. He reported on the trial of Thompson and Venables and wrote a best selling book about it afterwards, entitled *As If*. He argues strongly that the killers of James Bulger were in some ways innocent despite their crime. What does he mean by innocence? What do those who claim that Venables and Thompson were guilty mean by this? Do you think that innocence and ignorance are the same thing? How convincing are his arguments?

I have a four-year-old who believes the man in the moon is real – who believes the moon *is* a man. Other four-year-olds have similar beliefs. They think the mannequins in shop windows are dead people. They think the sea's there because someone left the tap running. They wonder who the sun belongs to, and whether heaven has a floor, and why people aren't in two all the way up. I know seven-year-olds who believe in the Easter Bunny and the tooth fairy. I know nine-year-olds who believe in Father Christmas. (I know forty-year-olds who think God lives in the sky and wears a white gown.) Long may it live, this belief in magic ... But don't tell me four-year-olds know the difference between right and wrong.

And eight-year-olds, ten-year-olds? They understand the difference better, but can they act on that understanding? Did I? At ten I stole a Ferrari – a Dinky toy belonging to my cousin Richard ... I knew I was doing wrong but desire – such a good feeling, which as a child I hadn't learnt to distrust – made it feel right ... I had moral sense but not moral conviction. How could I have conviction? I was a child.

Rousseau writes of a boy killing a bird *without knowing what he does*. The phrase is reminiscent of Christ's: 'Forgive them father, for they know not what they do.' Special pleading from the cross: that people sometimes kill in ignorance, even innocence, and should not be eternally punished for their sin.

The basis of *doli incapax* is similar: that before the age of reason, children can't be held responsible. When does the age of reason begin? Every country has its own answer, its own baseline: it's eight in Scotland, ten in England, Wales and Northern Ireland, twelve in Canada, thirteen in Israel, fifteen in Norway, sixteen in Cuba – and in Romania eighteen. The mad arbitrariness. And see how low the British come. Low is the word. Maybe Rousseau was right, or no less wrong than we are, to measure reason in inches rather than years: 'Childhood has its ways of seeing, thinking and feeling which are proper to it. Nothing is less sensible than to want to substitute ours for theirs, and I would like as little to insist that a ten-year-old be five feet tall as that he possess judgment.' Robert [Venables] is four foot six, Jon [Thompson] four foot eight.

[...]

God knows, adults find it hard enough to act on their knowledge of right and wrong. Can children, whose sense of right and wrong is newer but dimmer, fresher but fuzzier, act with the same clear moral sense? Do they grasp that badly hurting someone is much more wrong

than stealing and truanting (which T & V had got away with for months)? Do they have a sense of the awful irreversibility of battering a child to death with bricks? Can death have the same meaning for them as it has for an adult? I submit, your Honour, that the answer to these questions is no, no, no
and no.

(Morrison, 1998, pp. 99–101)

COMMENT

Morrison argues that, as children of ten, James Bulger's killers could have had no real sense of the consequences of their actions and that therefore they cannot be seen as truly guilty or held responsible. He is arguing from a belief that all children are innocent because they do not know the difference between wrong and right. Others, in the media and the justice system saw the learning of knowledge, especially about right and wrong, as a continuum and that by ten, children should know not to kill and what the consequence of beating and abusing a smaller child will be. The nature of the debate however centres on the notion of innocence. Morrison and many like him argue that all children are naturally innocent and therefore incapable of evil while others, such as the newspaper editors quoted earlier, suggest James's killers were innately evil and that normal children, the innocents, had to be protected from these aberrations.

Morrison's comments are eloquent and persuasive but they also need to be examined critically and analysed with caution. His comparison of stealing a Dinky toy with a brutal murder may strike many people as absurd in the same way as comparing petty theft to brutal murder by an adult would be. In Chapter 1 you were given several comments concerning the age of criminal responsibility and there is a wide range of opinion about the moment when children should have to take responsibility. In this instance, Venables and Thompson were judged as being able to understand the difference between right and wrong, between murder and letting James go.

Trondheim, Norway: the Raedergard case

A year after James's death, a child was murdered by children in the small Norwegian town of Trondheim. In 1993, five-year-old Silje Marie Raedergard was playing with two boys aged six when the game turned violent. They stripped her, beat her unconscious and then ran away leaving her to freeze to death in the snow. Despite the shock the case caused, the people of Trondheim, including Silje's mother, reacted very differently to Silje's killers. Although many people in the town knew who the killers were, their names were never published and they were protected from the media. The boys lived on the same housing estate as Silje and her family, and as soon as news of her murder was made public, the police and the local school teacher opened up the school that both boys and Silje attended and talked to both children and parents, stressing how safe the children were and appealing for calm and no vengeance. Meanwhile the mother of one of the boys who had killed Silje said 'Please remember that we are dealing with small children here. I cannot continue living here if my son is to be called a killer for the rest of his life' (Franklin and Petley, 1996, p. 148). Two days later, the killers went back to this school, accompanied by psychologists. There were no protests and no parents withdrew their own children. The *Guardian* reported the local paper's attitude; 'the culprits were just six years old; how did they know what they were doing? In Norway, where the age of criminality is 15 – as opposed to 10 in Britain – they were treated as victims not killers' (Hattenstone, 2000).

Silje's mother's reaction was also extraordinary. The day after the murder she appealed that the boys should be left alone and not subjected to a witch-hunt. She said: 'I forgive those who killed my daughter. It is not possible to hate small children. They do not understand the consequences of what they have done ... I can sympathize with the boys' parents. They must be going through a lot now. I do not know all of them yet, but they are welcome to contact me if they so wish' (Franklin and Petley, 1996, p. 148). Despite the fact that she still suffers from post-traumatic stress as a result of her daughter's murder and rarely goes out, she maintains that the boys should not be imprisoned 'No they were punished enough by what they did. They have to live with that. I think everybody has got to be treated like a human being. The children had to be educated, had to learn how to treat other people so they could get back into society' (Hattenstone, 2000). 'If these boys would have been treated like adults and locked up, they would have lost out on so much; their grasp of reality, how society works. They wouldn't cope with being put on the streets at 18. Would they have learnt anything? I don't think so' (Sturton, 2000).

There is a difference of course in the age of the killers. At six, Silje's killers were too young to be tried in either Norway or Britain. It may also be easier to accept that children of six do not know what they are doing while children of ten do. However, a comparison of these two cases reveals that ideas about children's innocence are not simply tied to ideas about age and social expectations, what children can be expected to know and how far and at what ages they have developed a moral consciousness and ability to reason. If Thompson and Venables had been Norwegian, there would have been no question about whether or not they would have stood trial, they simply could not, because the Norwegian legal system does not recognize that children under the age of fifteen can be guilty.

The biggest difference between the cases was the discussion that they provoked about the very nature of childhood. The killers in Trondheim were seen as much as victims as Silje herself and were counselled and reintegrated into society as soon as possible. The crime, while shocking, occasioned no great debate about childhood. In Britain, however, the murderers became symbolic of evil children out of control. On their release in 2001, the killers of James Bulger were not reintegrated into their communities, they were given new names and identities and moved away from Liverpool. Their case led to much soul searching about the nature of society and of childhood. Were these killers straightforwardly evil as the police had believed? Were they an aberration or was there something pathological in the nature of childhood itself?

Childhood became a dangerous state that had to be controlled and regulated by parents and adults. Others have taken this further, arguing that: 'Children everywhere were "described in terms reserved for hated enemies" ... ; they were subject to a relentless "outpouring of rage and hatred" ... ; the air was saturated with ... the "ideological whiff of child-hate". The cumulative impact of child contempt has reached its crescendo. The demonization of children was symbolically established.' (Goldson, 2001, p. 39.)

These two different cases show the two extreme views of childhood apparent in contemporary Western thinking. In Trondheim, the children were seen as entirely innocent because they were children and therefore did not, and could not, know what they were doing. In Liverpool, they were condemned as evil, precisely because they did. In so many Western images and understandings of children, as this chapter has explored, this dualism is inherent in studies of children. Their childhood is based around their innocence, whether that is defined as sexual, emotional or based on their lack of knowledge. Once their innocence has gone, so has their childhood and they are entitled to no protection, no sympathy and no special pleading. They are no longer children.

SUMMARY OF SECTION 4

- Children who participate in acts of criminality disrupt notions of childhood innocence. The behaviour of such children is seen as aberrant and becomes newsworthy. Media attention may turn individuals into symbols of delinquency.

- The ways that children who commit serious crimes are conceptualized have profound implications for the ways in which they are treated.

- In Norway, the killers of Silje Raedergard were seen as innocent because they were children.

- In the UK, the killers of James Bulger were demonized and seen as fully aware and fully knowing the consequences of their actions. They were not innocent and therefore could not be treated as children.

5 CONCLUSION

This chapter has explored several meanings of children's innocence. Innocence and childhood are strongly linked in contemporary Western constructions of childhood although evidence from cross-cultural studies indicates that this is not a universally shared assumption. In the West however, ideas about children's innocence come from many sources and it has only been possible to touch briefly on a few – in particular those that come from fiction, photographs and advertising. In these examples, however, complex and sometimes contradictory ideas about children's innocence are apparent and these can have an impact on children's lives. If childhood is constructed as a time of innocence, then children who are not innocent, because they have experience of sex, because they have committed crimes or because they have 'guilty knowledge' become problematic. It is unsurprising therefore that ideas about innocence are strongly tied to the age of the children under discussion. Teenagers are rarely seen as innocent because they have the wrong sort of knowledge and consequently are as likely to be seen as threatening and disturbing as innocent. The link between innocence and evil, and innocence and guilt is an unstable one, shown clearly in discussions of children and sexuality, and children and criminal responsibility. It is also highly dependent on social and cultural circumstances and constructions of childhood – an idea that has recurred throughout this chapter.

REFERENCES

BARNARDO'S (1999) *Giving children back their future*, Ilford, Essex, Barnardo's.

BLAKE, W. in STEVENSON W. H. (ed.) (1989, 2nd edn) *The Complete Poems*, London, Longman.

BROCKES, E. (2000) 'Chronicle of a death foretold', *Guardian G2*, 15 May, pp. 2–3.

DAVIS, H. and BOURHILL, M. (1997) 'Crisis: the demonization of children and young people' in Scraton, P. (ed.) *Childhood in Crisis*, London, UCL Press.

COUTURIER, M. (1996) *The Poerotic Novel: Nabokov's Lolita and Ada.* http://www.libraries.psu.edu/iasweb/nabokov/coutur1.htm (accessed 25 September 2001).

CROCKER, W. and CROCKER, J. (1994) *The Canela: bonding through kinship, ritual and sex,* Fort Worth, Texas, Harcourt Brace College Publishers.

FOUCAULT, M. (1976) *The History of Sexuality, Volume 1*, trans. HURLEY, R., Harmondsworth, Penguin.

FRANKLIN, B. and PETLEY, J. (1996) 'Killing the age of innocence: newspaper reporting of the death of James Bulger' in PILCHER J. and WAGG, S. (eds.) *Thatcher's children? Politics, childhood and society in the 1980s and 1990s*, London, Falmer Press.

FREUD, S. (1965) 'Infantile sexuality' in KESSEN, W. (ed.) *The Child*, New York, John Wiley & Sons.

GOLDSON, B. (2001) 'The demonization of children: from the symbolic to the institutional' in FOLEY, P., ROCHE, J. AND TUCKER, S. (eds) *Children in Society: contemporary theory, policy and practice,* Basingstoke, Palgrave.

HATTENSTONE, S. (2000) 'They were punished enough by what they did' *Guardian,* 30 October.

HOLLAND, P. (1992) *What is a Child?,* London, Virago.

JACKSON, S. (1982) *Childhood and Sexuality*, Oxford, Basil Blackwell.

KEMPADOO, O. (1998) *Buxton Spice*, London, Orion.

KESSEN, W. (1965) *The Child*, New York, John Wiley & Sons.

KITZINGER, J. (1997) 'Who are you kidding? Children, power and the struggle against sexual abuse' in JAMES, A. and PROUT, A. (eds) *Constructing and Re-constructing Childhood: contemporary issues in the sociological study of childhood*, London, Falmer Press.

MAYHEW, H. (1861) *London Labour and the London Poor*, London, Griffin, Bohn & Company.

MORRISON, B. (1998) *As If*, London, Granta Books.

NABOKOV, V. (1955) *Lolita*, Harmondsworth, Penguin.

THE OPEN UNIVERSITY (2003) *U212 Childhood,* Video Cassette 1, Band 4, Milton Keynes, The Open University.

PERISTIANY, J. G. (1966) *Honour and Shame,* Chicago, Chicago University Press.

PODHORETZ, N. (1997) ' "Lolita," my mother-in-law, the Marquis de Sade, and Larry Flynt', *Commentary,* **103**(4), pp. 23–36.

SMITH, D. J. (1994) *The Sleep of Reason*, London, Random House.

STAINTON ROGERS, W., ASH, E., HEVEY, D. and ROCHE, J. (1992) *Child Abuse and Neglect: facing the challenge,* London, Batsford.

STURTON, E. (2000) 'Our childhood', *Correspondent,* BBC 2, 25 April.

WARNER, M. (1994) *Managing Monsters: the 1994 Reith Lectures,* London, Vintage.

WHITE, P. (ed.) (1986) *Memoirs of Many in One*, Harmondsworth, Penguin.

Little angels, little devils: keeping childhood innocent

Marina Warner

In 1828, a young man was found in the market square of Nuremberg; he could write his name, Caspar Hauser, but he couldn't speak, except for a single sentence, 'I want to be a rider like my father.' He had been kept all his life in a cellar alone in the dark until his unexplained release that day. Though he was in his teens when he suddenly appeared, he seemed a symbolic child, a stranger to society, a *tabula rasa* in whom ignorance and innocence perfectly coincided. In his wild state, Caspar Hauser offered his new minders and teachers a blueprint of human nature – untouched. And in his case, his character fulfilled the most idealised image of original innocence.

He was sick when given meat to eat, passed out when given beer, and showed so little aggression and cruelty that he picked off his fleas without crushing them to set them free through the bars of his cell.

[...]

Caspar Hauser was an enigma, and after his mysterious return to the world, his life was never free from strange, turbulent incident ... His innate gentle goodness couldn't save him: he was attacked, seduced, betrayed, and abandoned by his would-be adoptive father, the Englishman Lord Stanhope. And finally he was murdered, in still unsolved circumstances, in 1833.

There'd been other wild children who'd inspired scientific experiments into human development [for example the Wild Boy of Aveyron described in Chapter 3], but Caspar Hauser more than any other foreshadows this century's struggle with the question of the child's natural character. And his fate still offers a timely parable about the nostalgic worship of childhood innocence, which is more marked today than it ever has been: the difference of the child from the adult has become a dominant theme in contemporary mythology. In literature this has produced two remarkable dream figures living in voluntary exile from grownup society – Kipling's unforgettably vivid Mowgli, and J.M. Barrie's cocky hero, the boy who wouldn't grow up, Peter Pan. Both reveal the depth of adult investment in a utopian childhood state. This can lead to disillusion, often punitive and callous, with the young as people.

[...]

Children are [seen as] the keepers and the guarantors of humanity's reputation. This has inspired a wonderfully rich culture of childhood, one of the most remarkable phenomena of modern society – from an unsurpassed imaginative literature for children today to deep psychoanalytical speculation on the thinking processes and even language of the foetus. But it also has social consequences for children themselves that are not all benign.

Childhood, placed at a tangent to adulthood, perceived as special and magical, precious and dangerous at once, has turned into some volatile stuff – hydrogen, or mercury, which has to be contained. The separate condition of the child has never been so bounded by thinking, so established in law as it is today ...

[...]

The nagging, yearning desire to work back to a pristine state of goodness, an Eden of lost innocence, has focussed on children. On the map of contemporary imaginative pathways, J.M. Barrie stands as firmly as the statue of Peter Pan gives West London children their bearings in the park. He truly became a founding father of today's cult of children when in his famous play of 1904, he made the audience responsible for the continued existence of fairyland: the fairy Tinkerbell drinks poison and Peter Pan cries out to the audience, 'Do you believe in fairies? Say quick that you believe! If you believe, clap your hands!' ... Adults applaud their loyalty to the world of pretend and children follow. The statement of faith in fairies signals collusion with Peter Pan, the boy who never grew up – it affirms the connection of the adult with that childhood Eden in which the Lost Boys are still living; it defies the death of the child within ...

[...]

Yet, even as I speak, I can hear objections flying thick and fast: for every dozen wonderful innocents in literature or popular culture, there are unsettling figures of youthful untruth and perversity ...

We call children 'little devils', 'little monsters', 'little beasts' – with the full ambiguous force of the terms, all the complications of love and longing, repulsion and fear. Jesus said 'Suffer the little children to come unto me', and Christianity worships its god as a baby in a manger, but the Christian moral tradition has also held, simultaneously, the inherent sinfulness of children.

Original sin holds up the spectre of innate human wickedness: whatever glosses theologians put on it, Christian children have been raised to believe that without divine help the species is bound for hell. Grimly, parents and carers confronted child wickedness: in New England, Cotton Mather used to beat his daughter to drive the demons of sin from her, and recommended the practice to his fellow Americans; in 1844, a German pastor wrote the terrifyingly punitive *Struwwelpeter*, with its scissor man and other bogeys for making little boys and girls be good ...

But the Child has never been seen as such a menacing enemy as today. Never before have children been so saturated with all the power of projected monstrousness to excite repulsion – and even terror ...

[...]

Today, such doubts match widespread fears, and public grief focusses obsessively on the loss of an ideal of children, of their playfulness, their innocence, their tenderness, their beauty ... Children are perceived as innocent because they're outside society, pre-historical, pre-social, instinctual, creatures of unreason, primitive, kin to unspoiled nature. Whether this is seen as good or evil often reflects the self-image of the society ...

[...]

Although the cultural and social investment in childhood innocence is constantly tested by experience, and assailed by doubts, it's still continued to grow. As psychoanalytical understanding of children's sexuality has deepened, so have attempts to contain it. The duration of the age of expected innocence has been greatly extended since Victorian times, for instance: a good thing, if it can prevent exploiting child labour and adult molestation but perhaps not, in other cases.

Most teenagers will have broken at least one of the many laws that forbid them adult behaviour – like smoking, drinking, clubbing, watching 18-rated films or having sex – thus placing them willy-nilly outside the law, and helping to reconfirm their identity as intrinsically delinquent anyway (something they don't find entirely uncongenial, of course).

At the same time, the notion of child sexuality is encoded in upbringing at a much younger age than before. The modern emphasis on sex difference, on learning masculinity and femininity, begins with the clothing of the infants, and has developed markedly since the end of the First World War. A boy who was dressed in pink ribbons by his father today would very likely be taken away from his care. Yet Robert Louis Stevenson, whose character was hardly disturbed, appears in a daguerrotype around the age of three dressed in fur-trimmed cape, full skirts, hair slide and spit curls ...

Yet even if children today aren't titillatingly dressed, they can still be looked at salaciously. It's we who have lost innocent eyes, we who can only be ironical children. Lewis Carroll's friends were undisturbed by his photographs of their children, while some pederasts today, it seems, are kept very happy by Mothercare catalogues.

Pornography clusters to the sacred and the forbidden like wasps' nests in chimneys: and children have in many ways replaced women. The very term child abuse, of recent, highly symptomatic coinage, implies that there's a proper use for children, and it is not sexual. Yet at the same time, there circulates more disguised kiddie porn than at any other period in history, and more speculation about their internal lives of fantasy and desire. The nineteenth century used *femmes fatales* with bedroom eyes and trailing tresses, wetlook drapery and floating chiffon on the official buildings and advertisements, but the late twentieth century has seen children emerge as the principal incitements to desire: the nymph or the vamp has yielded pride of place to the nymphet, the urchin and the toddler.

There's probably no way out of this maze of mirrors, at least on this side of eternity, unless, like Islam, we were to ban graven images – especially of children as objects of desire. The consecration of childhood raises the real-life examples of children to an ideal which they must fail, modestly by simply being ordinary kids, or horrendously by becoming victims or criminals. But childhood doesn't occupy some sealed Eden or Neverland set apart from the grown up world: our children can't be better than we are.

Children have never been so visible as points of identification, as warrants of virtue, as markers of humanity. Yet the quality of their lives has been deteriorating for a good fifteen years in this country; one of the fastest growing groups living in poverty are children and their mothers. The same ministers who sneer about babies on benefit, and trumpet a return to basic values cannot see that our social survival as a civilised community depends on stopping this spiralling impoverishment of children's lives. The Child Poverty Action Group estimates that a third of all children are suffering from an unacceptably low standard of living ...

To add to the difficulties, economic individualism has brought us the ultimate nightmare – not just the child as commodity, but the child consumer. Plenty of dinosaur lunch boxes at school, not many books in the library. The wicked, greedy, knowing child grows in the same ground as the industry around childhood innocence: children are expensive to raise, anyway, but all the products made for them unashamedly appeal to their pester power – as consumers of films, hamburgers, the right brand of trainers, video games. The child, as a focus of worship, has been privatised as an economic unit, has become a link in the circulation of money and desire.

[...]

Many of these problems result from the concept that childhood and adult life are separate when they are in effect inextricably intertwined. Children aren't separate from adults, and unlike Mowgli or Peter Pan, can't be kept separate; they can't live innocent lives on behalf of adults, like medieval hermits maintained at court by libertine kings to pray for them, or the best china kept in tissue in the cupboard ...

We know by now that the man is father to the child; we fear that children will grow up to be even more like us than they already are. Caspar Hauser the innocent as murdered; now we're scared that if such a wild child were to appear today he might kill us.

Source

Warner, M. 'Managing Monsters: six myths of our time', *The 1994 Reith Lectures*, London, Vintage, pp. 33–48.

READING B

Buxton spice

Oonya Kempadoo

[...] Tamarind Grove had four mad people. Uncle Joe was the safe one, the soft madman. He could help you with any homework, sums or spelling. When school over, children in blue uniforms would clump up around him by the roadside. Soon as they read out the sum, he'd be whispering the answers. Grubby little hands, gripping stubs of lead pencils flying over the exercise page, would fill in the numbers. And spelling. Any word you call he could spell. Some children'd be poking him, prodding him, pulling his shirt, calling out words while others tried more sums.

[...]

People gave him food, cigarettes, money. He'd never take rum. Sometimes he'd come in the yard and sweep the whole bottom-house, wash down the open drains and, if nobody was around, he'd eat the rice left over in the dog's bowl. Made you shamed when he did that though, wished you was around to give him a sandwich or some sugar water.

Today he eat and done already. When we came down from lunch, the four a'we girls, he was sprawled-off under the house, snoring on the in-breath, he two knees crooked and flapped open, his stain-up khaki pants taut between them. In the middle of his crotch, where the stitching had bust, was a lovely big hole, just skinning up at us. Straight there we headed, pushing and jostling, gulping down our squeals and squeaks to get a better look, peeping down that hole into the darkness of his pants. Inside, the curve barely visible, was a wrinkled, wrinkled, thick dull brown almost black skin. A few glints showed was hair there too. Plenty behind the curve and some curling out of the balls. Wasn't like no skin I'd ever seen. Too thick and wrinkly, not smooth and shining like my brother's young balls. To see them good, you had to lean right down and hold your breath. One thing Uncle Joe didn't like doing was bathing. And from that hole, Uncle Joe's pure smell came straight at you. That real vagrant smell – sweat, pee, stale cigarettes and crotch smell. Was that made you know he was mad too. Gasping for breath and pushing to take turns, we skinned-teeth like fools, blubbering around on the ground. My hand clamped over Rachel's mouth, my sleeve wet from corking my own bawling. Judy collapsed, she couldn't take it no more. Stupidy grinning face, red and shaking, she jammed Uncle Joe's foot. His legs clapped shut so fast. One hand fly down to his crotch and he sitting up straight now, rubbing his booboo eyes with the other hand. We was just rolling. Stamping and slapping the ground. Running up and down in front of him. Holding on to each other and folding up laughing like we had hinges everywhere. When his red eyes could see, he started laughing too, legs straight out in front of him clamped tight. His sideways, shake-head laugh. Making five of us in the foolishness under the bottom-house.

The front room downstairs had a stale piano, a baby grand – the third leg a packing chest and the cover cracked. In this yellow room, even on the hottest, driest day the pungent smell of damp newsprint, books and mouse-eaten felt lay like a blanket floating at the height of the windowsills – sliding out when you opened the front doors. Piles of music books, cardboard boxes, wooden chests and crates were the piano's only audience. All underneath the piano was packed with audience. The only empty space left in the room was an L-shaped piece of pocky concrete floor.

'Ann, Uncle Joe. Ann. Remember she?'

'She coming back from Suriname just now you know.'

'You like she nuh, you wicked t'ing you.'

'Ow, Uncle Joe – how you could like a big-shot girl like dat?'

Uncle Joe's aroma wafted around the piano room, mixing with the book and mouse-eaten felt smell. Sammy stood gripping the lock of the front door, eye open big – supposed to be locking him in with us and everybody else out but looked like she was going to run away any minute. I guarded the other door that led to the middle room. We had him cornered in the far end of the L space, against the piano. We was the ones frightened though, while he was gently dreaming of Ann, shifting slowly from foot to foot, still holding his embarrassed crotch.

'Yes, Uncle Joe. You like she. Ah know you like she. Oh me gawd, what you would do wid a nice girl like dat?'

That tickled him by one of his kidneys. He ginched and giggled jerkily.

'Youall mustn't be talking bout Miss Ann like dat,' he squeaked. 'Miss Ann is a decent lady, I like Miss Ann too bad.'

'Well what you would do bout it, if she liked you too?'

He jumped again, smiling wider. 'Liked me? If she liked me?'

'Yes, Uncle Joe, she like you. I hear she say so already!'

'Marry she. She is a decent lady. I would marry she.'

He whispered it over and over softly, rocking himself.

'But Uncle Joe, what you would do *after* you marry she? What you would do, eh?'

His head snapped up and his eyes scanned our faces. The worried flash faded from his face and he grinned at us

'Youall are very wicked. Wicked chi'ren. Not nice.'

Wincing it out but smiling his shake-head smile all the time.

'We not asking you to do no wickedness, Uncle Joe. Just show we what you would do to Ann after you marry she. Just show we, dat's all.'

'You want to see what I would do to Miss Ann?'

'Yes. Yes ... the piano is Miss Ann.'

He turned round to the piano, leaning his waist against it, stroking the curve of its belly, muttering 'Miss Ann? Miss Ann?'

We touching the piano now too, crowded up by the keyboard end.

'Miss Ann?' He bent down slowly, rested his dry lips on the wood, rubbed them in an arc on her chest, stroking her side with his hand.

'Ow Miss Ann,' his voice trembling.

'What he doing?'

'Sssh! You can't see is kiss he kissing she?'

'Ow Miss Ann. Miss Ann sweet, eh?'

'You lolo, Uncle Joe, What you would do wid your *lolo*?'

'Un humh? Miss Ann is a nice lady, eh?' His head hung right down on his chest while he caressed that piano cover. We could see the bulge of his khaki lolo growing between him and the smooth wood – just kept pushing up till it was straining at the string tied round his waist. He kept polishing.

'Uncle Joe, what's dat? All dat's lolo? Miss Ann would like dat!'

'Ow Miss Ann. Miss Ann nice, eh?'

'Take it out, Uncle Joe, take it out!'

'Uh huh. Nice Miss Ann.' He was still stroking her and now himself too. Scrubbing down his pants from the top of his lolo, with the heel of his palm. The zip had long gone and the front only lapped over, held down by the string. He reached in and brought his hand back out holding one huge thing.

'Waagh! Donkey lolo!' Never seen a big man's lolo, much less one this huge, much less one this black, much less this close. Just kept looking. He held it like it didn't belong to him.

'Donkey lolo! Donkey lolo!' Wasn't far from donkey lolo, stretched skin, with a dark sheen, pulled back behind the head the same way. Nodding the same way too, but hanging up instead of hanging down. Looked like it was moving by itself. Uncle Joe didn't even know what to do with it, with his embarrassed self. He watched it like us. As we all stared, it went down slowly. Right there in his hand, it shrivelled and got more black, till he was weighing it, bouncing it with a smacking sound in his palm and smiling his shake-head smile.

'This is what Miss Ann would like? Nice Miss Ann?' Pinching in his bumsey, he pressed the end of his soft lolo against her, pushing the loose skin up with his fingers. We scrambled round the side to see the smudge it left on the wood. A new scent blended with that acid afternoon air. His dry hand rasping on mahogany was the only sound in the room now.

'Youall play the piano nuh? Come nuh, play. Make Miss Ann sing for me. Nice Miss Ann.'

We just had to. Made Miss Ann sing for one whole hour ...

Source

KEMPADOO, O. (1998) *Buxton Spice*, London, Orion, pp. 5–12.

READING C

Lolita

Vladimir Nabokov

... Now I wish to introduce the following idea. Between the age limits of nine and fourteen there occur maidens who, to certain bewitched travelers, twice or many times older than they, reveal their true nature which is not human, but nymphic (that is, demoniac); and these chosen creatures I propose to designate as 'nymphets.'

It will be marked that I substitute time terms for spatial ones. In fact, I would have the reader see 'nine' and 'fourteen' as the boundaries – the mirrory beaches and rosy rocks – of an enchanted island haunted by those nymphets of mine and surrounded by a vast, misty sea. Between those age limits, are all girl-children nymphets? Of course not. Otherwise, we who are in the know, we lone voyagers, we nympholepts, would have long gone insane. Neither are good looks any criterion; and vulgarity, or at least what a given community terms so, does not necessarily impair certain mysterious characteristics, the fey grace, the elusive, shifty, soul-shattering, insidious charm that separates the nymphet from such coevals of hers as are incomparably more dependent on the spatial world of synchronous phenomena than on that intangible island of entranced time where Lolita plays with her likes. Within the same age limits the number of true nymphets is strikingly inferior to that of provisionally plain, or just nice, or 'cute,' or even 'sweet' and 'attractive,' ordinary, plumpish, formless, cold-skinned, essentially human little girls, with tummies and pigtails, who may or may not turn into adults of great beauty (look at the ugly dumplings in black stockings and white hats that are metamorphosed into stunning stars of the screen). A normal man given a group photograph of school girls or Girl Scouts and asked to point out the comeliest one will not necessarily choose the nymphet among them. You have to be an artist and a madman, a creature of infinite melancholy, with a bubble of hot poison in your loins and a super-voluptuous flame permanently aglow in your subtle spine (oh, how you have to cringe and hide!), in order to discern at once, by ineffable signs – the slightly feline outline of a cheekbone, the slenderness of a downy limb, and other indices which despair and shame and tears of tenderness forbid me to tabulate – the little deadly demon among the wholesome children; *she* stands unrecognized by them and unconscious herself of her fantastic power.

Furthermore, since the idea of time plays such a magic part in the matter, the student should not be surprised to learn that there must be a gap of several years, never less than ten I should say, generally thirty or forty, and as many as ninety in a few known cases, between maiden and man to enable the latter to come under a nymphet's spell. It is a question of focal adjustment, of a certain distance that the inner eye thrills to surmount, and a certain contrast that the mind perceives with a gasp of perverse delight. When I was a child and she was a child, my little Annabel was no nymphet to me; I was her equal, a faunlet in my own right, on that same enchanted island of time; but today, in September 1952, after twenty-nine years have elapsed, I think I can distinguish in her the initial fateful elf in my life. We loved each other with a premature love, marked by a fierceness that so often destroys adult lives. I was a strong lad and survived; but the poison was in the wound, and the wound remained ever open, and soon I found myself maturing amid a civilization which allows a man of twenty-five to court a girl of sixteen but not a girl of twelve …

Source

Nabokov, V. (1955) *Lolita*, Harmondsworth, Penguin, pp. 16–18.

ACKNOWLEDGEMENTS

Grateful acknowledgement is made to the following sources for permission to reproduce material in this book.

Chapter 1

Text

p. 20: Taylor, D. (2001) 'The panel: the age of criminal responsibility' © *The Guardian,* 20 June; *pp. 37–40:* Stainton Rogers, R. (1992) 'The social construction of childhood' in Stainton Rogers, W., Hevey, D., Roche, J. and Ash, E. (eds) *Child Abuse and Neglect: facing the challenge,* Batsford/The Open University; *pp. 40–43:* Asquith, S. (1996) 'When children kill children: the search for justice', *Childhood,* **3**(1), Sage Publications.

Illustrations

p. 1: Martin Woodhead; *p. 3: (top left)* Martin Woodhead, *(centre left) Painted Babies,* BBC; *(bottom left)* Mike Levers/Open University, *(top right)* Rachel Burr, *(centre right)* Oswaldo Paez/Associated Press, *(bottom right)* Richard Vogel/ Associated Press; *p. 6:* Geoff du Feu/Bubbles; *p. 7: (top and centre)* Gloria Upchurch, *(bottom)* Christopher Walker; *p. 8: (centre)* Martin Woodhead; *p. 32: (top):* courtesy of Alternative Education, *(bottom)* Matthew Hearn/PA Photos.

Chapter 2

Text

pp. 75–9: Ribbens, J. (1995) 'Mothers' images of children and their implication for maternal response' in Brannen, J. and O'Brien, M. (eds) *Childhood and Parenthood: Proceedings of ISA Committee for Family Research Conference on Children and Families,* 1994, Institute of Education, University of London, by permission of Jane Ribbens, Julia Brannen and Margaret O'Brien; *pp. 80–83:* Holland, P. (1992) *What is a Child? Popular images of childhood,* Virago Press, reprinted by permission of Patricia Holland.

Illustrations

p. 45: David Macgregor; *p. 48: (bottom)* Mercia Seminara; *p. 49:* Gloria Upchurch; *p. 50: (centre left)* Gloria Upchurch, *(bottom right)* Hulton Archive; *p. 52:* Pitt Rivers Museum, University of Oxford; *p. 56: (left)* Uffizi Gallery, Florence/Archive Alinari/Giraudon, *(right)* © The National Gallery, London; *p. 57: (top)* The National Trust Photo Library/Derrick E. Witty, *(bottom)* Harrogate Museum and Art Gallery/Bridgeman Art Library; *p. 63: (top)* Archivo Iconografico S.A./Corbis, *(bottom)* The Kobal Collection; *p. 64:* Bettmann/Corbis; *p. 66:* Archivo Iconografico S.A./Corbis; *p. 69:* Bettmann/Corbis; *p. 71: (left)* Caroline Penn/ Corbis, *(right)* Peter Turnley/Corbis.

Chapter 3

Text

p. 91: Chisholm, J. S. (1996) 'Learning "respect of everything": Navajo images of development' in Hwang, C. P., Lamb, M. E. and Sigel, I. E. (eds) *Images of Childhood,* Lawrence Erlbaum Associates, Inc.

Illustrations

p. 85: copyright © 1996 PhotoDisc, Inc.; *p. 88:* Gahan Wilson © Punch Ltd; *p. 93: (top)* Sally Greenhill/Richard and Sally Greenhill, *(bottom)* Mark Edwards/Still Pictures; *p. 96:* English Heritage Photo Library; *p. 98:* Helen Deakin/Bubbles; *p. 99:* Herbert Gehr/Timepix/Rex Features; *p. 101: (top)* Popperfoto, *(bottom)* Heatherbank Museum of Social Work, Glasgow Caledonian University; *p. 104:* Mary Evans Picture Library; *p. 106*: Martin Woodhead; *p. 107:* Archives Jean Piaget/Université de Genève; *p. 114: (top right)* Frans Rombout/Bubbles, *(bottom)* John Walmsley Photography; *p. 116:* Frith, U. (1989) *Autism: explaining the enigma,* Basil Blackwell Publishers; *p. 118:* Lois Joy Thurstun/Bubbles; p. 121: Ryan Cooper.

Chapter 4

Text

p. 150: Archard, D. (1993) *Children: rights and childhood,* Routledge; *pp. 170–3:* Vylder, S. de (2000) 'The big picture', *CRIN Newsletter,* no. 13, November 2000.

Illustrations

p. 135: Martin Woodhead; *p. 138:* Mary Evans Picture Library; *p. 139:* courtesy of United Nations; *p. 141:* The Art Archive/Free Library Philadelphia/Album/Joseph Martin; *p. 145:* Professor Jeffrey Barlow; *p. 158:* courtesy of UNICEF, Bhutan; *p. 160: (top)* Mark Edwards/Still Pictures, *(bottom)* Howard Davies/Exile Images; *pp. 162–3: Colour in Your Rights and Responsibilities,* Molo Songololo, Cape Town, illustrations by permission of the National Children's Rights Committee.

Chapter 5

Text

pp. 215–20: © 1997 'Children and gender: constructions of difference' by Barrie Thorne in *Towards a New Psychology of Gender,* Gergen, M. M. and Davis, S. N. (eds), reproduced by permission of Routledge, Inc., part of the Taylor & Francis Group.

Illustrations

p. 179: copyright © 1996 PhotoDisc, Inc.; *p. 184:* Punch Ltd; *p. 195(top):* courtesy of Penrith First School/Milton Keynes Council; *pp. 201, 207:* Martin Woodhead.

Chapter 6

Text

pp. 248–9: Brockes, E. (2000) 'A child in crime: the life and death of a balaclava boy, chronicle of a death foretold', © *The Guardian,* 15 May 2000; *p. 252–3:* reprinted by permission of PFD on behalf of Blake Morrison, copyright © 1997 by Blake Morrison; *pp. 258–61:* extract from *Managing Monsters: Six Myths of Our Times* by Marina Warner published by Vintage, used by permission of The Random House Group Limited and Rogers, Coleridge & White Ltd; *pp. 261–4:* Kempadoo, O. (1998) *Buxton Spice,* by permission of Phoenix House and David Bodwin Associates.

Illustrations

p. 221: Getty Images/Anne Menke; *pp. 226, 227:* copyright © The Fitzwilliam Museum; *p. 231(bottom):* courtesy of Danone Waters and Euro RSCG BETC; *p. 233 and 234:* copyright © Barnardo's; *p. 237 and 243(bottom right):* copyright © Topham Picturepoint; *p. 243(top and bottom left):* the Collection of Morten Cohen featured in his book *Lewis Carroll,* p. 167; *p. 245:* copyright © Kobal Collection/Mario Kaddar/ Pathe.

Cover and title page photographs

top: Martin Woodhead; *centre left:* Mike Levers; *centre right:* copyright © 1996 PhotoDisc, Inc.; *bottom:* Mike Levers.

Every effort has been made to trace all copyright owners, but if any has been inadvertently overlooked, the publishers will be pleased to make the necessary arrangements at the first opportunity.

INDEX